C000183041

THE FIELD OF CLOTH OF GOLD

G LENN R ICHARDSON

The Field of Cloth of Gold

YALE UNIVERSITY PRESS
NEW HAVEN AND LONDON

For Olivia and Katherine

Published with assistance from the foundation established in memory of Oliver Baty Cunningham of the Class of 1917, Yale College.

Copyright © 2013 Glenn Richardson

All rights reserved. This book may not be reproduced in whole or in part, in any form (beyond that copying permitted by Sections 107 and 108 of the U.S. Copyright Law and except by reviewers for the public press) without written permission from the publishers.

For information about this and other Yale University Press publications, please contact:
U.S. Office: sales.press@yale.edu   www.yalebooks.com
Europe Office: sales@yaleup.co.uk   www.yalebooks.co.uk

Set in Adobe Caslon Pro by IDSUK (DataConnection) Ltd
Printed in Great Britain by CPI Group (UK) Ltd, Croydon, CR0 4YY

Library of Congress Cataloging-in-Publication Data

Richardson, Glenn.
The Field of Cloth of Gold / Glenn Richardson.
    pages cm
  Includes bibliographical references.
  ISBN 978-0-300-14886-2 (hardback)
  1. Field of Cloth of Gold, France, 1520. 2. France—Foreign relations—Great Britain.
3. Great Britain—Foreign relations—France. 4. Francis I, King of France, 1494-1547. 5.
Henry VIII, King of England, 1491-1547. 6. France—Court and courtiers—History—
16th century. 7. Great Britain—Court and courtiers—History—16th century. I. Title.
  DC113.5.R53 2013
  940.2'2—dc23
                                                                          2013023518

A catalogue record for this book is available from the British Library.

10 9 8 7 6 5 4 3 2 1

Contents

Illustrations

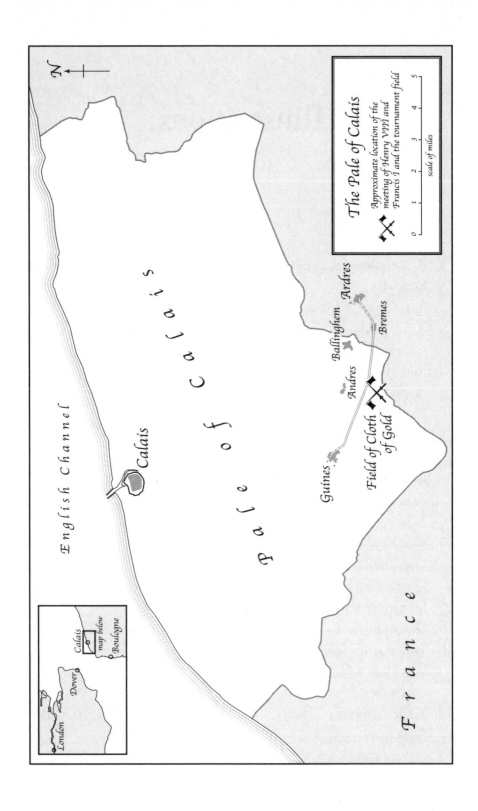

N

English Channel

Calais

Pale of Calais

Guines

Andres

Ballinghem

Ardres

Bremes

Field of Cloth
of Gold

France

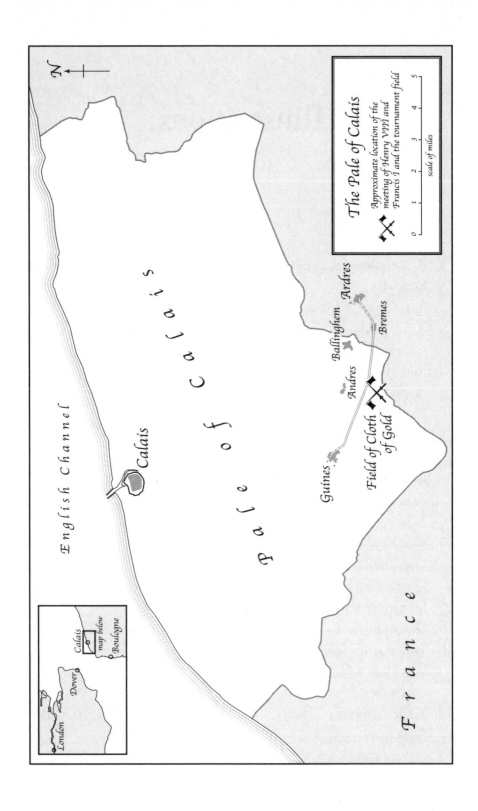

London

Dover

Calais

map below

Boulogne

The Pale of Calais

Approximate location of the
meeting of Henry VIII and
Francis I and the tournament field

scale of miles

0   1   2   3   4   5

Preface

THIS BOOK IS about an extraordinary meeting that took place in northern France in the summer of 1520 between Henry VIII of England and Francis I of France: the Field of Cloth of Gold. The two kings and their vast entourages were accommodated in tents and pavilions that were dressed in luxuriant fabrics, especially the cloth of gold that gives the event its name. At the Field each king strove to show his rival that he was a successful warrior, an effective governor and a great patron in a way that he hoped would secure the other's co-operation, or at least acquiescence, in his own plans. There has never been anything in the history of Europe since that quite equals it. So the Field offers a unique insight into many aspects of the world of Renaissance princes.

In contemplating writing a book on the subject it seemed me that, for all its extraordinariness, the Field of Cloth of Gold has recently been rather overlooked and certainly much misunderstood. It lives vaguely in public historical consciousness as some sort of medieval 'peace festival' or the occasion of a wrestling match between Henry and Francis. As we begin to approach its 500th anniversary in 2020, a new account is timely – particularly given the fact that the last book on the subject was published more than forty years ago.

For all their considerable antiquarian scholarship, the accounts of the Field of Cloth of Gold written to date have expressed a pronounced scepticism about the significance of the meeting. While devoting much care and attention to its details, they have characterised the Field as being either an elaborate sham designed by each side to deceive

the other as to its 'real', belligerent, intention, or 'merely an excuse for
a party on the grandest scale', as one historian has put it, which had
'no tangible result'. Such a view, however, raises more questions than
it answers. Why, for example, would two national elites whose
centuries-old rivalry had recently intensified even want to entertain
each other at a huge party merely for the sake of doing so? That medieval and Renaissance elites valued theatrical 'extravagance' is beyond
doubt, but this was a very different thing from pointless frivolity. It
seems to me important, then, to interpret the Field in ways that would
have meant something to those attending it but that are also, hopefully,
understandable to a modern reader.

Proceeding from the premise that people do not generally spend
huge amounts of money on major social and political events unless they
really mean something to them, this book tries to make better sense of
the Field. The description of its organisation, provisioning, its various
set-piece encounters and activities, is based on the relatively large
amount of primary source material that survives. Much of this has,
naturally, been used in previous accounts, but a reasonable proportion,
especially on the French side, is newly presented here. In reinterpreting
the Field, this book draws on the wide body of research into Renaissance
political and material culture which has been done since the 1980s. New
evidence and perspectives have changed our view of the conduct of
international politics and its relationship to domestic politics in general
and Anglo-French relations in particular. Whole new discourses and
debates relevant to the Field have emerged in recent decades. These
include discussions on the nature and role of the royal court, its presentation of monarchy and of royal political and artistic patronage. New
insights have been gained into forms of entertainment and public spectacle, display and hospitality in Renaissance society. Important research
has been done on gender, gender relations and particularly on concepts
of masculine honour and chivalry among sixteenth-century social elites.
This list is very far from exhaustive, but, as far as possible, I have tried
to bring new insights gleaned from these discussions to bear on the
evidence about the Field. The book gives a much fuller account of the

political, diplomatic and cultural contexts of the Field than has yet been offered. In so doing, it also offers a wider (although necessarily concise) account of Anglo-French relations during the first half of the sixteenth century.

Some of the research for the book was conducted in Paris in 2008 with the aid of a Small Research Grant from the British Academy. A Scouloudi Foundation Historical Award in 2010 enabled me to visit a number of French regional archives and libraries. Support from St Mary's University College Research Fund enabled me to present a paper on the Field at the Sixteenth Century Society Conference in St Louis, Missouri, USA in October 2008. I am grateful to the School of Theology, Philosophy and History at St Mary's University College for a Research Grant that helped me to visit the Folger Shakespeare Library in Washington DC in 2011, and for a partial sabbatical during 2012.

The scholarly debts I owe to the many historians whose work has inspired and guided my own will be clear from the endnotes and bibliography. A number of colleagues and friends offered useful advice in the course of helpful discussions. Sidney Anglo, Joseph Bispham, Andrea Clarke, Judith Curthoys, Brett Dolman, David Grummitt, Alasdair Hawkyard, Julian Munby, Kent Rawlinson and Jennifer Scott all generously shared their expertise in response to my enquiries about different aspects of the staging of the Field and its subsequent representation. Susan Doran, Daniel Grey, Steven Gunn, Maria Hayward, Robert Knecht, Simon Lambe, Roger Mettam and Dominic Omissi all read and commented helpfully on drafts of the book at various stages. David Potter also offered advice on archives and, with Mark Greengrass, kindly supported my funding applications. I am particularly grateful to John Murphy who helped me to clarify my ideas and who made many perceptive suggestions about the book's content, structure and style.

Thanks are also due to my colleagues at St Mary's University College who have shown generous and supportive interest in my work. I am grateful for invitations to give papers about the Field to the Society for Court Studies and to the Tudor and Stuart Seminar at the Institute of

Historical Research, University of London. My work over the years has benefited a great deal from conversations with students at St Mary's and with those attending the various study-day lectures and summer schools I have offered through Oxford University Department for Continuing Education. I would like to thank David Beard, Christine Jackson and Shirley Fawdrey at OUDCE for these opportunities. My particular thanks go to Heather McCallum at Yale University Press for the opportunity to write this book and to Rachael Lonsdale and Tami Halliday whose gentle but insistent guidance in all stages of production was helpful in completing the project. I am also grateful to Yale's anonymous readers who offered constructive advice on the initial proposal and on a first full draft of the book. The dedication is to my two beautiful daughters.

Introduction
Why the Field of Cloth of Gold?

IN THE EARLY evening light of 7 June 1520, in a narrow field in northern France, two richly dressed horsemen spurred their mounts and set off towards each other. As they gathered speed, both men raised their right hands as if about to draw their swords to attack. Instead, each reached for his feathered hat and doffed it as their cantering horses closed rapidly together. Amidst the cheers of a crowd of onlookers, they saluted each other, then dismounted and embraced like brothers – for that is what their meeting that evening proclaimed them to be.

The men were two of the greatest kings of the European Renaissance, the 25-year-old King Francis I of France and King Henry VIII of England then aged 29. They met for just over a fortnight between the towns of Guînes and Ardres in what is now the Pas-de-Calais in northern France. Together, they hosted a tournament held to celebrate peace between England and France, which was, itself, part of a wider Universal Peace among all Christian princes that had been agreed in London in October 1518. The event which this meeting inaugurated soon assumed mythic status in the annals of English and French history. It is known as the Field of Cloth of Gold. This book explains why the meeting took place, how it was organised, who its participants were and why it is important in the history of Anglo-French relations and in the broader history of Renaissance Europe.

Written against the background of nineteenth-century conceptions of diplomacy, the prevailing view of the Field of Cloth of Gold is that it was a colossal waste of time and money. This is largely because Francis and

Henry swore to be at peace in 1518, met as allies in 1520 and yet were at war by 1522. The event has been characterised as an entertaining instance of curious, theatrical medievalism of little ultimate significance. Nineteenth-century writers and artists exploited its dramatic and comic potential.[1] Writing in the aftermath of two world wars, twentieth-century commentators have generally viewed the Field with deep scepticism, even disappointment, as it failed to bring about a genuine peace. They regarded it as explicable, if at all, only as a deceptive cover for 'real' plans for war on each side.[2]

This book offers a very different view. It argues that in 1520 war was the very thing that both sides hoped to avoid – and to profit immensely by doing so. It also shows why those hopes were to be disappointed. The Field of Cloth of Gold was, first and foremost, a tournament held to inaugurate peace and alliance between France and England, two ancient enemies. That being so, the event gave physical expression, as it were, to genuine hopes of peace between many other 'ancient enemies' among European rulers at a moment of crisis and profound change across the Continent.

Our knowledge of the Field of Cloth of Gold comes mainly from the voluminous diplomatic correspondence about it and from administrative records drawn up by French and English court officials. The first narratives of the Field appeared in France in the early autumn of 1520. Most were comparatively brief, but celebratory and optimistic. They presented the Field as exceptional and were avidly read in Western Europe and beyond.[3] It is comparatively rare to find a major sixteenth-century event about which so much information survives. The Field of Cloth of Gold therefore provides important, and hitherto largely untapped, sources for the history of sixteenth-century material culture. It reveals much about subjects as varied as food preparation and banqueting, building techniques, tapestries and furnishings, horses, armour, transport and shipping. It also shows how royal courts worked and the effect of monarchy upon the lives of the gentry and working people of England and France. It offers striking insights into the mentality of the period, especially about ideas of masculinity and kingship and shows us how peace-making actually worked in an age of 'personal monarchy'.

For it to reveal its true meaning, the Field of Cloth of Gold has to be seen against the background of nearly two centuries in which most European states, large and small, monarchical, princely and republican, had experienced prolonged periods of foreign or civil warfare. England and France had fought the Hundred Years War between 1337 and 1453. No sooner had that conflict ground to an unresolved halt than the internecine strife of the Wars of the Roses began in England and lasted, off and on, until the middle years of the reign of Henry VII, the first Tudor king. A generation of similar dynastic conflict in Iberia was only ended by the marriage of Ferdinand of Aragon and Isabella of Castile and their joint conquest of Granada by 1492. Meanwhile, the kings of France, having got rid of the English, had also to face down aristocratic challenges to their authority in the 'War of the Public Weal' in 1465 and 'La Guerre Folle' in 1485. They then turned their military might against the Italian states in pursuit of various dynastic claims to the duchy of Milan and the kingdom of Naples. Into these 'Italian wars' as they became known, the papacy and the king of Aragon were routinely and destructively drawn, to the despair of commentators like Machiavelli. As if all this were not enough from Christendom's collective point of view, in 1453 Constantinople fell to Mehmed II, called the Conqueror, Sultan of the Ottoman Turks.

For most late-medieval rulers, war was, first and foremost, a way of asserting personal power and military prowess in order to became famous. Few of the wars fought during these years were motivated by purely strategic considerations. Conflicts between monarchs pursuing dynastic territorial claims were often referred to as wars of 'magnificence, honour and profit', reflecting their very personal nature. As nobles and as crowned heads of state, kings were expected to fight in defence of their national patrimony and to do so successfully, sharing the profits of conquered lands with their leading supporters. Modern sensibilities shy away from rejoicing at most military victories and warfare in general, but in the early sixteenth century the defeat of an enemy in a decisive battle fought in an apparently 'just' (or at least reasonably justifiable) cause with a minimum of casualties and civilian trauma was the *raison d'être* of kings.

Yet this was not quite the whole story. There were a number of constraints upon the ambitions of rulers. Leaders had, at the very least, to be seen to respect Christian injunctions against lawless violence. War in any age is also astoundingly expensive. No sensible monarch would, without good prospects of success, jeopardise the lives and livelihoods of his subjects in a reckless war. Keeping the peace when there was no reason for war was as important as being a warrior. The resolution of the paradox between the duty to practise war and that to maintain peace lay in the 'just war' doctrine and in the code of chivalry. Chivalry defined a set of ideals and aspirational behaviours that regulated the expression of violence and hostility among those entitled to bear arms.[4]

Against the background of apparent danger from without, the ancient ideal of peace within Christendom brought about by rulers acting in concert began to be articulated anew. Somewhat ironically, the accession, within a few short years of each other, of three young and well-educated monarchs further stimulated these hopes. The great biblical humanist, Erasmus of Rotterdam, longed for an end to endemic European warfare. His plea for rulers to show leadership through peace rather than war was expressed in three of his most famous works. His *Institutio principis christiani* (The Education of a Christian Prince) was published in 1516. It argued that the true glory of princes lay in the peaceful stewardship of their lands rather than in expensive and destructive wars. More explicit condemnations of war followed in 1517: *Dulce bellum inexpertis* (War is sweet to those who know nothing of it) and *Querela pacis* (The complaint of peace). For Erasmus, war was profoundly sinful unless undertaken in the last resort to punish or restrain evil-doing. Sir Thomas More took a similar line in his book *Utopia*, which also appeared in 1516. In treatises directed towards Francis I, Guillaume Budé, France's leading biblical humanist, had emphasised the importance of peace and good government as proof of great monarchy. These publications were read in ecclesiastical, courtly and academic circles and the hopes they expressed were widely shared. The rhetoric of peace as a noble Christian virtue worthy of the greatest princes came into its own in 1518. In the late summer of that year, news of plans to create and maintain international peace and co-operation began to reach European courts and capitals.

The two men responsible for this attempt to create a European-wide peace were not secular rulers, but princes of the Church. They were Pope Leo X and Cardinal Thomas Wolsey. Giovanni de' Medici, the scion of the great Florentine house, became pope in 1513. He was alarmed at the Ottoman conquest of Persia, Syria and Egypt and the potential threat to Hungary. During a meeting with Francis I at Bologna in 1515, Leo asked him to attack Sultan Selim I, but received an equivocal reply. In November 1517, Leo first called for a campaign against the enemies of Christendom, just as Urban II had done at Clermont in 1095. This military campaign was to be led by the Holy Roman Emperor Maximilian and the king of France. England, Spain and Portugal were to supply ships for an attempt to reconquer Constantinople. For this to happen, however, the rulers of Europe had to be at peace with each other. On 6 March 1518, therefore, the pope published a plan for a Europe-wide five-year truce. He would arbitrate on all existing disputes between rulers and thus bring about a basis for co-operation. Papal legates were dispatched to proclaim the truce to the rulers of England, France and Spain and to Emperor Maximilian.[5]

Thomas Wolsey had first entered royal service in England under Henry VII and was made almoner to Henry VIII in 1509. His appetite for hard work, command of detail and his personal charm enabled him to become, within three years, the dominant force in Henry's council. By 1514, Wolsey was Lord Chancellor of England and Archbishop of York. He was made a cardinal by Leo X in 1515 and incorporated the pope's personal badge of the red lion in his own coat of arms. His intelligent insight and his high dignity in the Church gave Wolsey an international perspective and an awareness of interests beyond those of England and its king. Supported strongly by Henry, in 1518 Wolsey insisted that Leo make him a papal legate *a latere* (literally one sent from the pope's side) of equal status with Leo's appointed legate to England, Cardinal Campeggio. Wolsey then rather hijacked the papal plans brought by his Italian colleague. He made London, not Rome, the centre of attention.

Instead of the planned five-year truce between princes that Leo envisaged, Wolsey wanted to create a multilateral treaty which would be the basis of a permanent European peace. Under this plan, all participants would commit themselves not to attack any other signatory to the treaty. Disputes likely to provoke war were to be referred to Henry, not Pope Leo, for arbitration and if no resolution could be arrived at, the rest of the signatories would attack the aggressor and prosecute war against him until peace had been restored and reparation made.

Incredible as it may seem to modern eyes, Wolsey's ambitious scheme was widely and rapidly accepted. By October 1518, all the major European sovereignties and a host of minor ones had committed themselves to the treaty of London, also known as the treaty of Universal Peace. The linchpin of the international league was a set of subsidiary treaties of peace and alliance between England and France, also formally sworn to in October 1518. The Anglo-French alliance was secured by the marriage of the Dauphin François to Henry's heir, Princess Mary. One of the terms of the treaty was that the two kings were to meet personally to affirm their alliance and their commitment to the Universal Peace. That is why the Field of Cloth of Gold was held and why Cardinal Wolsey was deeply involved in planning and organising every aspect of the event.

Given the important roles that Wolsey envisaged for Henry and Francis as chief maintainers of Christian peace, the way they related to each other as allies was to be the example to all the other adherents to the Universal Peace. Never before had a display of amicable Franco-English relations had such important implications for the rest of Europe. Never before had a meeting been required to be quite as spectacular, as impressive and compelling to the minds of fellow princes, as that in 1520. There were, nevertheless, several important precedents in medieval Anglo-French history that were drawn upon in preparing the Field of Cloth of Gold.

In 1254, King Henry III of England had crossed the Narrow Sea to meet his French counterpart, Louis IX, who was anxious to secure peace with England. He came to meet Henry at Chartres after Henry had visited the shrine of St Edmund Rich at the Cistercian abbey at Pontigny.

From Chartres the two kings rode to Paris where Henry III gave a huge banquet in the Hall of the Old Temple. The chronicler Matthew Paris affirmed that it was one of the grandest ever held and one by which 'the honour of the king of England and, in fact, all the English, was much increased and exalted'.[6] In November 1259 Louis IX once more received Henry in Paris. After some last-minute wrangles, a treaty of peace was proclaimed at the royal palace in early December. Insofar as the 1259 treaty of Paris was designed to end Anglo-French conflict and secure French financial support for the king of England, it somewhat anticipates the 1518 treaty of London. The hospitality provided during its signing in Paris also anticipates that offered in 1520.[7]

Even closer in spirit to the Field of Cloth of Gold, and in virtually the same location in a large encampment made especially for the occasion, was the meeting on 27 October 1396 between Richard II and Charles VI. They met to confirm an Anglo-French peace agreed in March the same year which it was hoped would bring an end to over half a century of Anglo-French conflict precipitated by the failure of the 1259 treaty of Paris. It was secured by Richard's marriage to the six-year-old Princess Isabelle of France. He came to Ardres to meet his bride. Just as Henry and Francis would do in 1520, Richard and Charles advanced over an equal distance to greet each other before their assembled courts. They shook hands, kissed, and presents were exchanged. The meeting was characterised by the same strict reciprocity and protocol as that of 1520. There were no paramilitary games at the 1396 meeting, but the banquets and masques held were as lavish as any at the Field. Prompted by his love of personal display, in which Henry would prove to be more than his equal, Richard appeared in steadily more splendid outfits of velvet and presented yet more expensive gifts to Charles and his entourage. He spent nearly £15,000 on the event, almost as much, in relative terms, as Henry would spend in 1520. As Nigel Saul has observed of Richard, he 'was determined to make a vivid and lasting impression on those present. Massive spending on gifts and fine clothing ensured that he did so.'[8] Exactly the same thing was true of the two kings who met in the same place over a century later.

As these meetings demonstrate, peace could be a perfectly acceptable alternative to war for most rulers, provided that it, too, had a chivalric and ennobling quality about it. Whether at war or at peace, monarchs had always to respond to the demands of the 'magnificence, honour and profit' mentality. For this model of 'chivalric' peace to work, one thing was essential. Each king had to feel that his status had at least been protected, and may even have been enhanced by it. Despite the idealistic and somewhat abstract rhetoric with which it was enacted, peace-making between princes was never done for its own sake. It had always to result in peace 'with honour' or advantage. A successful peace treaty made room for each participant to assert his own status and power in activities other than war between them. In 1518, for example, Francis got back the city of Tournai lost to the English in war in 1513. For his part, Henry secured increased annual payments from Francis that he regarded as 'tribute' for 'his' kingdom of France. Thus, each monarch gained something from the other that strengthened his status among his fellow princes and the nobles of his own realm. In making peace with the king of France, Henry always strove to appear the magnanimous friend, bestowing peace upon his fellow sovereign. Francis responded in kind, as the great lord and even the patron of his English counterpart. Thus assured of his own status, each monarch could take part in a joint enterprise whereby they, together, displayed their power to the rest of the world.

In 1520, there was between Henry and Francis a deeply felt ambivalence, ambivalence in the true sense of countervailing strengths. Each man felt a mix of positive and negative feelings towards the other. He admired his rival but did not easily trust him. Each man could welcome the other as friend and ally while still resenting his potential as an enemy. At the Field of Cloth of Gold, this ambivalence expressed itself in a spirit of demonstrative masculinity, articulated through the chivalric code. At the heart of that code of male bonding and service to the honour of God and women was, paradoxically, aggressive competition between elite men for each other's approval.[9] Displays of friendship and peace made between the two kings were, therefore, as much warnings against aggression as apparent invitations to co-operation.

Relatively rarely in the history of Western European monarchy have there been two sovereigns better able to use their own bodies, adorned and unadorned, as a means to express their personal power. The 1520 tournament acted as a metaphor for the agreement of peace and alliance between them. Thundering down the lists in full armour, displaying spectacularly colourful heraldic devices, Henry and Francis presented a compelling spectacle to the assembled elite audience, to the world beyond and to each other. Simultaneously celebrating his capacity to wage war while forsaking it in the interests of chivalric brotherhood, each knight gave what he considered to be manifest proof of his own exceptionality as man and monarch. Evidently, these kings knew how to act out war. Wolsey was determined that the Field of Cloth of Gold should teach all princes anew how to enact peace.

One European sovereign who Wolsey was most anxious should learn this lesson of glamorous peace-making was Charles, King of Aragon. He was the grandson of Ferdinand of Aragon and of the Habsburg Holy Roman Emperor, Maximilian. In June 1519, Charles was elected emperor in succession to his grandfather. Born in 1500, Charles was younger than either Henry or Francis and was still in the process of acquiring that immense collection of kingships and lordships in Germany, Austria and elsewhere that would finally constitute his empire at its widest extent. For ease of exposition in what follows, however, he will be referred to by his highest dignity as Emperor Charles V.[10] Francis I and Charles V were keen rivals with many territorial claims against each other. Between them there was already deep and lasting suspicion and hostility, quite different from the ambivalence between Francis and Henry. This hostility was widely known throughout Europe, not least at the English court. Although by his marriage to Katherine of Aragon, Henry was Charles's uncle, he barely knew the younger man. For his part, Charles was happy to style himself 'nephew' in correspondence, but had hitherto paid only formal respects to his English relative. Charles was, however, genuinely alarmed at the Anglo-French reconciliation under the treaty of London and was extremely anxious about the proposed meeting. He was deter-mined to wreck it if at all possible or, failing that, to make the other two kings take proper account of him and do nothing together to his prejudice. Knowing that the emperor's participation was vital to the success of the Universal Peace, Wolsey encouraged friendship between Henry and Charles as much as between Henry and Francis. While he could not prevent the Field, Charles ensured that he met Henry immediately before and after it. Throughout its duration, Charles remained within his Flemish territories, a little more than a day's ride from the scenes of luxury at Guînes and Ardres. His near presence effectively turned what was originally conceived as a meeting between two new allies into a tense encounter between three rivals.

As all these protagonists understood, one ruler could conduct a generous and equal friendship with another only if he had sufficient personal and material resources. Both Francis and Henry were determined that they should not be seen as inferior to their rival. The words and actions with which they interacted, either directly or through their courtiers, at the event were expressions of each man's sense of his own honour and 'their need continually to be acknowledged as honourable by fellow nobles', that is, each other.[11] The stakes were high for both kings and with so many of their subjects involved, there was a palpable sense of excitement, but also danger, at the Field. Strict security arrangements were put in place by both sides to guard the two royal families. The very tight protocols agreed for every aspect of the Field were designed to reduce the potential for embarrassment, or worse, to be inflicted by one side upon the other. Tensions reached fever pitch in the days and hours immediately before the kings' first meeting on 7 June and barely subsided thereafter.

Kings were seen to be at their strongest and safest when in the midst of an impressive entourage. Each monarch eventually brought with him a retinue of around 6,000 people. The royal court was the institution designed to protect and display the king to his people and to his fellow sovereigns in ways that would compel acknowledgement of his honour. This, and the fact that the Field was a tournament, meant that it fell to high-ranking court and army officers to prepare and conduct it. French participation was overseen by Gaspard de Coligny, seigneur de Châtillon.

As a Marshal of France and a knight of the Order of St Michael, Châtillon was one of France's most senior military commanders. He was commissioned to agree with the English representatives a place for the initial meeting of the kings and a site for the construction of lists for the projected tournament, and to oversee preparations to lodge Francis I and his court at Ardres.[12]

The English preparations were entrusted to a team headed by Charles Somerset, Earl of Worcester. Born Charles Beaufort in about 1460, Worcester became Lord Chamberlain in 1508. He fought in the war in France in 1513 and was made earl in February 1514. In October the same year he escorted Mary Tudor to France for her marriage to Louis XII. Four years later, he received Francis I's ratification of the Universal Peace. Worcester's status and recent experience in France made him the ideal man to arrange the meeting.[13] Worcester was assisted by three men who arrived in Calais on 17 March 1520, nine days before Francis formally ratified an agreement to meet Henry. They were Sir Edward Belknap, Sir Nicholas Vaux and Sir William Sandys.[14] All three were experienced administrators and soldiers who had served Henry VII in various capacities and gone on to senior positions under Henry VIII. Sir Edward Belknap had been Surveyor of Crown Lands and Master of Wards since 1514.[15] Sir Nicholas Vaux was Lieutenant of Guînes in 1520. He had participated in the 1518 ratification embassy to France.[16] Sir William Sandys had been Treasurer of Calais since October 1517. At the king's command, he worked with Wolsey at the Calais conference of 1521. In April 1523 he was made Baron Sandys. Three years later, he succeeded the earl of Worcester as Lord Chamberlain and exchanged the treasurership of Calais for the lieutenancy of Guînes. He is principally known for his fine manor house, 'the Vyne', near Basingstoke where the king visited him several times.[17]

The Field of Cloth of Gold set the tone for Anglo-French relations for the remainder of the reigns of Henry VIII and Francis I. During long periods in the 1520s and 1530s the rivalry between them was, paradoxically, expressed in extravagant demonstrations of 'peace-making' and of royal brotherhood. From Henry's initial point of view it seemed that the

Field of Cloth had worked like a charm. After some years of political isolation, he was now allied to the two most powerful monarchs of Western Europe. He held the balance, or perhaps more accurately the imbalance, of power between them. Both Francis and Charles appeared respectful of his potential as an ally and the leader of a Europe-wide non-aggression compact. In championing Christian peace, Henry appeared at his strongest and seemed to have everybody where he wanted them. But this was something of a hope-filled delusion. For all their rivalry and suspicion, Henry and Francis did not lack peaceful intentions towards each other, but the emerging power of Charles V threatened to make a lasting equilibrium between them virtually impossible. This was because it was all too likely that, in pursuit of claims against each other, the king of France or Charles would take it into his head to test Henry's capacity to maintain the Universal Peace. This is, of course, exactly what both of them immediately proceeded to do, with profound and destructive consequences for the harmony of Christendom.

All that lay in the future. In the summer of 1520 the kings of England and France were intent upon making dramatic gestures and statements to show that they were exceptionally great kings. They sought thereby to secure the loyalty and affection of their own subjects and the respect and co-operation of their rivals. This approval and this respect were their greatest sources of security and energy and the intense desire for them resulted in the extraordinary display of human and material resources mounted between Ardres and Guînes at the Field of Cloth of Gold.

CHAPTER 1

European War and 'Universal Peace'

The two kings,
Equal in lustre were now best, now worst
As presence did present them; him in eye,
Still him in praise; and being present both
Twas said they saw but one, and no discerner
Durst wag his tongue in censure.
HENRY *VIII* ACT I, sc. I

THUS WILLIAM SHAKESPEARE evoked the spirit of the Field of Cloth of Gold. By the time they met, Henry VIII and Francis I had already done a great deal to gain reputations as exceptional monarchs. They had frequently compared themselves with each other and had, themselves, been compared by others. The Venetian ambassador Niccolò Sagudino, spoke for many. Writing from England in 1515 shortly after arriving there from the court of France, Sagudino had observed:

> The like of two such courts and two such kings as those of France and England, have, I fancy, not been witnessed by any ambassadors who have gone out of Venice these past fifty years.[1]

Sagudino saw both men at close quarters and clearly thought them exceptional because of the compelling image each projected. Since their earliest years, both men had been imbued with the glamour of chivalric kingship. Each was a young, charismatic male at the head of a strongly patriarchal and militaristic elite. Their awareness of each other developed into an intense personal rivalry. It is with the context of that rivalry firmly in mind that their meeting in 1520 is best understood.

Henry had succeeded his father Henry VII on 21 April 1509. His accession was greeted with a mixture of carefully choreographed ritual and spontaneous public rejoicing. One of his first decisions was to marry Katherine of Aragon. After their wedding on 11 June, they were crowned together on 24 June 1509. Henry inherited a kingdom at peace. Although he did his best publicly to distance himself from his father's unpopular regime, Henry certainly benefited from it. Henry VII had quietened, if not entirely removed, the competitive ambitions among the nobles of England that had marked the Wars of the Roses. The most recent estimates are that at his death, his annual income was between £100,000 and £110,000.[2] This wealth, though modest by Continental royal standards, had been safeguarded in part by Henry VII's avoidance of war and his conduct of financially successful diplomacy with France.[3]

Henry VIII's attitude to France differed from his father's. He determined immediately to emulate the deeds of Edward III, of Edward the Black Prince and of Henry V. These predecessors seemed to incarnate an ideal of heroic kingship that appealed strongly to him. To Henry's youthful and conservative cast of mind, this meant nothing less than renewing the Hundred Years War with France. From the outset, he made no secret of his bellicose ambition. His coronation procession displayed his territorial claims in France more explicitly than had the coronations of his father or Richard III before him. He impressed the Venetian ambassadors who had come to congratulate him on his accession as already being a great enemy of the French.[4]

Somewhat frustrated by his council's more pacific instincts, the king continued to hone the martial skills first developed in him as a boy and otherwise busied himself in the 'pastyme with good company' of which he wrote in song. Day succeeded day in an apparently endless round of banquets, disguisings, music-making and hunting. As the chronicler Edward Hall's many descriptions of him attest, Henry's physical and sporting prowess as a young man had impressed observers at his father's court.[5] Henry was 6 feet 2 inches tall, physically strong and ideally suited to the paramilitary sports of hunting and archery at which he excelled. He loved the competitions of the tournament – although he did not joust until *after* he became king. He was also a very enthusiastic and athletic dancer, performing no less dramatically in the banqueting hall than he did on the tournament ground. The Venetian ambassador Giustinian summarised the 29-year-old king's talents and demeanour thus:

> He was very fair, and his whole frame admirably proportioned. Hearing that King Francis wore a beard, he allowed his own to grow, and as it was reddish, he had then got a beard which looked like gold. He was very accomplished and a good musician; composed well; was a capital horseman, and a fine jouster; spoke good French, Latin, and Spanish; was very religious; heard three masses daily when he hunted, and sometimes five on other days, besides hearing the office daily in the Queen's chamber, that is to say, vespers and compline. He was extremely fond of hunting, and never took that diversion without tiring eight or ten horses, which he caused to be stationed before-hand along the line of country he meant to take. He was also fond of tennis, at which game it was the prettiest thing in the world to see him play; his fair skin glowing through a shirt of the finest texture. He gambled with the French hostages to the amount, occasionally, it was said, of from 6,000 to 8,000 ducats in a day.[6]

The ambassador's emphasis on the king's physicality and handsomeness would have pleased Henry deeply. He lost no opportunity to demonstrate his strength in order to impress and intimidate his courtiers, female and male alike, and to reassure them that he had the makings of a fine king. Henry's height and strength seemed to prove his aptness to lead other men, not just on the tournament field but, when the time came, in war against England's ancient enemy.

On New Year's Day 1511 Queen Katherine gave birth to her first child, Prince Henry. The king and queen were ecstatic – the realm no less so. Siring a male heir apparently proved Henry's fertility and fulfilled one of the first duties of a king. It also demonstrated his potential to have yet more children by whom the succession would be further secured. Extravagant celebrations followed, including a tournament at Westminster at which Henry, as the proud father and husband, jousted as 'Sir Loyal Heart'. Henry's display of his athletic talents to celebrate the getting of a male heir was no accident. His prowess in one activity evoked his success in the other. Both achievements attracted the admiration and approval of his nobles and of foreign ambassadors. The 'Great Tournament Roll of Westminster' recorded this occasion. Lavishly illuminated, the roll depicts the king charging down the lists in full armour – the very incarnation of the dashing knight. It remains *the* iconic image of the young Henry to set against the more famous Holbein portrait of his later years. Sadly for Henry and significantly for English history, Prince Henry died barely six weeks after his birth.[7]

As Thomas Wolsey rose to prominence, he progressively relieved the king of much of the tedium of government with which the older generation of councillors had tried to saddle him. It was in no small measure due to the king's almoner that Henry's enjoyment of sports and games in the 'summer sun' of his own accession was so prolonged. With Wolsey's help, he eventually overcame the objections of his own council to war. In October 1511, following a series of disputes between himself and Louis XII of France, Pope Julius II formed a Holy League against France which Henry promptly joined. In March 1512, Julius excommunicated Louis, recognised Henry as king of France and spoke privately of crowning him at Paris. The following month Lancaster Herald defied Louis in Henry's name. Yet, for all his preparations and personal bravado, Henry's first attempt at Continental warfare in a joint invasion of Gascony in alliance with Ferdinand of Aragon was little short of disastrous. Fortunately for him, the Holy Roman Emperor Maximilian soon also declared war on Louis. The spring of 1513 saw naval action off the Breton coast and Henry spent the summer on active campaign in command of a well-equipped army, the like of which had not been seen in France for sixty years.[8] The English invasion did not culminate in another Agincourt, but Henry did take the town of Thérouanne and the city of Tournai. On the morning of 16 August, during the siege of Thérouanne, Henry's forces won the only recognised battle of the campaign, a cavalry skirmish at Guinegatte, known as the 'Battle of Spurs'. Henry celebrated his debut with banquets and jousts following a triumphal entry to Tournai in September. Wolsey, who had masterminded the turn to war and then acted as quartermaster-general for the English army, was rewarded with nomination as bishop both of Tournai and Lincoln.

Unfortunately for Henry's plans, in the opening months of 1514 Louis XII was reconciled to the newly elected Pope Leo X, who accepted him as legitimate king of France. This removed Henry's principal cause for war. Louis quickly made peace with Henry's two allies, leaving him effectively isolated once more in Europe. Although galled at this duplicity, he had no option but to accept initiatives for peace from France opened by Louis d'Orléans, duc de Longueville, then in England, a prisoner of the 1513 campaign.[9]

The only direct evidence we have of Henry's attitude to peace with France in 1514 is contained in a letter which he sent to Wolsey describing the audience he gave to Louis d'Orléans. This interview may justly be described as the most important that Henry ever gave to a representative of the French king because it was an important precedent for the 1518 treaty of London, and thus the Field of Cloth of Gold. The desire for recognition by his fellow princes had driven him to attack France in the first place and now peace with France would have to achieve the same thing. Henry demanded that Louis should publicly acknowledge his claim to the French crown by paying him a yearly 'tribute' of 100,000 crowns. He had also to acknowledge Henry's military success, its costs and his subsequent magnanimity in stopping the war.[10]

All this was agreed under the treaty of London signed in August 1514. The treaty of peace and alliance was secured by Louis XII's marriage to Henry's younger sister, Mary. Louis still had no son with whom to secure the succession and so the prospect of marriage to a young English princess already renowned for her beauty doubly delighted him.[11] The peace settlement of 1514 and the grand embassy which escorted Mary to France in October that year became the models for future contacts between the courts of England and France. It became a dialogue about making peace between two quasi-feudal elites, conducted in the language of international brotherhood and chivalry, but whose theme was intense competition between French and English courtiers, focused on the persons of the two sovereigns. This competitive spirit directly anticipates that of the Field of Cloth of Gold.[12] As one Venetian observer reported:

> In truth the pomp of the English was as grand and costly as words can express; and the princes and nobles of France, and the ladies likewise vied with them for the whole French court sparkles with jewels, gold and brocade.[13]

The French nobleman charged with meeting this impressive English embassy and marshalling the grandeur of the French court in response was none other than the future king, Francis, Duke of Brittany. He spent huge sums on his personal adornment for receptions to meet Mary and escorted the English princess to her wedding to Louis XII at Abbeville on 9 October 1514.[14] He attended her at her coronation at Saint-Denis and at her formal entry to Paris as Queen of France. Francis also hosted the tournament held there in Mary's honour. Louis showed scant gratitude for these efforts, saying of Francis more than once, 'this big boy will ruin everything'.[15] The marriage might indeed have proved disastrous to Francis's hopes of the crown. Instead, within just a few months, it was Henry's hopes of dominating the French king in this alliance that were ruined when the news reached England that Louis was dead.

Like Henry, Francis had been educated and cared for as a young boy by strong women. Francis's mother, Louise de Savoie, had taught him to read and write his own language (which he always admired), together with Italian and some Spanish. He was also very close to his older sister Marguerite and the three of them were said by contemporaries to form a kind of 'trinity'.[16] As an adult he was certainly regarded as well read and capable of intelligent discourse. He appreciated the talents of humanist scholars and became an assiduous collector of Greek and Latin manuscript and printed texts.

At the age of fourteen, Francis had moved to the royal court where his apparent good looks and ease of manner secured admirers. He was praised in Castiglione's *Book of the Courtier* as the embodiment of French nobility and the hope for its future. Magnifico Giuliano says of him:

> ...for it is not long since I, being at court, saw this prince, and it seemed to me that besides his handsome looks, there was such an air of greatness about him, accompanied, however, with a certain gracious humanity, that the kingdom of France on its own must always seem limited for him. And subsequently from many gentlemen, both French and Italian, I heard a great deal in praise of his noble courtesy, his magnanimity, his valour and his generous spirit; and among other things was told that he greatly loved and esteemed learning and respected all men of letters and that he condemned the French themselves for being so hostile to this profession, especially as they have in their midst as magnificent a university as Paris, where people flock from all over the world.[17]

In 1512 Francis had formally commanded the French army sent to meet the English invasion in the south-west and he was charged with the recovery of Navarre. Being young, however, Francis was escorted by the actual commander, Odet de Foix, seigneur de Lautrec with whom he gained his first military experience. Though the campaign ended in failure, a medal was struck bearing his effigy with the words *MAXIMUS FRANCISCUS FRANCORUM DUX 1512*. In 1513 Francis was once again in the field against the English, in defence of Thérouanne and his banner was one of those captured at the Battle of the Spurs although he did not himself participate in it.

In May 1514, Francis had married Louis XII's daughter, Claude de France, and was thereafter openly acknowledged as Louis's heir presumptive with the courtesy title of 'Dauphin'. It was in the course of hosting Mary Tudor that the young French duke first properly came to the attention of Henry VIII and his advisors. He did so in such glowing terms as to lay the foundations in Henry's mind for a lifelong rivalry with Francis. As the duke of Norfolk wrote of him to Wolsey in November 1514:

> Here is nothing done but the said duke is made privy and doer thereof by the French king's commandment ... My lord, I assure you this prince can speak well and wisely.[18]

Francis was of an equivalent height and physical strength to Henry. Hall's *Chronicle* describes him at the Field of Cloth of Gold as being: 'a goodly Prince, stately of countenance, merry of cheer, brown coloured, great eyes, high nosed, big lipped, fair breasted and shoulders, small [i.e. thin] legs, and long feet'.[19]

Francis's accession at the age of 20 on the morning of 1 January 1515 was greeted by the nobility of France with exactly the same kind of jubilation that five years earlier had greeted Henry's accession in England. Francis was crowned at Reims on 25 January 1515 and acclaimed by the ecclesiastical and lay peers of the realm. He made his formal entry to Paris as sovereign on 15 February.[20] Blessed with a relatively stable and prosperous kingdom, the new sovereign was determined from the outset to rule as well as to reign. Prominently presented on his entry to Paris was Francis's personal badge, the salamander amidst flames, and his motto, *Nutrisco et extinguo*. According to Ovid, the salamander could live in fire and also extinguish it. This device and motto had a double meaning: 'I am nourished by flames and I extinguish them' and 'I nourish good and extinguish evil'. The symbol was designed to show that the new king was of a passionate nature, that he would sustain his friends and his kingdom, that he could endure adversity and would overcome his enemies. More widely, the propaganda favoured by the new regime emphasised, on the one hand, legitimacy and political stability at home, manifested in orderly government; and, on the other, youthful vigour focused on the king, expressed through chivalrous display and channelled outwards towards the goal of a reinvigorated political nation.[21]

Francis I's monarchy was to be as personal in style, as much a 'kingship of participation', as that of his English counterpart. He was keen to hunt, to feast and to make plans for war. Like Henry, Francis showed little interest in the dull mundanities of government and sat for only a short time each day with his council, but he was not as much in thrall to his predecessor as Henry had been. As 'Dauphin' from 1514, Francis had served a brief apprenticeship in government even if, as some at the time noted, his mother's predominant tutelage over him continued unabated into the first years of his reign. Nevertheless, far more quickly than Henry, Francis began setting his own agenda.[22] His primary ambition was to make his name as a great French monarch by securing the dynastic claims of all his predecessors. In practice this meant, first and foremost, taking the duchy of Milan, whose Orléanist duke Francis claimed to be in his own right and as Louis XII's successor.[23] He also inherited Charles VIII's claim to the kingdom of Naples, which included Sicily and most of southern Italy. Francis also had claims to certain territories along the permeable border between France, the Netherlands and the Empire. In July 1515 a Holy League was formed between the pope, the duke of Milan, Ferdinand of Aragon and Emperor Maximilian to defend the Italian states from him.

Henry used every means possible to attract attention to himself as a potential opponent to the new French king. He was fiercely determined to sustain his place as Europe's most illustrious, if no longer youngest, sovereign. Henry contributed money to pay for Swiss mercenaries taken on by the emperor to oppose any French move into Milan. Yet behind his bravado lay the king's gnawing anxiety that the new French monarch would isolate him once more in Europe. The Venetian ambassadors recognised this anxiety and understood that Francis was the real audience for Henry's display of his horsemanship, and even of his legs, to which he famously treated them. This is clear from their description of Henry jousting strenuously at the May Day tournament in 1515:

more particularly on account of Pasqualigo (who is returning to France today), that he may be able to tell King Francis what he has seen in England, and especially with regard to his Majesty's own prowess.[24]

So far as they could, Henry's demonstrations of his physical skills got the desired reaction. Francis did take notice of Henry's potential and even admired him personally, but he never let the king of England stop him making his own name internationally. In striking contrast to Henry's long-postponed debut as a warrior king, Francis achieved his first aim with remarkable speed and élan. In the summer of 1515, barely seven months after his accession, he led a royal army of some 23,000 infantry, cavalry and a huge artillery train, over the Alps into the Italian duchy of Milan.[25] At the Battle of Marignano on 14 September 1515, Francis led his mounted heavy cavalry, the *gendarmerie*, to victory over a mercenary Swiss army hired by Duke Massimiliano Sforza to defend his duchy. A few days later, Francis entered Milan as its victorious conqueror and new duke.

The news of Francis's military success spread through Europe like wildfire. Such a spectacular military debut seemed to lay everything at the feet of the dashing young Frenchman. Francis stayed in Italy for the remainder of 1515, sought by Italian princes, all eager to ingratiate themselves with Europe's new *wunderkind*. Francis, who loved all things Italian, was delighted to receive them and took many Italian courtiers and guests into his entourage, including Sforza, the former duke of Milan, and Federigo Gonzaga, the future duke of Mantua and ally of Charles V. Their presence further heightened the reputation of Francis's court as the new centre of international exchange and patronage.

By the end of 1515, the papal coalition against Francis disintegrated and Leo X came to Bologna to meet the French king, and agree a Concordat formally confirmed the following year. Francis's over-whelming victory made him the foremost military leader of the time and Pope Leo obtained a promise that he would make war on the Ottoman Sultan once he had secured the succession with the birth of a son.[26] The political mood in the north-west corner of Europe was rather less sunny than that south of the Alps. Henry VIII was utterly furious. He was reportedly close to tears when a French envoy brought him news, not just of Francis's overwhelming victory, but of the king's personal leadership of the elite of his army in the heat of the action – exactly what Henry had craved in 1513 but never achieved.

The 1518 Treaty of London:
the Prelude to the Field of Cloth of Gold

On 11 March 1517, Francis agreed to the treaty of Cambrai with Charles of Aragon and the Emperor Maximilian, by which they all promised to assist each other if any one of them was attacked. Once more, Henry was left isolated. In order to overcome this, he and Wolsey promoted various anti-French schemes and on 5 July 1517 agreed a league between Henry, Charles and Maximilian designed to nullify the Cambrai league. It was celebrated in London with tournaments and extravagant banquets.[27] By late 1517, Wolsey had been informed of Pope Leo's plans for an international truce as a prelude to a crusade against the Ottomans. His quick intelligence saw that a high-profile Anglo-French alliance, which was also the linchpin of an international league and peace, might be a more effective way of restraining Francis than a more conventional bilateral agreement. Better still, if it could be arranged, Henry's de facto leadership of the whole enterprise would catapult him back to centre stage in European affairs and displace Francis from the triumphant position he had enjoyed since Marignano. It was an article of faith upon which Wolsey's meteoric rise was based that what was good for the king was good for the cardinal, and so wresting control of the implementation of the Universal Peace agreement and placing it under Henry's aegis became the driving force in Wolsey's conduct of England's international relations.[28]

In March 1518 Normandy Herald arrived in England to announce the birth of the Dauphin François. By his recently affirmed promise to the pope at least, Francis was now committed to war against the Ottomans.[29] Henry was gracious yet restrained in his congratulations, but Wolsey saw this news as a providential endorsement of his plans once more to unite England and France under a Universal Peace. The English had found the city of Tournai expensive to maintain and of limited strategic use. Since his accession, Francis had wanted to regain the city lost under Louis XII. Its sale to the French and the marriage of the dauphin to Henry's two-year-old daughter Mary therefore became the focus of negotiations during the early summer of 1518 between Wolsey and the representatives of the king of France.[30] Sebastian Giustinian, the Venetian ambassador in England in 1518, reported his response to Cardinal Wolsey's assurance that he would unite England and France once more in a marriage alliance:

> I lauded this excellent project, and told him he could do nothing more glorious in the world, or that could add greater splendour to his eminent qualities than in the midst of such great strife amongst princes to prove himself the *lapis angularis* which joined the two detached walls of the temple.[31]

A renewed alliance, the French re-purchase of Tournai and the marriage agreement formed the basis of the Anglo-French alliance which was finally concluded, subject to final royal approval, by 22 July.[32] It also provided that Francis and Henry should meet personally.

No sooner had that agreement been reached than Wolsey began pressing for France's inclusion in his plans for a proposed multilateral alliance. Initially, Francis gave no more than limited and conventional support to the idea.[33] As negotiations continued in England, however, and as the scale of the project became clearer, Francis became increasingly enthusiastic about the idea of an international non-aggression pact. In some ways this may seem surprising. On the one hand an alliance with England and the return of Tournai were both welcome developments that Francis had been seeking since 1515. On the other hand, such a dramatic restructuring of alliances threatened to disturb the 1517 status quo, which was decidedly in his favour. Of course this was exactly what Wolsey intended but Francis had his own ideas.[34]

As early as 1516 the French king had made agreements with the arch-bishops of Trier and Mainz, two of the Electors of the Holy Roman Empire, that when Emperor Maximilian died they would vote for Francis to succeed him as elected ruler of the German peoples. In June 1517 the margrave of Brandenburg also agreed to vote for him and the Elector Palatine followed suit. As a result, by early 1518, Francis felt he could make a plausible claim on the Empire. In these circumstances, a leading role in the enterprise of international peace of the kind Wolsey was engi-neering for him suited Francis's purposes rather well. Then at the Diet of Augsburg in August 1518, Emperor Maximilian secured the promises of five Electors for his grandson Charles.[35] Faced with such competition, Francis anticipated that Henry's political (and perhaps financial) support might prove useful and might also bring papal support in its wake. Alternatively, any prospect of Henry joining a new Habsburg emperor against him threatened a return to the bad old days of 1513. Accordingly, Francis instructed his ambassadors to co-operate fully with Wolsey and to assure the cardinal of his trust.[36] He began putting together a magnifi-cent embassy, designed to impress Henry with the calibre of his kingship and the value of his friendship. He was doing in 1518 exactly what Henry had done four years earlier when his sister had been sent to France.

William Sandys, the governor of Calais, received the great French embassy in the town, from where it crossed the Narrow Sea to England. He told Wolsey that he thought 'the very purpose and intent of their coming is for good . . . and as goodly and well appointed company they be as I think ever was sent to any prince'. After a false start on 14 September due to contrary winds, the French delegation, led by Admiral Guillaume de Bonnivet, arrived on the English coast on 18 September.[37]

Thomas Howard, Earl of Surrey, accompanied by 160 gentlemen, met the French embassy at Blackheath on 23 September. Each of the French gentlemen was matched by an Englishman of equivalent status and, as Hall reports, they 'accoupled themselves with the Frenchmen lovingly together, and so rode to London'.[38] Prominent among the members of the embassy were the young *gentilshommes de la chambre*, the personal friends and body servants of Francis. Their status at the French court presented an immediate challenge to Henry and Wolsey because each of them had to be entertained as generously as possible. The chief ambassadors were accommodated at the Merchant Taylors' Hall and the remainder in neighbouring merchants' houses.[39] No sooner had the great embassy arrived in London than its leaders received urgent instructions from Francis. He had received further promises of support from certain Electors, 'principally, Monsieur the marquis of Brandenburg'. Francis ordered the ambassadors to keep him informed of events in London and to assure Wolsey of his full co-operation.[40]

Dressed as splendidly as one Venetian envoy had ever seen him, Henry formally received the French ambassadors at Greenwich on 26 September and greeted them individually, a process which took some fifteen minutes.[41] Over the following month, the king displayed the kind of ostentatious and self-regarding generosity which quickly became the hallmark of his dealings with Francis and his representatives. On 2 October the treaty of London was sworn to by its signatories and the Anglo-French alliance followed suit in the days after. The dauphin was betrothed to Princess Mary on Tuesday 5 October and this was celebrated two days later with a tournament and a banquet at Greenwich. The centrepiece of the entertainment was a pageant featuring a rock planted with the symbolic flowers of the European dynasties and on which were masquers dressed in some exotic fashion. At the top sat a young woman holding a dolphin in her lap – an obvious allusion to Mary's betrothal and thus the alliance with France. The rock opened to reveal knights who fought a tournament against a group of 'Turks', before those on the rock descended and danced a masque. A figure called 'Reaport' explained the pageant as a presentation of Henry's greatness as the protector of the Universal Peace.[42]

The same message had been delivered more explicitly during High Mass on 3 October at which the Universal Peace was spiritually inaugurated. It was celebrated by Cardinal Wolsey with all possible solemnity and the royal secretary, Richard Pace, delivered an oration. Entitled *Oratio Ricardi Pacei in pace nuperrime composita et foedere percusso*, the oration was immediately printed by the king's printer, Richard Pynson.[43]

By December 1518 the Latin text and an anonymous French translation had been printed in Paris by Jean Gourmont.[44] At first sight, Pace's oration seems a rather conventional Christian humanist praise of peace, of a kind that Erasmus would have endorsed.[45] When one looks closer, however, it is really nothing of the kind. Pace's oration is actually a lecture to the French in general, and Francis I in particular, about the roles of peace and war within effective and honourable kingship. Pace's primary concern is not to flatter Henry into deciding that peace with France is a more honourable alternative than war, as first appears. He praises Henry as a ruler who loves peace but who is not afraid of war. Henry is also presented as a highly educated and highly religious monarch, who understands that the keeping of good faith between kings is essential:

> for if faith be kept inviolably – and this is what a treaty entered into and struck in holiness most ensures – it removes all dissension and discord, and all tearful and ruinous war.[46]

After expatiating on the horrors of war and deploring the cruel ingenuity of contemporary warfare, Pace lauds Henry as the instigator and Wolsey as the designer of the Universal Peace. He declares that Henry is an expert tactician and a brave warrior. Far from being embarrassed by Henry's bellicose nature, he recalls 'how gloriously and marvellously' the king conducted himself in the war of 1513 and goes on to reflect that nature herself has fashioned Henry as a consummate general. The king's masculine virtues of bravery and skill are evidenced in his body:

> He who looks closely upon you cannot but see that the beauty of your splendid body, the incomparable aptness and compactness of your limbs, all breathe war: you are tall, brave, active, powerful, and so strong that you leave far behind all who seek to display their bodily strength in earnest or in play.[47]

For Pace, Henry's prowess is proof of his masculine nature and therefore of reliability. It demands an equal response from Francis if he wishes to

secure Henry's friendship and thus avoid war. Not only is Henry personally famous, but so too is his 'warlike nation'. From this position of
apparent strength, Henry chooses peace as proof of his real power and
status. In so doing he has provided the means for an effective opposition
to the Ottomans. Other princes, chiefly Francis, now also recognise
Henry's qualities and seek to join the League.[48] For Pace, Henry's kingship is already of such a compelling and authentic kind that he is equally
honourable whether he is at peace or at war. Both options are open to
him. The sign of Henry's honour is his faithfulness. As noted above, the
speech begins by emphasising princely fidelity. Pace returns to this
theme throughout his remarks and towards the end of the oration sets
out in order of importance the three things being sworn to at the Mass.
These are:

> To the treaty, that it shall be entered into in holiness;
> To faith, that it shall be sincere and inviolable;
> To peace, that it shall be perpetual – that is, not only shall all war be
> removed but suspicion of any war shall totally be taken away.[49]

In other words, peace is not an end in itself; it is the fortunate consequence of honouring treaties. Pace ends with an exhortation to both
kings: 'look to the giving and taking of your faith', he tells them,
'persuade yourself that nothing can be more alien from great princes
than to violate their faith'.[50] Perhaps Pace is, in true Erasmian humanist
style, pleading with Henry to keep his promise and maintain peace.
More likely, however, he is stating that Henry will honour his word and
that he has given himself greater freedom against France. If Francis
breaks the treaty, Henry's universally acknowledged intelligence and
military potential will allow him to bring moral and military force to
bear on France, just as he did in 1513.

Every attempt by Henry to impose himself on Europe during the
previous ten years had been thwarted by agreements dishonoured by his
ostensible allies. These broken pledges had cost him dearly in money
and prestige. Pace, who was no pacifist Francophile, had spent two of

the three previous years engaged in complex negotiations with Emperor Maximilian, Ferdinand of Aragon, the Venetians and the Swiss. All of these talks had come to nothing.[51] Now, thanks to Wolsey, the king was where his virtue demanded he should be – at the head of the international community. At heart, Pace's oration is a forceful assertion of Henry's personal and moral superiority over Francis, a warning to the French against discounting the significance of the treaty of Universal Peace and challenging the new status quo.

Francis knew well enough that the embassy that Henry would send to receive his ratification of French inclusion in the Universal Peace would be as splendid as possible. He prepared to meet the challenge. This embassy was led by the earl of Worcester.[52] He was accompanied by Bishop Nicholas West of Ely and Sir Thomas Docwra, Prior of the Knights of St John of Jerusalem. The latter's inclusion emphasised the fact that, in theory at least, the European peace presaged an anti-Ottoman campaign. The total party numbered some 400 and included several of Henry's close personal friends, the equivalents of the young men sent to England by Francis. The embassy left England on 27 November and travelled by stages to Paris, receiving conspicuous hospitality at every point. As Worcester told Wolsey, at Amiens the seigneur d'Orval invited them to stay a day longer than planned on Francis's orders because:

> The king's highness and your Grace had made them so [much] cheer
> in England, that he would in no wise we should pass [any] town
> within his realm but we were honourably feasted.[53]

A more mundane explanation may be that the court in Paris needed more time to complete its preparations. Francis received the English ambassadors in the richly decorated Salle Saint-Louis in the Louvre, embracing each of the English gentlemen 'in acknowledgement of a similar compliment paid by the king of England to the French courtiers at Greenwich'. Two days later he swore to maintain the treaty of Universal Peace and the espousal ceremony for Mary and the Dauphin François took place on 16 December.

The spirit of competition between Francis and Henry as to who would be the best guarantor of European peace was expressed in an oration which may have been given at that ceremony and which was, in effect, the French counterpart to Richard Pace's oration at St Paul's in October. Written by Bernardino Rincio, a Milanese physician and philosopher at the French court, the *Oraison en La Louenge du marriage de Monsieur le Dauphin de Gaulles* is an important indication of how Francis's participation in the Universal Peace was explained in France.[54] Like Pace's speech, the *Oraison* is ostensibly about peace but ascribes to Francis the same kind of warrior qualities with which Pace had credited Henry. Francis's recent conquest of Milan is compared to the deeds of Scipio, Caesar and Alexander, but it also demonstrates the king's magnanimity as conqueror. Much of the *Oraison* then conjures up the frightening 'domino theory' of continued Ottoman advance before reintroducing Francis as the one king in Europe who has the courage, proven ability and resources to fight back. It notes that it was on 7 December that Francis had accepted from the papal legate to France, Cardinal Bibbiena, leadership of the enterprise to regain the sacred city of Jerusalem.[55] In other words, the events in London in the autumn were really only the prelude to the main event which would see Francis unite in his person the imperial heritage of Rome with the French national tradition of defence of the Catholic faith.[56]

The same message was delivered at the most spectacular entertainment Francis offered to the English ambassadors during their stay in Paris. This was a banquet held in a specially constructed theatre in the Bastille on the night of the winter solstice. The whole event was executed as a propaganda piece that celebrated the achievements and potential of Francis's reign.[57] A description was published immediately afterwards. The design of the temporary banqueting house built in the central courtyard of the old fortress was deliberately designed to invoke a classical temple or arena. The whole area of the inner courtyard had been covered with a canvas roof, under which hung an azure blue ceiling or 'sky' decorated with a constellation signifying 'great happiness for the present and time to come'.[58] At the moment of the setting of the sun on the shortest day of the year, the king entered the banqueting hall. As he did so, 600 torches were lit 'which banished the night . . . in the way that the king at his joyous advent had joined the night with the day'. He was a sun king, whose advent banished the darkness of the winter evening, just as his rule apparently brought light, warmth and prosperity to France and to the whole of Christendom.[59]

The spectacular embassies and receptions of late 1518 are best seen as the conscious preludes to the Field of Cloth of Gold itself. At the time when they were hosted it was expected that the two kings would meet in little more than six months' time, during the summer of 1519. In this context, each side did its best to impress the other and claim the high strategic and moral ground in the rivalry between the two kings.

Francis and Henry did not meet in 1519 after all. This was largely because in January that year Emperor Maximilian died. This prompted the long-anticipated imperial election in which both kings were candidates. In these circumstances, there was no real appetite for an immediate meeting. They did, however, exchange resident ambassadors for the first time. The first resident French ambassador in England was Olivier de la Vernade, seigneur de La Bastie, who arrived in London in February 1519.[60] Sir Thomas Boleyn, the father of Anne, was appointed to the equivalent position at the French court the same month. Working in concert with Wolsey, Boleyn helped to facilitate the return of Tournai to the French. Certain formalities of exchange were insisted upon by the English, whereby they wanted the French to acknowledge the city's return as a gesture of royal magnanimity to an ally. Nevertheless, its return to French hands was a genuine achievement for Francis as a warrior king and protector of his realm. It was also, in effect, the precondition for his willingness to meet Henry in person. The transfer took place in February 1519 after a number of disputes had arisen about the status of the French hostages that Henry was to hold against Francis's full payment for Tournai. On 8 February 1519, the English commissioners acknowledged receipt of the first instalment of 26,315 *livres*, 30 *sous tournois* as part payment of the full price of 600,000 *écus* or crowns.[61]

As the transfer of Tournai proceeded, the pace of the imperial electoral race quickened. When Sir Thomas Boleyn arrived at the French court as English ambassador, Francis greeted him effusively, complimenting Henry on the hospitality shown to his friends sent to England the previous autumn and saying that it had inspired his own efforts in entertaining the English delegation. This flattery contained a kernel of truth, but it was primarily designed to remind Boleyn and Henry of Francis's recent co-operation in establishing the Universal Peace. He then assured Boleyn that in the imperial election he already had the votes of four Electors and hoped for those of two more. Francis had sent Admiral Bonnivet to Germany and, as Boleyn reported, 'practises what he can . . . to win them by any means'. Francis thought that Henry should declare his support, considering 'he is advertised [that] your highness will help and aid him in this matter . . . as your grace pretends not to it yourself, as his ambassador [writes] to him'.[62] Francis knew well enough that Henry also 'pretended' to the imperial throne. By late March 1519 Boleyn was fielding further demands from Francis and Louise de Savoie for more overt support and he noted their disguised threats of retaliation should that support be found wanting.[63]

Once it was clear that Francis had not been elected emperor, Henry 'made believe, especially to the French hostages that he greatly regretted that King Francis had not been elected'. Thoughts turned once more to the planned meeting and both sides made efforts to improve relations between them.[64] On the first Sunday in June 1519, Boleyn stood proxy for Henry as godfather at the baptism of Francis's second son Henry, duc d'Orléans, who was born on 31 March. He presented the duke with a gold salt cellar, cup and ewer and gave money to the child's nurses.[65] This goodwill gesture Francis accepted and assured Henry of his continuing desire to meet. Francis shortly afterwards compensated some English merchants robbed by French privateers the previous autumn. Henry sent Francis a brace of hunting dogs as a gift. In October Princess Mary received a gold cross from Queen Claude, valued by the Venetians at 6,000 ducats, and a portrait of the dauphin – her betrothed. Henry allowed Francis to send ambassadors to Scotland

and agreed, at Francis's instigation, to extend his truce with Scotland agreed in 1518.

As recently as the middle of March 1519, Francis had expressed the determination to meet Henry though he should come only 'himself with his page and his lackey'.[66] In July, Henry made a similarly extravagant gesture of his own, saying that although it was now too late that year for him to meet Francis, he expected to do so the following year. He would not, he said, shave his beard off until he and Francis met. Hearing this, Francis made the same promise. In November, Louise de Savoie confronted Sir Thomas Boleyn with the news that Henry had in fact shaved off his beard and demanded an explanation. Boleyn, thinking on his feet, explained that it was almost certainly at Queen Katherine's instance as it was well known that she preferred her husband clean shaven. He assured Louise that Henry loved her son as no other king, the altered state of his facial hair notwithstanding. Apparently reassured, Louise replied, 'Th[eir love] is nat in the berds but in the harts.'[67] In December 1519, Louise once again raised the prospect of the two kings meeting in the spring or summer of the following year either in Calais or some place between there and Boulogne. With numbers being talked about already in the thousands, the French felt that Calais was too small. Besides, as Francis and Louise both observed, with the meeting in summer, the two entourages might lodge in pavilions in the fields; and so they eventually did.[68]

In February 1520 Henry appointed Sir Richard Wingfield as his new resident ambassador in France. His instructions, probably drafted by Wolsey, who always worked to give Henry the upper hand, strike a new, expansive and personal chord in Anglo-French dealings. Clearly written with the prospect of a meeting of the two kings now very much in mind, they state that Henry could not be satisfied until he had sent to Francis one of his

> right trusty and near familiars ... to the intent that by the renovelling [renewing] of ambassadors, new testimonies may be found as well of the perseverance of fraternal love on both sides, as also

by such means to further the augmentation thereof from time to time.[69]

Wolsey evidently intended that the new ambassador should help him to build a rapport between the two kings. Wingfield had been carefully chosen for the task. He then held the position at court of a 'Knight of the Body in the King's Privy Chamber'.[70] As such he was one of Henry's closest personal servants with regular access to him in his private apartments and also one of his councillors. This meant that he could represent Henry far more personally and effectively than had his predecessor, Sir Thomas Boleyn. Sending such a 'right trusty and near familiar' was a great compliment to the French king. It was also an assertion of Henry's own claim to be an honourable 'friend and brother' to Francis and it implicitly challenged him to demonstrate a like regard for the king of England.

Francis responded in the only way he could: with an equal or greater gesture of chivalric magnanimity. When Wingfield was first introduced to the king at Cognac on 8 March, Francis expressed pleasure that Henry had decided to renew his representative. Then, as Wingfield told Wolsey, Francis invited the new ambassador to enter his own royal 'chambre', his private apartments, 'at all times, as I was accustomed to do with my master, and also the queen's and my lady's'.[71] Such an invitation had never been extended to his predecessor. In effect, Francis accorded Wingfield the honorary status of one of his own close personal servants, the *gentilshommes de la chambre* in his own household. The freedom of access Wingfield was accorded initially disconcerted him, aware as he was of the importance attached to entering the monarch's private space in England. He wrote home several times that he had not presumed to act upon the invitation until French courtiers insisted that he should do so.

The resident French ambassador in England by this time was Jean de Sains, seigneur de Marigny. He had arrived in December 1519 and remained until mid-1521.[72] While he did not receive exactly the same kind of free access to Henry as Wingfield did with Francis, his compatriots, the hostages then in England, certainly did. Alongside the ambassador, these young men constituted, in the months prior to the Field, a very tangible and lively French presence in the English court. They were often the centre of attention at court banquets, in hunting parties and the like. Treating them well allowed Henry to display a princely generosity on which he prided himself and of a kind directly parallel to that which his own man at Francis's court was then experiencing. Some of the hostages evidently accompanied Henry to France where, according to one witness at least, they were exchanged for others.[73]

By February 1520 detailed planning was under way for the meeting and news of it began to spread throughout the European courts. Emperor Charles V was first alerted to the realistic prospect of an Anglo-French summit by the French themselves. Since 1516, he and Francis had maintained an uneasy peace under the treaty of Noyon which was supposed to settle many of the competing territorial claims between them. Charles had not been much inclined to fulfil the terms of the treaty and a conference convened the previous year to sort out the competing claims to Navarre was inconclusive. Then, at Burgos on 20 February, Francis's representatives suddenly demanded the immediate execution of the terms of the treaty of Noyon and implied that England would support their claims under it.[74]

To this provocative gesture Charles reacted swiftly. Having, he thought, secured his Iberian dominions, he already planned to return to his native Flanders before going on to his German lands. Habsburg envoys in England had hitherto rather vaguely intimated that he might, so to speak, call in en route, to meet Henry on the Isle of Wight in response to an invitation Henry had made in 1519. Now, working in collaboration with his aunt, Marguerite de Savoie, his regent in the Netherlands, Charles expressed a fervent desire to meet his English uncle by marriage. Marguerite arranged a high-level delegation to England to be led by her old confidant Jean de Berghes (although illness finally prevented his travelling), together with Gérard de la Pleine, seigneur de La Roche, her secretary, Jean de la Sauch and Philippe

Haneton. They joined with Charles's envoy, Bernard de Mesa, the bishop of Elna and arrived in the first days of April to announce the emperor's imminent departure from Spain. They reminded Henry that he would therefore be the first European monarch to meet with Charles since his elevation to the imperial dignity almost a year earlier, a fact not lost on observers at the papal court in Rome.[75] The prospect of such international recognition immediately before a meeting with his great rival was too much for Henry to refuse. Happily, dynastic and diplomatic protocol gave him virtually no choice anyway.

On or about 7 April, at Blois where the court was for Easter, ambassador Wingfield presented members of the French royal council with Henry's request for a postponement of the meeting of approximately one week, urging the difficulty of making preparations. This they 'took amiss', thinking it would cause Francis 'to imagine many things'. Behind this rather oblique language was genuine anxiety about Henry meeting Emperor Charles. Uppermost in the minds of the French was the fear that Henry would cancel the meeting or perhaps concoct some sort of conspiracy to insult or even attack Francis, during the Field. Francis refused absolutely to delay the meeting, saying, with some justification no doubt, that Queen Claude's pregnancy was too advanced to allow him to do so. He had shown good faith in settling the date and this had now been agreed under treaty. Francis pointedly reminded Wolsey, through Wingfield, that whenever he, Francis, had wanted an alteration to arrangements, Wolsey had insisted on the letter of the treaty. Francis now chose to do likewise. The most he would concede was that Henry might be at Calais as late as 4 June. The king intended to start for Paris and the northern borders of the realm immediately after Easter and had appointed the Marshal Châtillon to work with the earl of Worcester. The Admiral Bonnivet also wrote in these terms to Wolsey that same day and in the evening the admiral and the royal secretary Florimond Robertet told Wingfield plainly that Francis knew that a delegation had left the Netherlands for England with the intention of preventing the Franco-English meeting.[76]

The French were quite right of course. A letter written by Jean de la Sauch in England to Charles's close advisor, Guillaume de Croy, seigneur de Chièvres on 7 April canvassed exactly the possibility of persuading Henry not to meet Francis, or at the very least to meet with Charles again immediately afterwards. De la Sauch thought this imperative because he was genuinely concerned at the potential of the forthcoming Anglo-French meeting. He recognised that, flattered as they were by the emperor's proposed visit, Wolsey and Henry had no particular confidence in Charles. 'If you think', he warned Chièvres, 'that they will labour for us and our beautiful eyes, then you will find yourself very much mistaken'. He evidently did not assume that Henry was already intent in the spring of 1520 on allying with Charles against Francis – and neither should we. De la Sauch took some comfort, however, from the fact that Queen Katherine was not in favour of the Anglo-French meeting and had told her husband as much. Negotiations continued and a treaty arranging two meetings between Charles and Henry, one before and one immediately after the Field of Cloth of Gold, was finally signed on 11 April.[77]

CHAPTER 2

Two Stars in One Firmament

And for as much as for the King's honour, it is behoofull [beneficial] and necessary to put everything in readiness, as well for the apparell of his noble person as for the garnishing of his lodgings, tents, pavilions and preparations of all other things requisite to so great an act and triumph, therefore not only the specialities of everything his hereafter articled, but also the persons appointed to execute all and singular the said articles and charges be particularly named and expressed in form following.

WITH THESE WORDS from 'A Memoriall of such things as be requisite', dating from early 1520, the English royal council began its detailed planning for Henry VIII's meeting with Francis I.[1] Its first three items provide a remarkably succinct summary of the purpose and spirit of the Field of Cloth of Gold and show that, for both sides, the event was first and foremost about displaying its sovereign as a nobleman and warrior king as magnificently as possible.

The first item specified that Henry's clothing for the Field was to be prepared as suited his 'high pleasure' and that Henry would himself decide on its design and look – to be the 'divisor thereof' as the 'Memoriall' puts it. The second specified that Guînes castle was to be refurbished and that lodgings where the English could entertain their French guests in appropriate splendour were to be built in or near the castle, according to a design drawn up in consultation with the king and Wolsey. The result was the famous temporary palace built for Henry just outside Guînes, acknowledged as the architectural masterpiece of the event. The third item specified that a site for a tournament was to be agreed with the French and that it should be located and 'assigned in egall [equal] distaunce betwixt the said Guysnes and Ardre'. Achieving these things, getting the two kings and their retinues to the site and having somewhere for them to stay that fitted the grandeur of the occasion were the principal tasks with which the chief officers of the French and English courts occupied themselves throughout the spring of 1520.

Given the kind of status brinkmanship in which both sides were engaged, the atmosphere in the eight weeks that followed was fraught with tension and mutual suspicion. This was heightened still further as both sides began to expend huge sums of money on preparations while uncertain as to whether or not the other side was also preparing or instead leading them into a diplomatic – or even a military – trap.

Ardres: the French Royal Encampment

Formal French preparations for the Field of Cloth of Gold began on 22 February 1520 when, at Cognac, Francis signed letters patent author-ising the preparation and transport to Ardres of tents and pavilions to house the French court. The two men charged with overseeing the French preparations were both high-ranking military officers: Gaspard de Coligny, seigneur de Châtillon, whom we have already met, and Jacques *dit* Galiot de Genouillac, the Great Master of the Royal Artillery. Genouillac was a member of a family who had served the French kings as Masters of Artillery since the reign of Louis XI. He became Great Master in 1512 and so was responsible for getting the artillery over the Alps for Francis's 1515 campaign for Milan and enabling it to play an important role in the French victory at Marignano.[2] He was paid 2,000 *livres tournois* per annum and headed a complex network of officials. Guillaume de Saigne, the treasurer and receiver-general of the *artillerie ordinaire*, drew up accounts for the preparations now preserved in the Bibliothèque Nationale. These show that the artillery was called upon not simply for its manpower and logistics expertise, but also for its own proper function of defence – should this prove necessary.[3]

The town of Ardres is about 10 miles (17 km) south-east of Calais and just under five miles (7.5 km) east and slightly south of Guînes. In 1520 it stood on the border with the English territory around Calais known as 'the Pale' and was quite close also to Habsburg territory in the counties of Artois and Flanders. This area had witnessed near-constant military activity in the early sixteenth century and Ardres had been partially burnt by the English in the war of 1513. The town lay within the province of Picardy whose governor in 1520 was Charles de Bourbon, duc de Vendôme. He closely supervised preparations for the meeting.[4]

Perhaps the earliest evidence of French activity in connection with the Field of Cloth of Gold is the set of surveys of armaments and ammunition in Picard towns undertaken by officers of the artillery in March and April of 1519 or 1520 (the accounts are unclear). The artillery accounts record that one Jacques Doussel, *commissaire ordinaire*, was paid for costs in going from Montreuil to Amiens and from there conveying to Ardres equipment for some 2,000 infantrymen or guards including body armour, some 4,000 pikes or halberds and 100 arquebuses.[5] Ardres was wrongly described by one observer in 1520 as 'long ago destroyed', but its fortifications were certainly degraded, as was its stock of housing. A letter which Francis sent to his ambassador in England in March 1520 is the first to mention the need for tents and pavilions to accommodate the king himself and his entourage at Ardres.[6] Francis ordered the repair of the town's castle and its defensive ditches. It was also rearmed to some degree.

To the south of Ardres and Guînes was the county of the Boulonnais, whose principal town was the port of Boulogne, which Henry VIII would successfully besiege in 1544. It was to Boulogne that the materials and equipment needed for the French camp were brought in late May 1520. At the time its governor and *sénéchal* of the county was Antoine Motier de La Fayette who, having been captured at the Battle of the Spurs in 1513, was already known to the English. In the intervening years of peace La Fayette had frequently entertained English envoys arriving on missions to Francis.[7] In 1517 the Council of Calais had reported that he was favoured by the king of France above other local gentry.[8]

To the south and east of Boulogne and Ardres on the route to Paris lay Montreuil, Hesdin, Abbeville, Péronne and Amiens. At Montreuil the governor was Antoine de Créquy, seigneur de Pont-Rémy. He had been captain of Thérouanne in August 1513 and had conducted a vigorous but ultimately unsuccessful defence against the English siege. Pont-Rémy would host the French king at Montreuil in the days immediately before his meeting with Henry.[9] At Abbeville two generations of the Harcourt du Huppy family held the governorship and at Amiens three generations of the Lannoy family succeeded each other in the post between 1495 and 1562. At nearby Péronne, Jean II d'Humières, a royal favourite, had just been appointed as governor and his influence probably enabled the town to escape a financial contribution towards the Field of Cloth of Gold.[10]

Given their proximity to Ardres and the English Pale, the French evidently decided that these towns also needed reinforcements of arms and ammunition. The aforementioned Jacques Doussel was paid 150 *livres tournois* for costs in going to Troyes in Champagne and there obtaining 300 pack horses and then taking 12 *canons serpentines* (2–3 tonnes); 10 *colverines bâtardes* (1.2 tonnes); 10 *colverines moyennes* (0.6 tonnes) and 200 *arquebuses à croq* and other munitions to Saint-Quentin, Péronne and Amiens 'for the fortification and defence of the same'.[11] This number and range of weapons is akin to what, according to one military protocol from the 1520s, was the usual strength of an artillery company. What proportion of the total armaments brought to Picardy this particular shipment represents the records do not allow us to say, but it suggests a reasonably serious effort to enhance the military capacity of the towns closest to the border with the Calais Pale and imperial territory. Inventories of weapons were also taken of available supplies in Brittany, Normandy and Champagne, indeed as far away as Languedoc, Provence and Dauphiné.[12] The French were clearly planning for all eventualities, including the possibility of an imperial attack during, or immediately after, the event itself.

The three English commissioners in Guînes kept a close eye on what the French were up to at Ardres and were unsettled by what they saw, or rather did not see, there. Informed by a network of observers and inform-ants, they reported as late as mid-April that little preparation had so far been made in the town.[13] On 21 May they reported that they were sure that Ardres was being fortified 'secretly' – not least because Marshal Châtillon had told them that it would be! They wondered whether, even now, the French were really serious about a meeting or planning a surprise attack on Henry and his entourage at Guînes or even in the open fields. They advised Henry to ship over 'the ordnance lying on the Tower wharf'; thus both sides talked of peace but still prepared for a fight.[14]

Happily for the story of the meeting, the appearances at Ardres were deceptive because work to assemble the accommodation for the French court had in fact already begun in earnest some 320 miles (520 km) away in the city of Tours. At first sight, Tours seems an odd choice, given its distance from Ardres. Yet Tours, lying on the lower reaches of the Loire river at its confluence with the Cher, had long been an impor-tant cloth town. Its location provided it with the water supply, albeit one with considerable seasonal variation, that was necessary for the silk, cloth and leather industries. These had reached their zenith under royal patronage in the later part of the fifteenth century, at which point it has been estimated that 85 per cent of the manual workers in Tours were involved in its fabric and clothing industries. Thereafter, however, the city's production of luxury cloth rapidly succumbed to international competition, especially from Florence, but the production of more mundane fabrics expanded.[15] In 1520, Tours's appeal as the venue for manufacturing the tents needed for the Field was almost certainly based on the availability at short notice of the materials and the skilled and semi-skilled labour needed for the tasks of dyeing, cutting and stitching canvas and other fabrics.

Preliminary work began in late February and the centre of opera-tions was the palace of Christophe de Brillac, the Archbishop of Tours.[16]

It was evidently chosen for its size as a suitable work and storage area. The project was under the direction of Briçet Dupré, one of six royal tapestry-makers in 1520.[17] He worked with the assistance of the officers and men of the artillery who supervised the gathering of materials and workers and maintained their security at Tours and Ardres. The scale of the operation was extraordinary. By May there were some 170 men and 120 women, described in the accounts as 'tantiers et couturiers', working in the great hall of the palace at Tours virtually around the clock in successive shifts in order to produce an estimated 300 to 400 tents, the tallest and largest of which were for the king and his immediate entourage. All the men were paid 5 or 6 *sous* a day, apart from those identified as 'masters' who received as much as 20 *sous* per day. Some of the women also received 5 *sous*, though others had only 3 *sous*. Although modest, these wages were in line with those paid for similar work across France at the time. Like their counterparts in Lyon, France's other great cloth manufacturing city, working women in Tours had a more limited range of trades open to them than their male counterparts. Training for work in stitching and sewing was comparatively easy for girls from poorer backgrounds to obtain and when times were good, as they were in the 1520s, large numbers made their living from day labour, although the scale of that offered on this occasion by the royal court was exceptional. During the French Wars of Religion the supply of silk, and with it the work of labourers and artisans, diminished severely. The years of Francis's reign would be recalled in Tours and Lyon as relatively good ones for day labourers in the cloth industries.[18] Master tent-makers were in fact brought from Lyon, and were paid the same daily rate as those from Tours. Some of the workers then travelled north to set up the French camp. Others, paid the same rate, were engaged at Boulogne and still others were brought urgently, 'en toute extreme diligence', to Ardres to dress the tents in the first five days of June. The tent-makers were paid 4,600 *livres* out of the total wages bill for preparations of 5,788 *livres tournois*.[19]

Lit day and night by torches, the hall of the archbishop's palace would have been organised into different areas of production. Cartload after cartload of materials would have arrived in the courtyard with lengths of dyed canvas or with finer fabrics carefully wrapped in serge or buckram to protect them. Once accounted for, the materials were assigned to teams of cutters and stitchers, who worked up sections which were then labelled in a variety of related alphabetical sequences for assembly on site. Once prepared, the canvas panels and their covering fabrics were carefully packed and loaded for carriage up to Ardres.

Not less than some 35,143 *aunes* of canvas were required. Most of it was supplied to Dupré by eight merchants of Tours at a cost of 18 *livres*, 10 *sous* per 100 *aunes*. Further amounts were supplied directly to the site at Ardres from merchants in Boulogne and Saint-Omer at the slightly higher price of 20 *livres* per 100 *aunes*. The rich fabrics needed to cover and decorate the exterior and interior of the pavilions were also supplied in or through Tours. One merchant, Jean Richard, had the lion's share of sales, supplying hundreds of metres of silk, taffeta, satin and velvet in the royal colours and in violet and deep blue, which was used to dress the tents. His business with the crown earned him almost 4,500 *livres* (£450).[20] The temptation to profiteer from the king's need for large amounts of expensive material evidently proved too much for some. In 1526 one Nicolas Lalemant and a number of fellow merchants and bankers were found guilty of fraud in the provision of pavilions at Ardres. Twenty years later, four councillors of the Parlement of Paris were commissioned to investigate allegations of fraud against 'des marchands qui avient fourni les tentes, pavilions, draps d'or et fleurs de lis' for the meeting with the king of England.[21]

After the Field, the canvas tents were stripped of their fine fabrics, retained by the artillery for military use and redeployed within twelve months. An inventory of those fabrics used to dress the king's pavilion and those of the queen and Louise de Savoie was drawn up as an appendix to De Saigne's account. This inventory, together with two of the royal 'garde-meuble' or warehouse in Paris made in 1542 and 1551, allows a significant number of items used at the Field of Cloth of Gold to be identified. The inventories list hundreds of *aunes* of cloth of gold, cloth of silver, damask, silk, satin, velvet and velour mostly of blue, violet and crimson, many of them 'strewn' (*semez*) with *fleurs-de-lis*, together with many lengths in the royal livery colours of white, tawny and black. The length of these items, most over three or four *aunes* long, indicates that they were used to cover the canvas walls and roofs of the pavilions. Some have specified purposes, such as twenty-three pieces of canvas faced with cloth of gold, used in the galleries of the king's pavilion or ten pieces of cloth of gold used on the walls and private chambers of the king within it.[22]

Similar entries present striking combinations of different fabrics stitched together or overlaid upon each other for decorative effect, just as they are described by contemporaries at the Field. One such piece combined cloth of gold with cloth of silver, overlaid with a band of violet velvet. Another piece combined lengths of cloth of gold and of silver backed with yellow buckram. Some 200 lbs of silk fringing of various lengths in the royal livery colours and others of white, black and violet were all stored in buckram wrappings. Many were apparently stored in the form in which they were used and not disassembled into their constituent elements afterwards. Even some of the streamers that flew from the masts of the tents and pavilions were stored. These included eighteen white *banderolles* painted with arms of Queen Claude and Louise de Savoie and another sixteen with those of the king's arms.[23]

A range of ancillary items were also purchased from merchants at Tours, including lengths of rope and cord, pegs, posts, various metal fastenings and pulleys, taffeta and leather for fastenings and straps of varying lengths and hundreds of large, medium and small nails. The purchase of these items alerts us to the fact that the French also required a good deal of timber for the king's accommodation at Ardres and for the pavilions. The largest individual items were great and smaller masts used to hold up the tents. One wood merchant in Tours, Bartélemy Grand, supplied some 412 feet (125.5m) of pine wood from the forests of the Auvergne.[24] Oak and walnut trunks were also cut into shorter planks to be used to support the structure of the pavilions in the form of skirting and runner boards, roof frames, supports for doorways, window frames and the like.

Once assembled, the materials were taken by cart or packhorse to the island of Saint-Gracian on the Loire. From there the river might, theoretically, have provided convenient means to transport the material at least as far north as Orléans but the accounts make no mention of boats or barges being used. They do, however, specify that over 400 packhorses and some 120 carters were contracted for service at a rate of 5 *sous* per day per horse.[25] They also specify the tax areas or *élections* from where these carters and the horses were contracted. They indicate that the route to Ardres was probably by land first to Blois and Orléans and from there along an established trading route via Chartres, Dreux and Evreux to Rouen, roughly in line with the present Route Nationale 154.[26] At Rouen, more wood was evidently collected and then the expedition moved on to Boulogne, probably via Abbeville. Final preparatory work, possibly also repairs and the final repackaging of the material for the return journey to Tours, was done at Boulogne where the cloisters and grounds of the Franciscan convent and those of a hospital had been taken over. The prior of the convent was compensated with 25 *livres* for the inconvenience and as thanks for the prayers of the community for the king's health and prosperity. The nuns of the hospital received 8 *livres*.[27] From Boulogne the finished tents were finally brought the relatively short distance to Ardres.

Two scraps of sentences in a mutilated section of a letter written by Sir Nicholas Vaux to Wolsey from Guînes on 18 May indicate that in addition to the tents prepared at Tours, Francis had taken over four houses in the town of Ardres and 'a great peace [piece] of the abbaye there called Anderne'. Dillon's survey of the Pale indicates that there was an abbey anciently located somewhere between modern Andres and Balinghem which would appear to be the one to which Vaux referred. The abbey was destroyed by the English in the war of 1544 which suggests that, despite the confusing description of its location within the boundary of the Pale, it lay outside it and so on French territory. If this was the abbey to which Vaux refers, it was probably used to house the higher members of the French entourage beyond the immediate royal circle.[28] Vaux was also informed that Francis intended to make 'great buildings' at Ardres. A large stock of timber, some of it 'redye framed', was waiting at Rouen. So, Vaux concluded, 'by soche meanes they be in a greate forwardness of thier provisions'.[29] Three days later the commissioners told Wolsey that their French counterparts 'work better than they did at the beginning' and now seemed convinced that the meeting would go ahead.[30]

In his description of the Field, Robert III de La Marck, seigneur de Florange, offers a little more detail, albeit somewhat confusing, about the king's accommodation. He states that:

> the king of France at Guînes, [*sic*] made three houses, one in the town of Ardres which was completely newly built and was fine enough for a town house; it had fairly spacious lodgings and in that said place was feasted the king of England.[31]

The other two 'maisons' to which Florange referred were Francis's tented pavilions and a banqueting house, all outside the town.

It is not clear whether the house in Ardres was built from scratch or was a fundamental renovation of some one or more of the four houses identified by Vaux. One possibility is that several of the houses abutted each other and were converted into one very large residence. *La Description* says that a house was made of bricks but was never quite finished because the meeting was 'so sudden'. Hall concurs: 'there was at the same toune of Ardre buylded the Frenche kynges lodgyng full well, but not finished, muche was the provisions in Picardy on every part through all'. Jacques Dubois's poem commemorating the event boasts: 'In the middle of the town he [Francis] establishes an immense, majestic, strong palace'.[32]

There is some evidence that the residence and/or the fortifications at Ardres were worked on by the Italian architect, Domenico da Cortona (*c.* 1465–1549), who had been brought to France by Charles VIII and remained in service throughout Francis's reign. A mandate from 1532 repaying expenses incurred over some fifteen years' work for the king mentions Ardres, alongside Tournai and Chambord, as one of the places at which he 'built in wood, in the town as well as the castle' – but gives no further details.[33] There are only a few snippets of information about Francis's lodgings from contemporary documents. Dubois's modern editors have concluded that in the absence of substantive evidence, his further description of it as 'magnificent with smooth- dressed stones', whose interior, 'in its entirety is of gold and gems', is pure poetic hyperbole. An unidentified Italian observer thought it 'very beautiful, but neither so beautiful nor so costly as that of England'.[34] *La Description* notes that when Henry dined at the French residence on 10 June, Louise de Savoie came to greet him 'a l'entrée de la grande cour de la maison', and that they then walked together to a reception room, suggesting a residence of the required grandeur to accommodate the king, the queen and Louise herself. Hall describes the king of England being received by Queen Claude a week later in a reception hall hung with blue velvet embroidered with gold *fleurs-de-lis*. From there he was taken into a second chamber, evidently the French king's *salle*, hung with cloth of gold and *cordelières* or 'friars' knots', one of the personal emblems of Francis and a punning allusion to St Francis of Assisi and the Franciscans. This room also had two sideboards of silver gilt plate, and here Henry dined.[35] Dubois describes a passage in the building adorned with arms of the kings and queens of France and England and the dauphin, in gold medallions.

Members of the king's close entourage also had accommodation in the king's house or elsewhere in the town. The journal of Louise de Savoie notes that at about 10.30 on the night of 17 June a suspicious fire broke out in the lodgings in Ardres of Jean d'Albret, seigneur d'Orval, then the governor of Champagne and a regular attendee in Francis's inner council.[36]

The location of the king's residence has never been established with certainty, but one suggestion may be offered. Several sources state that the residence was in the centre of the town. The 1832 survey map or *cadastre* of Ardres shows a street in the centre, then the rue du Château, now the rue de Lambert d'Ardres, which runs behind and to the west of the main town square, Place d'Armes, known in 1832 as La

Grand-Place. On the west side of the square, and thus between it and the former rue du Château, the *cadastre* shows two blocks of abutting buildings. One is a long range terminated at each end by two short wings. The other block has six dwellings grouped around three central courtyards. Given its dimensions and central location, this block of buildings *may* have been the site of the royal residence in 1520. If the royal residence was here or hereabouts, it would have been reached via the town's principal street which, then as now, led to the Porte de Calais and the road to Guînes.[37]

Francis had also prepared a large banqueting house in the French camp to which his residence was connected, according to Dubois. From the left side at the back of the royal lodging, 'a long gallery leads peacefully to a tower'. From here, a gallery made of elegantly cut box plants led to a 'pavilion situated at the foot of the little town'. Hall described this pavilion as a 'house of solas and sporte, of large and mightie compass'. It was held up by a huge central mast, ropes and tackle and featured a striking constellation ceiling which Hall described as: 'all blewe, set with starres of golde foyle, and the Orbes of the heavens by crafte of colours in the roffe, were curiosly wrought in maner like the sky or firmament ...'[38]

This banqueting house, the third of the 'maisons' to which Florange referred, reminded him of one built in the Bastille in December 1518 for the reception of the English embassy. Florange described it as being like a Roman amphitheatre, built on stone (Hall says brick) foundations, with rooms and galleries on three levels surrounding and above a central dancing floor. It may have looked something like the Globe theatre. Hall states that there was a 'creasant' or semicircular dais on the side of the rotunda closest to Ardres. Such a dais had also featured in the Bastille banqueting hall and, like it, the one in 1520 was decorated with 'frettes and knottes made of Ive bushes and other thynges that longest would be grene for pleasure'. Dubois alludes to the same occasion when a temporary cover of canvas had been stretched over the courtyard of the fortress and under it was hung a ceiling featuring an elaborate constellation for a banquet on the night of the winter solstice. Dubois confirms the ivy decoration hanging from galleries around the

1520 pavilion, then makes the connection to 1518 explicit: 'The French are wont to call it "festin", such as was recently held at the gates of Paris for the English ambassadors'.[39]

Evidently common by then in Francis's Milanese dominions, such temporary banqueting structures had never been seen or used in France prior to 1518, but the custom of building them was rapidly established thereafter. For the baptism of the Dauphin François, on 25 April 1518, Domenico da Cortona built a banqueting pavilion in the courtyard of the royal château at Amboise to house the celebrations after the ceremony. It remained in place or was perhaps re-erected for 2 May when the court celebrated the marriage of Madeleine de La Tour d'Auvergne to Lorenzo de' Medici, the duke of Urbino.[40] It seems that in 1520 Francis was ready to reprise his earlier successes with this kind of dramatic entertainment space but, perhaps because it was not finished in time, Florange tells us that the banqueting house was never used.[41] The next occasion when a temporary banqueting house was used in Anglo-French diplomacy was at Greenwich in 1527. There, the astronomer royal Nicolaus Kratzer and Hans Holbein designed an astronomical ceiling for the space intended to make a very detailed and pointed English response to the French efforts of 1518 and 1520.[42]

Lesser nobles and their servants were accommodated in the camp Francis built which Edward Hall describes as 'out of the toune of Arde in the territorie of an old castle, whiche by the war of old time had been beate[n]'. *La Description* indicates that the camp was near a little river or stream and the Mantuan ambassador Soardino states that Francis set up his camp of tents and pavilions 'outside the walls of Ardres, near his dwelling house'.[43] The camp would have to have been sited reasonably close to the 'foot of the town' in order for Francis to have reached the banqueting house via the gallery described by Dubois and, given the high levels of insecurity, in case of emergency. The 1832 *cadastre* shows the canalised 'Riviere de la Fontaine de la Ferme', likely to be the watercourse to which the *Description* refers, flowing across an area just beyond the western entrance to the town, the Porte de Calais and to the south side of the road.[44]

The general estimate from eyewitnesses is that there were between 300 and 400 tents erected on the site below the walls of Ardres. Some were single structures, but most were actually pavilions comprising a large central tent, square or round in shape and three or four additional sections, not unlike those provided for Henry's entourage at Guînes.[45] Of these, the principal pavilions naturally belonged to Francis and his immediate family. The king's main tent was 120 feet (36.5m) high supported by the two ships' masts lashed together. It was dressed overall with cloth of gold and three broad stripes of blue velvet strewn with gold *fleurs-de-lis*. This was the centrepiece of a complex incorporating three more accommodation pavilions. Here were housed the king's private chambers, his chapel and *garderobe*. Some 1,055 *aunes* of cloth of gold were required for the exterior of these pavilions, in addition to that used on the main one. Seven sailors were paid 40 *livres tournois* (about £4) between them for erecting 'with ropes and wooden ladders' the masts of the royal pavilion and hauling the canvas tents into position so they could then be dressed with the rich outer fabrics and other decorative flourishes.[46] At the pinnacle of the royal pavilion, standing on a large golden ball or 'pinot', was a statue of St Michael, six feet tall, carved from walnut, for which Guillaume Arnault was paid 70 *livres tournois* (about £7). In common with most depictions of the patron saint of the French monarchy and its order of chivalry, St Michael held a lance or dart in one hand and a shield in the other. At his feet was the overthrown Lucifer (described as in the form of a 'serpent'), whom he trod down in defeat.[47]

Closest to the king's pavilions were those of Queen Claude and Louise de Savoie dressed predominantly with *toile d'or* and *toile d'argent*, both lighter and finer than cloth of gold. The queen's pavilion also featured *fleurs-de-lis* in gold thread strewn on violet together with heraldic ermines, her emblem as duchess of Brittany in succession to her mother, Anne. Louise de Savoie's pavilion had crimson rather than violet satin and, in addition to strewn *fleurs-de-lis*, also featured some 14,280 white crosses, the heraldic emblem of the house of Savoy. The accounts also list, but do not describe in such detail, smaller pavilions in appropriate livery colours provided for leading members of Francis I's entourage including the duc d'Alençon, his uncle René de Savoie, the Admiral Bonnivet, Anne de Montmorency and the king's chief financier Jacques de Beaune, seigneur de Semblançay.[48]

The figure of St Michael on the king's pavilion had been painted in gold and blue by the royal painter Jean Bourdichon, who also painted in fine gold 117 large apples carved from walnut which were used as pinnacles for the lesser masts of the royal tents and pavilions. From them flew banners, also painted in gold and blue with the arms of the king, the queen and Louise de Savoie. A further 211 smaller carved apples, also painted in fine gold, were used as decorative devices on the pavilions of other members of the entourage. Some of these painted wooden apples at least were retained and taken back to Paris where they were stored in Francis's *garde-meuble* and also appear in the inventories referred to earlier. One final statistic: a staggering total of 72,544 gold *fleurs-de-lis* on blue velvet were used in the decoration of the pavilions of the king, the queen and Louise de Savoie.[49]

Unfortunately for them, the French perhaps underestimated the changeability of the weather in the north-western part of what Shakespeare would later call 'the best garden of the world', and many of their tents came crashing down during a succession of squalls and storms in the middle days of June. Although sources are silent on this point, Francis and his immediate entourage presumably retreated to the royal *hôtel* and houses around it in Ardres for shelter. The tents and pavilions for the rest of the entourage had to be repaired and set up again as best could be.[50]

Guînes: the English Royal Encampment

On 13 April 1520, the earl of Worcester, who was responsible for overseeing English preparations,

> landed at Calais, for to go to Guînes and the camp of the king's council of Calais, for to meet with divers lords of France for to appoint the ground at the camp, where the jousts and tournaments

should be kept most convenient for such a triumph for so noble kings and queens.[51]

Guînes lay in the Pale of Calais, a piece of terrain conceded to England after the fall of Calais to Edward III in 1347. It remained in English hands until retaken by the French in the winter of 1557–8. It extended inland some 8 miles (13 km) from Calais and about 12 miles (19 km) along the coast south towards Boulogne. Its total area was about 86 square miles (*c.* 138 square km). The area's geological character is a transition from downland at the coast (in fact a continuation of Kent downland) to a large mixed area of peat fenland with marsh, woodland and very fertile arable land, settled with villages. Guînes was the second town of the territory, some six miles (9.5 km) south-east of Calais. To the north of Guînes lay large areas of open water, 'plashes' as the English called them, the pools left after the peat had been dug out during medieval times. They are shown clearly in a painting, *The Field of Cloth of Gold*, now in the Royal Collection and on display at Hampton Court Palace. Water was an important means of transport in this landscape. Guînes was linked to the centre of Calais, and thus to its port, by the river Guînes.[52]

Shortly after his arrival at Calais, the earl of Worcester met Marshal Châtillon. The two men had first encountered each other a little over twelve months earlier when the marshal handed Tournai over to Worcester. As on that occasion, each man was acutely conscious of representing the honour and reputation of his master. Neither ever missed an opportunity of scoring a point at the other's expense – even as they also tried to co-operate in order to achieve their appointed tasks. Very little of their correspondence to their respective masters survives, but what does attests to sometimes protracted and frequently heated discussions between them.

For the English commissioners, as for their French equivalents, time was of the essence. They had barely three months to oversee the construction of necessary facilities and accommodation. The first task was to repair and refurbish the walls and towers of the castle at Guînes where the king and queen would lodge during the event. It had been described by Sir Richard Wingfield on his way to the French court in March as not being fit to be seen.[53] Their principal task was, however, to oversee the construction of a temporary palace 'before the castle gate of Guînes'. This building was awe-inspiring to those who saw it, even if no two sources agree entirely about its appearance, decoration, spatial arrangements or use. To build a structure of its size and ingenuity for an event of just over two weeks' duration was a bold statement of Henry's ambition to be ranked among European princes of the first order. It was conceived in the spirit of ostentatious rivalry that characterised the whole event, and reports of it in English, French and Italian circulated widely throughout Europe.

The palace was built just outside the walls of Guînes quite close to the castle, near a bridge which crossed the town's defensive moat. Wolsey kept in close contact with the English commissioners about its progress and this has led to the suggestion that he actually designed the palace.[54] The evidence for this, however, remains somewhat ambiguous and it is more likely that it was a joint project of king and cardinal. Wolsey had certainly taken a hand in the redesign of Bridewell Palace and by 1520 he was also working on renovations and extensions at both York Place, his London residence as archbishop, and at Hampton Court. Henry had made his debut as an architect with his designs for Newhall in Essex. On 26 March, Belknap and Vaux first reported to Wolsey their anxiety about its sheer scale, for according to the 'platt' or plan of it, evidently held by Wolsey and Henry, the building would be larger than Bridewell, Grenewiche or Eltham', the king's three principal metropolitan houses.[55]

When completed, the temporary palace at Guînes was 328 feet (100m) square and comprised four blocks, ranged around a central square court or atrium. It would have fitted snugly within the confines of Tom Quad at Christ Church, Oxford (another building associated with Wolsey), which is 382 feet (116m) square. The walls of Henry's palace were built on stone foundations and were of brick to a height of eight feet (2.5m). Above the brickwork, the timber-framed walls reached to a height of 30 feet (9.14 m). At the top of the walls was a cornice surmounted by frieze decorated in an Italianate classical style, or 'antique work' as it was known, featuring scrolls, strap work and leaf motifs. The palace was crenellated and had four brick-built towers at its outer corners. Its roof was of oiled canvas painted in lead colour to simulate slates.

The work on the palace began two days after the commissioners arrived but little progress was made in the first week. They lacked timber and sawyers. Nor, they told the cardinal, was there sufficient fallen or ready-sawn timber in London or near Dover to do the work before the end of May. Accordingly, they had sent William Lilgrave to Holland for timber and other necessities. Their panicky letter may be somewhat misleading, however, as wood was evidently found relatively quickly. Some or most of what was needed was apparently floated behind barges or ships along the coast to Calais and then transported to the construction site, probably along the river Guînes. One Henry Smith also supplied timber from England in April and May to a total value of £400.[56]

Even allowing for the fact that this was a temporary structure and that Tudor building projects could sometimes progress at speed, it seems unlikely that something the size of the Guînes temporary palace could have been made on site entirely from scratch in barely two months. Support for this view comes from Martin du Bellay's account of the meeting which states that Henry's palace was made in England and shipped across to Calais 'all made'.[57] This observation cannot literally be true of course, but what du Bellay probably meant was that sections of the building were prefabricated in England and transported to the site. Further support for this idea comes from an admittedly confusing phrase in the *Chronicle of Calais* immediately after it relates the floating of timber to Calais:

... all the tymbar borde that cowld be browght out of England, whiche *palays was framed in many places*, all the roves whereof was paynted canvas, and all the walls from the second plate downward.[58]

Partial prefabrication was in fact a common method of constructing a timber-framed building. It was used, for example, in the construction of the roof of Westminster Hall in 1395–6 when some 660 tons of the timber needed was worked at 'the Frame' near Farnham in Surrey, from where it was sent in sections by land to the Thames and then by barge to Westminster. It will be recalled that Sir Nicholas Vaux reported that the French had timber, some of it 'redye framed', at Rouen to be used in the king's residence at Ardres. The *Chronicle of Calais*'s oblique phrase 'whiche palays was framed in many places' perhaps alludes to this practice. Du Bellay also states that at the end of the festivities the English temporary palace was dismantled and taken back to England. Some years ago, David Starkey suggested that boards of the tiltyard at the Field ended up in the ceiling of the chapel at Ightham Mote in Kent. Subsequent study of the boards means that this suggestion is no longer accepted but materials from the palace, the tents and tournament site itself were recycled in a variety of ways through the Revels and other court offices.[59]

Given that plans for a meeting were in hand as early as 1519, the royal carpenters would have had ample time to calculate the number of sections or 'bays' needed to constitute each of the four ranges that eventually comprised the palace and then to assemble the necessary timber-frame walls and the beams for the roof. The main members of the walls, almost certainly of green oak, would have been hewn and laid out in sections on the ground according to a 'patten' or building plan, in a yard somewhere in England. Shipped to the site, they would have been set into the stone and brick lower walls by their groundsills, then morticed and pegged into each other. The main elements thus assembled, window frames could be incorporated and the smaller timbers which constituted the lesser framing, normally called 'studs', could be inserted. In a permanent structure, the framing would then be bricked or wattled and daubed. At Guînes, the timbers were instead covered with canvas, painted to look like brick.[60]

That this is most likely to have been what was done is also suggested by the speed of construction once it began in April. By 10 April, the commissioners reported that the stone foundations had been laid and that some at least of the lower walls of the temporary palace had reached their full height.[61] A month later, on 18 May, the commissioners reported that they anticipated finishing 'all the building that shall stand in the square court at Guînes' by the end of May.[62] They evidently did so, because Richard Gibson, who was responsible for the canvas roof of the building and the decoration of the palace, arrived in the nick of time towards the end of May and was able to do the required work. Only a week earlier, Vaux had asked Wolsey to dispatch him with all speed, 'so that the king be not disappointed of his roofs'.[63]

The preparatory work in England may well have been done in the vicinity of the Palace of Westminster. The office of the King's Works was located there under Henry VII, and although the palace was not used as an official royal residence after the fire of 1512, it was not totally destroyed. Many of the offices were repaired and the king still used it occasionally, such as on the eve of the Parliament of 1529. The work-shops at Westminster may have been located within the precinct of Westminster Abbey where the tombs of Henry VII and Elizabeth of York were constructed and some work at least was carried out on designs for tombs of Cardinal Wolsey and Henry VIII.[64] Certainly in April and May 1520 large items of wooden furniture for use during the king's visit were constructed in something identified as the 'worke house' at Westminster. They included display shelves for silver and gold plate, known as 'cupboards' and made from wainscot, a fine-quality oak imported from Russia, Germany and Holland. Folding tables, trestles and stools, made from 'deales', planks of pine or fir wood, were also made. Supplied by London merchants, the wood was loaded into lighters at Battle Bridge on the south bank of the river at Galley Key and the Vintery on the north bank (where a stevedoring crane was located) and carried down the Thames to Westminster. The furniture made there was then brought back and stored in a London cellar before being taken in a hoy to Sandwich. From there, it was moved in five carts to Canterbury for use during the emperor's visit at the end of May. It was then taken back to Sandwich and shipped across to Calais where it

was used in Henry's banqueting house and possibly also in the temporary palace at Guînes. The total cost for materials, wages and labour,
storage and transport was £48 7s. 4d.[65]

Those primarily responsible for constructing the temporary palace at
Guînes worked under the direction of Robert Fowler, who gave them
all advances, or 'prests' for which he accounted in May.[66] They were
William Vertue, the king's chief mason, and Humphrey Coke, the king's
chief carpenter. Vertue had worked at St George's Chapel, Windsor.
Coke was a member of the Carpenters' Company with a good reputation for imaginative and sound work. By 1520 he had worked for Eton
College and at Corpus Christi, Oxford, whose founder, Richard Fox,
described him as 'righte cunnynge and diligent in his werkes ... if ye
take his advice ... he shall advantage you large monee in the building
thereof, as well as in the devising as in the werkinge of yt'.[67] Vertue had
assisted Coke at Corpus Christi and together they now led a team of
many hundreds of craftsmen, artisans and labourers. In March the
commissioners had asked that Vertue be accompanied to Calais by 150
bricklayers. They also required 250 carpenters, 100 joiners and thirty
pairs of sawyers (to work double-ended saws) and forty plasterers. Henry
Smith contracted 100 carpenters, fifty glaziers and twenty-four painters
to contribute to the total. An unspecified number of labourers were
brought from England and Flanders to work alongside the craftsmen.[68]

Relatively little specific documentation survives about who these
people were or what they were paid at Guînes, so assessing their wages
and conditions is fraught with difficulty. In general terms, however, these
would have been similar to those on other prestigious royal building
projects in the period. The commissioners and workers were accommodated at the king's charge, according to status, at inns within Guînes,
probably within the habitable parts of the castle, even as they worked to
repair it, or under canvas in its courtyards and at the foot of its walls.
Under the terms of the 1495 Statute of Labourers, work was to begin
at 5a.m. in spring and summer. There was to be a half-hour break
for breakfast and one of an hour for lunch. For some of the period of
construction, after mid-May, half an hour's sleep was also allowed.

Thereafter work continued till between 7p.m. and 8p.m., perhaps with another short break about 4p.m.[69]

The majority of craftsmen in the building trade had no more than about £2–£5 in personal wealth per annum. The work of unskilled day labourers earned only half as much as that of a craftsman, at between 2d and 3d per day to a total of about £1 per annum.[70] Master carpenters and masons on a prestigious project such as this would be paid about 12d per day, foremen received about 7d or 8d and a carpenter from London or Oxford could earn 6d, all higher rates of pay than prescribed by the 1495 statute. Such master craftsmen might have annual incomes as high as £10–£19. Extra money might be paid when a project demanded overtime – as we know this one did from the costs of torches used for work into the night.[71] Allowances for the maintenance of specialist tools and clothing or 'livery' might also be included in remuneration. Particular industry might be further rewarded with incentives in cash – or drink.[72]

Demonstrating how far this money went for ordinary working people has perplexed economic historians for years. An authoritative study done in the 1950s established that 40d, or approximately seven days' pay for a building craftsman, was sufficient in the mid-fifteenth century to cover the food, fuel and clothing expenses for a week of a small household at Bridport in Dorset, of two priests and a servant. Extrapolating from that, the authors of the study showed that the purchasing power of a builder's daily pay had slipped a little by the 1520s, but it had collapsed catastrophically by the end of the century. The disparity between these workers' wage levels, estimated annual worth and conditions and the levels of income and expenditure among those attending the Field of Cloth of Gold is simply staggering.[73]

The basic structure and decoration of the temporary palace seems to have been as it is rendered in the Hampton Court painting.[74] The most prominent feature of the elevation was the ornate gatehouse with its scallop-shell pediment surmounted by a figure of St Michael between two monumental roses and capped with another smaller figure of St Michael above the entablature. The appearance of the patron saint of French chivalry as a decorative feature on an English palace was certainly unusual, but

it is most likely to have been intended as a compliment to the French king
and his nobles who entered and left the palace through this gateway. The
English were also aware that too dominant a display of St George, the
patron saint of English royal chivalry, might have conveyed rather too
strong anti-French sentiments on this most sensitive of occasions.

According to Hall, the gateway was also 'set with compassed [that is,
round] images of auncient Prynces as Hercules, Alexander and other by
entrayled woorke, rychely limned with golde and Albyn colours'. They
do not feature on the gateway in the painting but these polychrome
figures of classical heroes evidently had some sort of interwoven or
interlaced decoration about them.[75]

One of the most striking features of the palace beyond the gateway
was the amount of high-quality glass with which it was lit; the French
nicknamed the building 'the crystal palace'. A series of double-paned
clerestory windows lit the first floor, running all the way around the
outer walls and the inner walls around the courtyard as well. Dubois's
poem describes the palace as 'flooded with light on every side from
windows made of glass' that 'stretch to the very floor, displaying English
sovereigns'.[76] According to one source at least, there were also square
windows at the ground floor level. This glass was supplied from Flanders.
Although there was an established glass industry in the western Weald
of Kent in the 1520s, good-quality window glass was not made in significant quantities in England until the mid sixteenth century.[77] As much
as 5,000 feet (1,524m) of high-quality glass was purchased from two
merchants in Saint-Omer at a total cost of £48 15s. 4d under the direction of the king's Flemish-born glazier, Galyon Hone, who was paid a
total of £88 for work 'setting up the king's glass'. Florange and Du Bellay
confirm that the palace was an extraordinarily well-lit and airy building,
one for which there was no contemporary English equivalent, although
Du Bellay considered that it had been modelled on what he called 'the
merchants house' in Calais, by which he evidently meant the Staple.[78]

The internal arrangements of the palace are extremely difficult to
reconstruct with any certainty due to the many inconsistencies in the
observers' descriptions of them. Taken together, however, they indicate

that the front range carried the gateway itself which gave access to the inner court and at the ground floor to an entrance hall. To the left of the 'principal entry' on the first floor level were three apartments for Cardinal Wolsey, 'two halls and a chamber' in lodgings which extended from the gatehouse around the angle of the building and about halfway along the left side wing. To the right of the main entrance were the same arrangements for Henry's sister Mary, Duchess of Suffolk.[79] The remainder of the two ranges at right angles to the main façade contained the royal apartments. Henry had three chambers in the left-hand range and Katherine had the same number in the right-hand range. Their quarters were connected by a passageway under the floor. A gallery led from the king's side back to the castle which Hall noted was designed 'for the secrete passage of the kynges persone into a secrete lodgying within the same castle the more for the kings ease' and which the commissioners described to Wolsey in their letter of 26 March.[80]

The fourth range, opposite the gateway, housed a large hall on the upper level which Hall specifies to be 328 feet (100m) and occupying a quarter of the entire building space. One source describes the space as 'two halls', and another notes that it was sometimes divided in two by hangings. This became the palace's banqueting hall when it was eventually decided that there was not time to build both a separate banqueting house on the site as originally intended and also a chapel.[81]

The hall was reached from the ground floor by a wide staircase which Dubois says was made of oak and had ten steps. Its base can be glimpsed through the main gateway in the Hampton Court painting and it seems to have been the sort of broad, shallow-stepped, straight staircase found in the ducal palaces at Urbino, Ferrara and Venice, which were then starting to come into fashion in English palaces. Hall's description indicates that the staircase itself was highly decorated with 'images of sore and terrible countenaunces, all armed in curious work of argentyne'. At the top of the stairs, according to Dubois, there was 'the figure of an armed foot-soldier, with a great missile who threatens a mortal wound to all who would enter'. This figure may have been a statue or perhaps painted on the wall or ceiling above the stairs.[82]

Hall also specifies that the ground floor of the palace contained offices for household officials: the Lord Chamberlain, the Lord Steward, the Treasurer, Comptroller and the Board of the Green Cloth, together with those for the keepers of the wardrobes and the jewel house. It also housed the service departments: the Ewery, Pantry, Cellar, Buttery, Spicery, Poultry, Pitcher and Larder. All these offices, together with others in nearby villages and under canvas, served as the kitchens in which, Hall notes proudly, the staff 'did marvels in the craft of viands'.[83] Real stone chimneys rose from them and the living quarters of the palace.

The roof of the palace and its overall decoration were in the hands of Richard Gibson, Sergeant of the Tents, and the king's painter John Brown, who was paid £333 6s. 8d for his work. They were assisted by Henry Saddler, John Rastell and one 'Clement Urmeston' or Armstrong. Henry Saddler provided £700 worth of canvas and buckram, most likely to have been used for the roof. He, with Clement Armstrong, was paid £366 13s. 4d 'for making buttons and other garnishing' for the roof of the temporary palace. Armstrong was a London grocer and decorator, a friend of Rastell's, by whom he was almost certainly brought to work at Guînes. Armstrong worked with him on a number of royal decorative projects in the 1520s. John Rastell was a lawyer, known to Sir Edward Belknap, who had employed him to assist in organising the movement of royal artillery in the war of 1512–13. By 1520 Rastell was in London and married to Sir Thomas More's sister Elizabeth. He was also by then a printer, a publisher of legal textbooks, and a playwright.[84]

This trio seem to have worked not only on the canvas roof of the palace but in its main rooms and the halls as well. They painted decorative motifs, mottos and those cryptic sayings so beloved of the age, apparently provided by Alexander Barclay, the Benedictine monk and author, whom Vaux asked Wolsey to send over, in his letter of 10 April. Barclay wrote his most famous work, *The Ship of Fools*, when he was priest at Ottery St Mary in Devon, but from 1513 he was based at Ely Cathedral priory where he completed a number of works related to France. He wrote a critique or satire entitled *Alex. Barclay his Figure of our Mother Holy Church Oppressed by the French King*, now lost. It may have been directed against either Louis XII in 1512–13 or perhaps against Francis I following his invasion of Italy. At about the time of the Field, Barclay produced an English translation of Sallust's *History of the Jurgurthine War*, an edition of which was dedicated to Bishop John Veysey of Exeter. His appearance at the Field may indeed have been at Veysey's instigation. The bishop almost certainly knew Barclay from his time at Ottery St Mary, and Veysey was a patron of the revived interest in classical literature.[85]

In his letter, Vaux also asked to have sent over one 'Master Mayuu'. Joycelyne Russell suggested this was Nicholas Maynwaring, a young man in the household (probably as a chaplain) of Bishop Veysey, although what his connection with the decoration of the palace was remains unclear.[86] An alternative suggestion is that it was the Tuscan sculptor Giovanni da Maiano who was responsible for the classical figures which Hall described as decorating the gateway of the palace. The description of them certainly recalls the set of terracotta roundels of the so-called 'Caesars' now at Hampton Court, paid for by Wolsey in 1521. A number of them still bear evidence of painting in the colours which Hall describes.[87] Garter King of Arms was also called upon to advise on the accurate rendering in a variety of forms of the arms, badges, beasts and devices of members of the Tudor and Valois royal families.

If the exterior of the palace was calculated to impress with its scale and ingenuity, its interior was intended to be nothing less than a spectacular showcase of Henry VIII's personal wealth and taste. The ornate rooms, galleries and hall on the upper floor of the temporary palace impressed all observers as much by their size as by their ingenuity but are confusingly described. The most evocative description is, not surprisingly, by Dubois and is usefully quoted in full:

> The interior of the palace, for its part, brilliant with kingly pomp, is to be extolled above all triumphal palaces. Its suspended terrace is everywhere green with great quantities of rushes; the whole edifice is fragrant with the scent of flowers of every kind. The walls are everywhere cloaked with golden hangings, or else with every variety

of embroidery an embroiderer has fashioned with skilful needle. With cloth of silk in lattice work, interspersed with golden rivets, the inner chambers of the English palace are magnificent.[88]

More prosaically, Hall informs us that the ceilings were sealed and covered in silk, white in the apartments, green in the hall. The ceiling space in the apartments was divided by patterned strips and bosses formed of silk 'knitt and fret with cuttes and braides'. Some of the mouldings may have been supplied by the duke of Suffolk, and the ceilings are likely to have resembled those now to be seen in the 'Wolsey rooms' at Hampton Court, which date from 1526. Around the walls ran a wide cornice decorated in antique fashion, the elements of which were gilt and set against a background of blue material somewhat like enamel.[89]

Like Dubois, Hall emphasises how, in every room, the wall spaces below the cornice were decorated with woollen, silk and gold hangings and tapestries, featuring 'many auncient stories'. Tapestries were the single most costly items of furnishing in sixteenth-century noble and royal houses, designed for ostentatious display. Portable, they could be used to divide, decorate and insulate large and small spaces as needed. The gold and silver threads with which they were woven reflected light from windows in the daytime and from candles at night. Their imagery and themes, usually theological or historical in inspiration, could be used as propaganda on particular occasions, associating the sovereign who owned them with the ideas and ideals represented by the classical or biblical episodes they depicted.

By 1520, prompted not least by the Field of Cloth of Gold, Henry had begun amassing what was, by his death, the largest collection of tapestries and hangings ever owned by a European monarch. In December 1517 he had paid £1,481 16s. 3d for sets of 'arras' of 'King David and Saint John the Baptist', purchased on his behalf by the earl of Worcester and probably woven in Brussels. In April 1520, £410 5s. 9d was paid to the Florentine merchant Giovanni Cavalcanti for another 'David' set. The following month, £971 5d was paid through Cavalcanti for 272 square yards of 'arras' from Pieter van Aelst.[90] It is probable that the 1520 set of 'David' tapestries was the one noted as hanging in the great hall in Dubois's description of the temporary palace. Thomas Campbell has tentatively suggested that the *David* set at Guînes was an early weaving of an identical set also woven for Henry in 1528, now in the Musée de la Renaissance at Ecouen.[91]

The chambers of the other principal members of Henry's entourage were also decorated with an impressive array of new hangings. Queen Katherine's displayed nine tapestries of gold and silk in floral and foliage, or 'millefleurs', design estimated by a Venetian observer to be worth 7 ducats per yard.[92] The duchess of Suffolk's rooms had tapestries that featured Louis XII's 'porcupine' emblem and 'LM' motifs, both allusions to her status as dowager queen of France. No detailed description of Wolsey's apartments survives beyond an observation that the first two chambers were hung with 'silken tapestry without gold, of astounding beauty'. Campbell has suggested that these hangings may have been at least part of a set of the *Triumphs of Petrarch* that appear to have been made for the cardinal in 1520, to a design first presented to Louis XII by Cardinal George d'Amboise in about 1503.[93]

As the commissioners had reported, all of these living rooms and spaces were 'caste aftyr a square courte', that is contained within the main square of the building 'except the chapel and oone gallery'. One Italian observer notes explicitly that the chapel was 'behind the building, adjoining it' and another describes it as 'outside this palace'.[94] Evidently the chapel projected from the range opposite the gateway and so was, in effect, at the back of the building, reached via a short gallery leading out from the middle of the banqueting hall in the range opposite the gateway.[95] Nothing of the chapel is shown in the Hampton Court painting.

In its size and arrangements, the chapel of the temporary palace somewhat anticipated the Chapel Royal now at Hampton Court Palace, with the main liturgical space on the ground floor and two royal 'oratories' or 'holyday closets' upstairs overlooking it. The chapel and oratories were decorated in gold and silver and the high altar was dominated by a massive pearl-studded crucifix over four feet high. The chapel had its own organ which an anonymous Italian observer heard played admirably. Apart from daily and Sunday services, the chapel is likely to have been used for ceremonies marking two of the major annual Christian festivals which fell during Henry's time at the Field. The first was Corpus Christi on 7 June (the day the two kings first met) and the second was the Feast of St John the Baptist, on 24 June.[96]

The temporary palace was the major item of English expenditure on the Field. Unfortunately, the complete lack of records of the Office of the King's Works for these years means that we have only isolated items of expenditure on materials and some wages for work on the palace paid out by the Treasurer of the Chamber, who was exclusively responsible for financing the royal works from 1509 until the late 1530s. The work on the palace as specified in the Chamber accounts of 1520–1 comes to perhaps £2,000 but this cannot represent anywhere near the total cost. In May, Robert Fowler advanced £4,079 for materials and labour on the project. The comparison which the English commissioners at Guînes made with Bridewell Palace may be helpful here. Like the temporary palace at Guînes, Bridewell was a timber-framed structure standing on a brick base. A total estimated cost of around £21,000 was given for Bridewell in or about 1516, including £2,033 for the cost of foundations, £450 for timber and £1,083 for bricks. Glazing came to £686 13s. 4d. Wages of masons, bricklayers, carpenters, joiners and other workmen together came to at least £4,640. Although the temporary palace was larger, Bridewell was a more complex building. It had no hall but was set around two brick-built courtyards and it had a long gallery ending in a watergate on the Thames. The royal lodgings were stacked, rather than horizontally arranged as they were in the temporary palace at Guînes, but in both cases they were reached via a grand staircase.[97] The upper parts of the walls of the temporary palace and its roof were made of timber and canvas rather than brick and slate as at Bridewell, and this would have greatly reduced the cost. Given these considerations, perhaps an estimate of £10,000 for the total cost of the temporary palace is not unreasonable.

The largest element of the English camp at Guînes was the estimated 300 tents erected in the area just outside its walls to accommodate members of the Tudor nobility. For the English tents we have nothing like the detailed accounts we have for the French. There are, however, designs for royal pavilions, now generally accepted to be those for the Field, in the British Library.[98] These indicate that the pavilions consisted of a variety of square, rectangular and circular tents, laid out in a line or set at right angles to each other and linked by smaller galleries. The spaces thus created by the tents, or by hangings within them, provided a range of public and private areas and approximated the sequence of rooms in Tudor palaces and manor houses.

One of the surviving designs for a pavilion gives an indication of their size and layout. The pavilion is entered through a main rectangular tent marked as 40 feet long and 19 wide which acts as a kind of 'great hall'. A short gallery then leads down to a second rectangular tent set at right angles to the first and measuring 30 feet long by 18 wide. This creates a second, semi-public, space something like a 'presence chamber' in a royal or noble manor house. A second short gallery leads from this room and is itself intersected by another gallery, at either end of which is a round tent each marked as 18 feet and serving probably as a private or 'privy' chamber or garderobe of some kind. A final short gallery along the main axis leads to a larger circular tent marked as 20 feet, which was probably the bedchamber and private space of the occupant.[99]

Among the most impressive of the surviving designs is one for a quadrilateral pavilion. It comprises no fewer than eight (and possibly as many as fourteen) large rectangular tents linked vertically and horizontally into six intersecting ranges. Some tents were dressed in blue or red silk embroidered with decorations in gold. The vivid colours in these drawings evoke the rich fabrics used to create visually impressive accommodation in the English camp, as in the French. The cost of these pavilions in total was considerable. An inventory of the possessions of William, Baron Sandys, taken at his death in 1541, lists a new pavilion consisting of three chambers, a hall, and appurtenances valued at £40. Henry spent large sums of money in the months before the Field on substantial amounts of material likely to have been used to decorate the palace and to dress these tents. These purchases include 1,050 yards of velvet at 12s. 8d the yard provided by Richard Gresham in June. In May he had also supplied sables to the value of £442, and £1,033 12s. 1d worth of velvet. In April, one Francis de Barde was paid £1,497 12s. 2d for cloth of gold and other fabrics, and Cavalcanti was paid £2,355 17s. 4d for cloth of gold and velvet.[100]

All the pavilions featured painted wooden ridge boards running along their tops decorated with carved *fleurs-de-lis* and Tudor roses. Many also sported polychrome 'king's beasts' such as lions, dragons, griffins, greyhounds, stags and royal antelopes seated on bases which covered the tops of the masts that held up the tents. The beasts held standards topped either with closed crowns imperial or *fleurs-de-lis* and flying pennants in a variety of heraldic designs which included the royal arms: the Beaufort portcullis and the Tudor rose. Tented pavilions dressed in the Tudor livery colours of green and white also feature in the Hampton Court painting of the Field of Cloth of Gold. Henry might well have smiled at the discomforture of the French when their tents blew down in the summer storms of mid-June, safe as he was in his sturdy temporary palace and his castle at Guînes, but many of the tents of his own entourage were also blown down in the wind and rains.[101]

The Tournament Lists

The English and French camps were the separate projects of each court. The preparation of the tournament field and the competition to be held there was, however, a joint enterprise.[102] As already noted, Francis had agreed to come into English territory for the first meeting with Henry on the understanding that he could determine the arrangements for the tournament. This being the case, the site of the tournament field was the first controversial issue for the two leading commissioners. Marshal Châtillon expected that it would be sited 'a little mile' from Ardres and thus in the neutral place of the boundary of English and French territory, exactly where the kings were originally supposed to have met. However, the 1520 English 'Memoriall' of the meeting stated that the site was to be equidistant between Guînes and Ardres. Worcester nominated a site that answered that description, but this meant that it was still within the English Pale. Châtillon refused the suggestion outright. This action Francis endorsed on 20 April. He could defer to Henry in small things, but not on this point and no agreement had been reached as late as 26 April when Worcester wrote seeking immediate instructions.[103] By 13 May, however, the English ambassador in France, Sir Richard Wingfield, wrote that Francis had now accepted the site originally suggested by Worcester. The immediate political context of this decision will be discussed in more detail in the following chapter, but it may be that practical considerations, such as the topographical suitability of Worcester's preferred site, were finally decisive.[104]

The place set out for the tournament, which the English called 'the Field', was rectangular in shape, covering an area 900 feet long and 328 feet wide (274.3m × 100m) roughly along an east–west axis, with Ardres at one end and Guînes at the other. The whole 'camp', as Worcester also called it, was surrounded on all four sides by an eight feet (2.4m) wide ditch. The earth dug from the ditch was then used to build a bulwark some nine feet (2.7m) high. In front of this bulwark was a railed area some eight feet across. Within this protected space was the 'Field' proper, laid out according to a ground plan or 'platt' designed by Henry himself, which was presented to the French commissioners by Worcester. The design included a proposed location, along the east–west axis, of the tilt, counter-lists and runs used for jousting. This also proved controversial. Given that the whole area was on English territory (and that Francis had already agreed to meet Henry initially on English soil), Châtillon wanted it to be located more towards the Ardres end, for his king's honour. Worcester understood the point and after a long discussion a compromise was reached in which the whole camp was extended 50 feet (15.2m) towards Ardres. Evidently satisfied with this, Châtillon then wanted the barriers to be used in the foot combats to be located nearer the Ardres end. This demand Worcester refused, saying that they would interfere with the location of the 'tourney' used in the tilting. Châtillon countered that the barriers would be removed when not required. As the whole camp was still on English territory, it would not diminish Henry's honour at all if the barriers were towards the Ardres end. Worcester refused to alter Henry's plan in this respect or even to seek further instructions on the point. He did, however, inform Henry of the conversation, noting that, this issue apart, the two sides were conscious of the time and were agreed on what now needed to be done.[105]

As it was eventually constructed, the tilt stood centrally along the main axis of the field. When this area was first marked out, it had been immediately realised that Henry's plan had put the tilt too far away from a proposed royal pavilion to allow those occupying it to get a good view of the action. It was therefore shifted back to the middle so that, on the right-hand side as one entered from Guînes, the stand contained within it a royal pavilion used sometimes by the kings, but mainly by the queens and ladies of the two courts. On the left was a larger stand, probably of some three tiers, used by general spectators. Henry wanted a ditch four feet deep and eight wide (1.2m × 2.4m) dug in front of this stand to prevent intrusions on to the field. In the end this was thought too time-consuming to excavate and a potential threat to the foundations of the stand in the event of rain. A railing in front of the gallery was built instead. At either end of the field stood a triumphal entry arch and Hall tells us that just inside the entrance at the Guînes end were two 'arming chambers' made of painted wainscot: one for each king with Francis's on the right and Henry's on the left.[106]

The area in which the Field of Cloth of Gold took place is still open space and farmland. It lies along the present D231 road between Guînes and Ardres although there is some doubt that the modern road follows the route between the two towns in 1520. A commemorative granite stela is located on the northern side of the road about a mile west of Ardres. This probably marks the site of the tournament lists, which contemporary sources indicate were on English territory but close to Ardres. Certainly this is the only section of the modern landscape between the two towns which is flat enough, long enough and wide enough to have contained the lists.

The work required was not begun properly until mid-May. Even as Châtillon and Worcester argued about the location of the camp in late

April, they had agreed that the French would build 'half the fortifications, scaffolds and tilts' at Francis's charge. One thousand pioneers were at Ardres ready to start building the camp and Worcester agreed that he would also supply workmen and timber. On 26 April he asked Wolsey to instruct the three commissioners at Guînes to arrange timber, bricks and carpenters for the work. This raises the intriguing and likely prospect that English and French carpenters, bricklayers and pioneers worked alongside each other. They would have been able, so far as their different languages allowed, to share, and probably argue about, different materials and building techniques. This situation, unique in the history of early-modern Anglo-French dealings, where technicians and labourers of both nations worked together on a joint civil project, would not be repeated until the construction of the Concorde aircraft and the Channel Tunnel in the twentieth century.

Worcester doubted that all could be finished on time and thought that, if required, work on the general spectators' stand could continue at night after the tournament had begun – which it evidently did. Marshal Châtillon, too, was concerned that all would not be ready in time. On 23 and 24 May, he wrote to Worcester reminding him that the artificial 'Tree of Honour' for the tournament had yet to be constructed. The tree stood upon a stage shaped to look like a mound called a 'perron' and upon the tree hung a set of shields, each of which indicated a different competition in the tournament. Knights who wished to participate, who were already starting to arrive, had to indicate by touching with their lances the appropriate shields. Their personal armorial shields would also be hung there to signify their entry to the tournament.[107] Originally two trees had been planned by the French but pressure of time simplified things.[108] The reports of Venetian ambassadors and the fact that detailed records of the materials used survive in Gibson's Revels accounts, show that the English took responsibility for setting up what was, in the end, a single Tree of Honour. It was located at the Guînes end of the field, between the two royal arming chambers. From the 'perron' long spars of wood were fashioned to represent the trunk and branches of a hybrid raspberry and hawthorn tree – symbolic of France and England. It was festooned with hundreds of hawthorn and rasp-berry flowers made of silk and satin and, rather curiously, some 2,000 cherries made of crimson satin. Its role in the ceremonies of the tourna-ment will be discussed in a later chapter.[109]

Worcester's brief reference in his letter alerts us to the fact that the 'Franco-English' encounter of the Field of Cloth of Gold permeated more social levels than might first be supposed. It also alerts us to the work required by thousands of ordinary men and women whose names are not, for the most part, recorded in accounts but whose skills were essential. Almost as many artisans, pioneers, bricklayers, carpenters, plasterers, painters, tailors, seamstresses and other cloth workers, carters, soldiers and labourers were employed in preparing the Field of Cloth of Gold as there were people attending the event itself.

CHAPTER 3

Equal in Honour

The four gentlemen hostages of France, daily resorted to the court and had great cheer and were well entertained and every time they moved, stirred and required the king to pass the sea and to meet with the French king their master, whom they praised highly, affirming that if the king and he might once familiarly commune together, that there should such a constant love rise and increase between them, which afterward should never fail.

Edward Hall[1]

THE IDEA OF a personal meeting between Henry VIII and Francis I eventually became an international event that involved enough people to make a respectably large early-modern army. Transporting, accommodating, ordering, feeding and watering, protecting and entertaining this vast concourse of people was certainly akin to organising a royal military campaign. Participating in it may well have felt like one too.

In February 1520 Cardinal Wolsey drew up a treaty for both kings to ratify, which set out the prospective arrangements for their meeting. He also issued a proclamation declaring that the two sovereigns would come together and prepare 'to do some fair feat of arms, as well on foot as on horseback against all comers'. Henry was to come with his wife Katherine and his sister Mary, Duchess of Suffolk, to the castle at Guînes by the end of May. Francis was to be at his town of Ardres with his wife Claude and his mother Louise within four days of the end of May. A copy of Wolsey's proclamation was sent to France.[2]

Given the extraordinarily detailed and expensive preparations and assembling of people to attend which were under way pursuant to Wolsey's proclamation, maintaining good relations between the two kings in the weeks leading up to the meeting was vital. In France, Sir Richard Wingfield was called upon not merely to be a cipher of the competitive spirit between them but to handle several issues which threatened to wreck the meeting altogether, even as plans for it were being finalised. The first problem that arose was where, exactly, the two kings were to have their first personal encounter.

Despite a tone of apparent neutrality struck by Wolsey's February proclamation on the purpose of the meeting, there was a definite, if initially covert, aggressiveness about the English approach to this issue. According to another 'memoriall', dating from 1519 for a meeting that was first projected for July that year, it had been agreed that the kings would meet on neutral ground, on the border of the Pale of Calais and France. The chosen place was Sandingfield. This ensured that, as had been customary since medieval times when two kings met to make peace, they would have equal status, neither being the host or guest on that occasion.[3]

Yet a second proclamation Wolsey made, on 12 March 1520, declared that because Henry had to subject himself to the labours, dangers and expenses of crossing the sea and 'leaving his realm and puissance for certain time', it would not accord with his honour to make the further concession of meeting Francis on neutral ground as originally envisaged. It declared, even before Francis had actually agreed to this, that the encounter would take place 'within the territory of the said castle of Guînes ... near the limits of France'. In other words, and as would be heavily emphasised to the English nobles summoned to the event, Francis had to come into *English* territory to meet Henry.[4] This would make him the first king of France in history, not then a captive, to enter English domains conquered from France during the Hundred Years War. Such a move was tantamount, in English eyes at least, to an acknowledgement of Henry's rights over those lands in succession to Edward III and Henry V. Only then, Wolsey declared, on the day after the initial meeting, would Henry and Francis meet again 'in some place indifferent between Ardres and Guînes'.[5]

Not surprisingly, the French council strenuously objected to this idea, as the Admiral Bonnivet informed Wolsey. Yet Francis chose to show princely magnanimity designed to set at naught the petty point-scoring played at by Henry and Wolsey. Having, he said, 'full confidence' in Wolsey, he agreed to come on to English soil to meet Henry, despite the advice of his council. In return for this gesture, he insisted that the style and formalities of the tournament being arranged should be in accordance with his preferences and according to French custom. The English grumbled at having to make even this concession, but Francis would not be gainsaid.[6]

No sooner had a final date for the meeting and the first encounter of the kings been agreed than Henry decided he wished to postpone the Field. This was ostensibly to allow him more time for preparation but was actually to allow him to meet Charles V in England in late May. On 16 April Francis told ambassador Wingfield that he knew that the forthcoming Franco-English meeting had prompted Charles's proposed visit to England. The ambassador rather lamely suggested that such a meeting was simply a contingency in case the winds blew Charles's ships into English ports. He didn't convince himself, much less Francis. Things maritime being in the conversation, the king then rather pointedly talked about his own 'grete shippes, whyche He had all redye', including a new one then being built, which was as big as Henry's largest ship. From a survey taken at the end of 1520 we know that Francis had about twenty-five great ships in ports in Brittany and Normandy and these included *La Grande Francoise*, which, at 1,500 tons, was indeed as large as Henry's flagship the *Henri Grâce à Dieu*.[7] The king asserted that he had good personal knowledge of ship-building but, as Wingfield tactfully put it when reporting this interview to Henry, 'He approchyth not Your Highness in that science'.[8] Wolsey eventually brought the issue to a conclusion by telling the French that Henry was hardly in a position to decline to meet with his relative as he passed by the realm and that the king would be at Guînes by 31 May.

During these difficult negotiations, Wingfield very effectively used the privileged access granted to him by Francis to establish a good rapport with the king. He frequently hunted with Francis and would introduce into conversations information about Henry's hunting and jousting abilities, talents upon which Francis also prided himself. Immediately after his conversation with Francis on 16 April, Wingfield was invited by the king to join a chase in the forest near Blois. He was close enough to the action to send Henry a detailed description of French boar-hunting techniques and of Francis's personal skill as a huntsman. After killing the boar and cutting off its right foot, as was customary, Francis remounted and at the suggestion of the seigneur de Lautrec, but with little evident enthusiasm, followed the flight of falcons against a heron. As he rode with Wingfield, the king said that the French were the only true masters of 'theyr hunting by force', that is, pursuit on horseback of a fleeing quarry. Wingfield defended his master and his nation, saying that it was hardly surprising that Francis was good at the chase given that it was the only form of hunting he really practised. Henry was as good, or better, at the chase proper and equally skilled at many other forms of hunting. He could therefore offer all those who hunted with him their preferred sport: 'In all whyche sortes of huntynge I shewed to know Your Grace to have no fellowe, for the assuryd and perftye knowledge of all that belonged to that arte'.[9]

Francis and Wingfield evidently enjoyed this sort of spirited repartee and towards the end of this letter, Wingfield reported that had he been one of Francis's own subjects, he could 'no more familierly use [treat] me, then he doythe contennually'. Francis had renewed the invitation for him to enter the private royal apartments whenever he wished to, 'with new and straycte commaundement . . . to all the huyssyers [ushers] to opyn unto me wheresoever he may be'. The ambassador recognised why this was so: 'All whyche, Sir,' he went on, 'I know wele procedythe onlye to do Your Highness singular honour and pleasure'.[10]

Written in the weeks immediately before the Field of Cloth of Gold, Wingfield's letter is important for the insights it offers into how the very personal rivalry between Henry and Francis operated and how it would be expressed at that encounter. Central to that rivalry were not only their various personal accomplishments in hunting, horsemanship, archery and so on, but, in the demonstration of those skills, the assertion of princely virtues of magnificence and generosity. In his conversation on hunting with Francis, the ambassador defended his master as the greater man because his wide-ranging proficiency enabled him to offer better hospitality to his guests. Francis's own hospitality in allowing the ambassador unprecedented access to the royal apartments was itself a compelling act of generosity, which was principally designed to assert his chivalric virtue in dealings with Henry. The generous treatment of the French hostages in England was offered in the same spirit, and news of it had reached the French court – just as Henry intended.

Nevertheless, the early days of April marked a high point of tension and uncertainty on the French side as to whether the meeting really would take place. Then, on 17 April, a reassuring indication of English goodwill arrived at the French court in the person of Thomas Benolt, Clarenceux King of Arms. He came to proclaim the June tournament in the names of the two kings who would be the chief challengers or 'tenans'. He announced the terms of the challenge from a place 'called the terrasse, whyche over loketh all the courte' at the château of Blois the following day. Meanwhile, at Greenwich, Orléans King of Arms, Clarenceux's French counterpart, also proclaimed the challenge in the name of the two kings. The ambassador thought that the news cheered Francis and was taken as a sign that the meeting really would go ahead, Charles V's planned visit to England notwithstanding.[11]

The presence in the French court of one of England's chief heralds also prompted Francis to raise, for the first time, the prospect of an exchange of royal orders of chivalry between himself and Henry. Having lost the imperial election to Charles in 1519, Francis sought to join him in the ranks of what was then the most eminent chivalric order in Europe. This quickly became yet another competitive issue between Francis and Henry. On 18 April Wingfield had enquired where Francis would be on 23 April, St George's Day. Mention of the Garter patron's feast day prompted the Admiral Bonnivet to request an exchange of orders in June. This, he thought, should be neither strange nor difficult to accomplish and intimated that Francis was bound to ask for such an exchange at the meeting. Wingfield confirmed that the place of the deceased Emperor Maximilian as a knight of the English order was vacant but, in contrast to his witty responses to Francis's other enquiries about Henry, on this matter he 'durst not touch in any wyse'. Francis reflected that it was honourable for Henry to have foreign princes in his order of chivalry and that he had many among the knights of the Order of St Michael. What better sign could there be of fraternal and chivalric love than that they make each other a member of their sovereign orders?[12] Henry duly marked St George's Day with the knights of the Order at Greenwich and in early May received Olivier de La Vernade, seigneur de La Bastie, who had been resident ambassador between February and December 1519, and who now returned to England as special envoy in the final weeks before Henry's meeting with Francis.[13]

It is worth noting that at exactly the same time as the prospect of an exchange of orders was being raised at the French court, Châtillon and Worcester were busy arguing about the location of the site of the tournament to be held at the Field. It will be recalled that on 20 April Francis had written from Chambord insisting that the marshal's preferred site should be accepted as he had agreed to enter English territory for the first meeting with Henry. Yet by 13 May, the king had changed his mind. Wingfield wrote from Beauvais that he had received a letter from a servant of Sir Nicholas Vaux indicating that Worcester and Châtillon had now agreed that the tournament would be held on the place originally proposed by the English commissioner and that this had been at Francis's behest. The French marshal was apparently still resisting, but Francis had now written to him confirming his second order to accept the site chosen by Worcester.[14] Practical considerations about the suitability of the site may finally have determined his decision, but Francis may also have acquiesced on the location of the tiltyard as yet another gesture of what he saw as chivalric generosity in the hope of being admitted to the Order of Garter at the event. He was to be disappointed on this occasion but Francis renewed his demand a number of times in the years that followed and finally succeeded in 1527.[15]

The Royal Entourages

Pursuant to the March 1520 'Memoriall', the English began drawing up detailed lists of those who were to be summoned to the Field, in what capacity and with what number of attendants, so we have very nearly a complete listing for Henry's train. The principal consideration in these preparations was to ensure parity of numbers with the French because neither king wished to incur greater expense than was necessary, but nor did he wish to be outshone by his opponent's having a more splendid retinue. When the idea of the meeting was first talked about in 1519, it had originally been agreed that Henry and Francis were to be escorted to their meeting by the members of their respective households and guard and a further 100 nobles, of whom forty were to be at their first personal encounter. In accordance with this plan, on 5 March 1519 Sir Thomas Boleyn reported that 'Francis desires to know what number the King and Wolsey will bring over, that he may appoint an equal number to meet them'. By 19 March he reported that the French would order their entourage according to a roll of the English attending, of which they now had a copy.[16] When, a year later, the English began planning in earnest they specified that neither king should 'bring with theyme a mor number of Noblemen and women servants and horsis than is contenyned in a bill indented, enterchangeably delyverd and subscribed with their handes'.[17] This may refer to the 1519 agreement whose total numbers were already projected to be about 6,000 on the English side.

Given this determination to achieve numerical parity, it follows that the French entourage would have been of an equivalent order to the English one. Similar French lists must once have been made, but only one memorandum of those who were to attend Francis and his first meeting with Henry survives.[18] From this we know that the French retinue comprised the realm's greatest nobles and prelates, each with his own large retinue. The officials and servants of Francis's household, who numbered about 450 in 1520, were also there with the king. So too were those of Queen Claude and Louise de Savoie. We know from eyewitnesses that beyond the household, the French entourage was headed by the great territorial magnates, the great officers of the crown and the knights of the Order of St Michael. There are also records of those who jousted at the tournament in June and some individual names of other participants are given in the many descriptions of the event. A good deal of work has, however, been done in the last thirty years on the personnel, structures and functioning of the French royal court. This research, set alongside what is known about the English party, enables us to get a better impression than we have had hitherto of the size and disposition of both royal entourages at the Field.

But who, exactly, was meeting whom in 1520? The members of the French nobility as a whole were more numerous and more broadly defined than those of England. The population of France itself was about fifteen million whereas that of England is thought to have been around two and a half million.[19] Therefore the 1,130 or so principal members of the English party constituted virtually the entire English peerage and a sizeable proportion of the gentry, whereas the equivalent number on the French side represented a very much smaller proportion of the total number of their nobles. There are reckoned to have been approximately 25,000 noble households in France by c. 1560–80. Although they constituted a tiny proportion of the total French population, this number was still vastly more than the total number of both nobles and gentlemen in England combined. Moreover, although there was a rough equivalence between them at each social level, the French upper nobility was more highly stratified than the English peerage, while English gentry status was much more tightly circumscribed than French 'nobility' at its lower levels.[20]

The overall parity of numbers upon which both sides were so insistent in 1520 is, perhaps, somewhat deceptive. This is because parity did not extend to particular ranks or degrees. Given limited numbers, each king is likely to have summoned to him those nobles whose own high status best reflected his pre-eminent authority. Francis simply had more nobles of all ranks to choose from and consequently brought more individuals from the higher nobility (*haute noblesse*) and fewer, proportionally, of his middle-ranking nobles (*moyenne noblesse*) to the Field. This is borne out by the various lists and descriptions which indicate that whereas, for example, Henry was escorted by two dukes, only one of whom claimed royal blood, Francis was escorted by four dukes, three of whom were of royal blood. Whereas Henry brought eleven other peers with him, Francis had some twenty-one counts and princes (the equivalent of English peers but not themselves French *pairs*) in attendance.

The same is true among the ecclesiastical peers. The highest-ranked members of the French party after the king and queen were the fifteen prelates of France, several of whom were members of peerage families. In answer, as it were, to Wolsey as papal legate *a latere*, Francis brought four cardinals: Adrien Gouffier, Cardinal de Boisy, himself a papal legate; Amanjeu, Cardinal d'Albret; François Louis, Cardinal de Bourbon; and Jean de Guise, Cardinal de Lorraine. Etienne Poncher, the Bishop of Paris, led nine other bishops together with François de Moulins, the Great Almoner (*Grand Aumônier*) of France, who also headed the Chapel Royal. It was a similar story at the other end of the secular hierarchy. Whereas Henry was accompanied of necessity by knights from nearly all the shires in England, whatever their relative wealth and importance in his regime, Francis would have been able to summon, from among the middle-ranking nobility, those to whom he was personally close and those who were of greatest importance in their locality. Given the comparatively large travelling distances in France, he may also have chosen more of those whose lands lay closest to the venue and to England, in Picardy, Normandy and the Île-de-France.

Such variations in status among individuals at the Field did not go unnoticed in the mentality of the period and created some interesting disparities within and across the two national entourages. In time of conflict, the aristocrats of Francis's court disparaged the recent elevations and short pedigrees of even the highest English nobles, especially the duke of Suffolk. Cardinal Wolsey's lowly origins were not infrequently commented upon. The greatest French duke and an unassuming English knight would have had very little in common. Yet the bonds of chivalry and the concept of *noblesse* would have given them a basis for greeting and interacting with each other as gentlemen at the Field, the difference in their ranks notwithstanding.

The English 'Memoriall' confirms that Henry's entourage consisted of the great officers of state, the royal household (organised in its three departments of the Chapel, the King's Chamber and the Household proper), together with the king's guards. It specifies that 'bokes' of the names of those attending, with 'their nombres, traynes, and horses', were to be made, principally to ensure that sufficient shipping was prepared for them and that all could be accommodated and fed once they arrived at the event.[21]

The 'Memoriall' also states that nobles and gentry in the country were to be summoned to attend by individual letters written by the king's secretaries and sent out under the direction of the Master of the Posts. The fullest of three English lists which survive is in the Bodleian Library and is reproduced as Appendix A.[22] It details the entourages of the king and queen separately, showing the numbers of peers and barons, knights, esquires, noblewomen and gentlewomen in each, together with bishops, chaplains, secretaries, musicians, physicians, heralds and others in attendance. Each of the principal members of these entourages was himself entitled to bring a specified number of attendants, according to rank, so that the dukes of Buckingham and Suffolk were each able to bring ten gentlemen, fifty-five servants, five chaplains and fifty horses. Each of the ten earls and four bishops with Henry could have six gentlemen, thirty-three servants, three chaplains and twenty horses, and so on.[23] Perhaps predictably, the number of Wolsey's personal attendants as Cardinal Lord Chancellor and papal legate exceeded even those of the dukes. He was able to bring fifty gentlemen, twelve chaplains and 237 servants; that is 299 men in total and 150 horses. The Bodleian list indicates that there were 994 principal persons in Henry's retinue (excluding two named foreign ambassadors). When all the attendants, servants and horses allowed to all the principals and all the clergy, officials and servants of the king's and queen's households and stables proper are added together we reach a total English entourage of 5,832 people and 3,217 horses.

Impressive though the size and calibre of Henry's entourage was, it did not include two of the highest-ranking nobles of England. The first was the four-year-old Princess Mary. Although Mary did not accompany her parents, she did emulate them in welcoming and entertaining French courtiers. In late June, three French gentlemen arrived in England directly from the Field to greet her on behalf of the Dauphin François, whose betrothal to her had been confirmed at the event. Attended by her governess, Margaret Pole, Countess of Salisbury, by Agnes Howard, Duchess of Norfolk, and by Eleanor, Countess of Worcester, Mary greeted the Frenchmen in the Presence Chamber at Richmond Palace, 'with most goodly countenance, proper communication and pleasant pastime'. She also played the virginals for them and, as the royal council proudly told her father, 'greatly marvelled and rejoyced the same, her young and tender age considered'.[24]

The other great noble who was not at the Field was Thomas Howard, second Duke of Norfolk. He presided over the royal council in England assisted by Richard Fox, Bishop of Winchester, William Atwater, Bishop of Lincoln and the Lords Berners and Darcy among others. Their main responsibility was for the governance and security of the realm in the king's absence and they sent regular reports informing Henry that England was peaceful and that no threatening news had come from Ireland or Scotland.[25] Another, perhaps surprising, absentee was Howard's eldest son, Thomas, Earl of Surrey. He had recently been appointed Lord Deputy of Ireland and had taken up duties in Dublin. The family was represented solely by the duke's younger son Lord Edmund, who participated successfully in the tournament.[26]

Like its English counterpart, the French court was at the heart of the king's entourage. It was divided into three main departments: the *chapelle*, the *chambre*, the king's private living space and the *hôtel*, with its various sub-departments. In addition there was the *écurie* or stables, and departments responsible for hunting equipment, animals and birds, the *vénerie* and *fauconnerie*. Finally there were several companies of mounted and foot guards.[27]

The *chapelle* was formally the head of the royal household hierarchy. In 1520 its twenty-two senior members ministered to the spiritual needs of king and court and some of them at least were present at the Field. They included the king's confessor, Guillaume de Paruy, Bishop of Troyes, Symphorien de Bullioud, Bishop of Glandève (in the Alpes-Maritimes), Pierre de Montigny, Bishop of Castre, and Jean de la Baulme, Bishop of Auxerre. They were themselves attended by chaplains and clerks. With them came the men and boys of the chapel who sang at liturgical ceremonies and entertainments during the event. Although the members of the court clergy were not directly involved in policy-making in the way of the prelates mentioned above, they still maintained some spiritual influence over decision-makers, including the king himself, and interpreted royal policy to the court and the nation in religious terms that glorified the monarchy.[28]

In overall charge of the royal household was the *Grand-Maître* (Great Master) of France, René de Savoie, comte de Villars and Beaufort, governor of Provence.[29] His nearest equivalents in England were the earl of Worcester as Lord Chamberlain and the earl of Shrewsbury, the Lord Steward. Each year the *Grand-Maître* drew up a wages roll of the king's household, showing the names and ranks of royal attendants. These noblemen usually served the king personally for a quarter or perhaps half a year at a time and the rolls therefore provide a reasonably reliable guide as to who was actually with the king for at least a part of each year. The upper section of the household payment roll for 1520 is given at Appendix B.

The department of the *chambre* was the true heart of the court and its members accompanied the king in significant numbers. Early in Francis's reign it was presided over by an honorary officer, the *Grand chambellan* (Great Chamberlain), who, in 1520, was the thirteen-year-old Claude d'Orléans, duc de Longueville. His duties would therefore have been nominal. Immediately below him was the *premier chambellan*, Louis II de La Trémoïlle, vicomte de Thouars. He was a veteran of the Italian wars and the king's lieutenant-general or governor of Brittany and is listed as part of Francis's retinue at the first meeting with Henry. So, too, was his grandson François, prince de Talmont.[30]

At his accession in 1515, Francis had created the office of *gentil-homme de la chambre du roi* which, over time, replaced the older and more widely held office of *chambellan du roi*. Their nearest antecedent would appear to be that of the *écuyer de la chambre* in the household of Charles the Bold of Burgundy. Olivier de la Marche's account of his household, written in 1474, describes the duke as having a group of sixteen young men who were:

> Men of great houses who serve as companions to the duke whether he goes on foot or on horse, and look after his person and his clothes. They sleep near his chamber to aid in the security of his person. When the duke has worked all day on his business and given audi-ence to everyone, and then retires to his chamber, these sixteen go with him to keep him company. Some sing, others read stories and short tales; others discuss arms or love and all make the prince gracious pastime. These squires may be in the prince's chamber all hours when he does not hold council. They have *bouche* of court like the *maîtres d'hôtel*.[31]

The evidence is that Francis I's *gentilshommes de la chambre* had very similar duties and their most important privilege was access to their master's *chambre* outside the times of his formal interactions with the court. In 1520, Francis had twenty-one *gentilshommes de la chambre*, virtually all of whom were beginning important careers in his service as local governors and officials, as ambassadors and military commanders. Seven of the *gentilshommes* are known from the records to have been with the king in June, but we might reasonably expect that, on such a grand occasion, more of them were in attendance.

The activities of the *chambre* and its *gentilshommes* were actually co-ordinated on a day-to-day basis by the *premier gentilhomme de la chambre* (First Gentleman of the Chamber), who, in 1520, was Anne de

Montmorency, one of the king's childhood friends, then known as the seigneur de La Rochepot after one his family's lordships in Burgundy. A number of *gentilshommes* were named participants in the tournament, including Montmorency himself and his younger brother François. Philippe de Chabot, seigneur de Brion, another childhood companion of the king, who eventually succeeded Bonnivet as Admiral of France, also jousted. He and Montmorency were to become great rivals in power at the French court in the 1530s. Other *gentilshommes* known to have been at the Field were François, seigneur de Saint-Marsault, René d'Anjou, seigneur de Mézières, whom Wingfield later described as being 'in the king's chamber here and in singular good favour with him' and Michel de Poysieu, seigneur de Saint-Mesme *dit* Capdorat. So too were Adrien de Tiercelin, seigneur de Brosse, and Antoine de Raffin, *dit* Poton, whom Henry rewarded with gold chains. All had made favourable impressions on Henry when they participated in the 1518 embassy to London and had helped to entertain English ambassadors in France thereafter. Also at the Field was Charles du Solier, seigneur de Morette, eventually one of Francis's longest-serving *gentilshommes* and a future ambassador to England, who was superbly portrayed by Holbein in the 1530s.[32]

Although the *gentilshommes de la chambre* were already of great significance in the court by 1520, they did not yet formally outrank the other personal servants of the king as they would do later. Francis was also attended by considerable numbers of these officers, responsible for household organisation, serving his meals and caring for his clothing and possessions. Among their ranks were men who participated in the tournament in 1520, including two of Francis's sixteen *échansons* (cup-bearers, responsible for the king's wine service), several of his nineteen *pannetiers* (table servants) and at least two of his sixteen *écuyers d'écurie* (esquires of the stable). One very successful participant in the tournament was Antoine de Hallewin, seigneur de Piennes. He was one of twenty-five young men in training in the royal household, known collectively as the *enfants d'honneur*, the French equivalents of Henry VIII's 'henchmen'.

The French king's military establishment at the Field was led by Charles III, duc de Bourbon-Montpensier, the Constable of France, the realm's chief military officer after the king. He sponsored one of the companies of jousters at the tournament, although he does not appear to have participated personally.[33] The *Grand Écuyer* (Master of the Horse) was the Milanese nobleman Galeazzo da San Severino who, together with the Constable, was principally responsible for the king's security at the Field. The French Admiral, Guillaume Gouffier, seigneur de Bonnivet, also attended. He was an early favourite of the king who had already been prominent in relations with England. Finally there was . Galiot de Genouilhac, Great Master of the Artillery, whose officials, as we have seen, organised the French camp.

Ranking as peers because of their military office and entitled to address the king as 'mon cousin', were the four marshals of France, all of whom seem to have been at the Field. They were, in addition to Gaspard de Coligny, seigneur de Châtillon, whom we have already met, Jacques II de Chabannes, seigneur de La Palisse, the governor of the Lyonnais, and Odet de Foix, seigneur de Lautrec, the governor of Guyenne and of the duchy of Milan.[34] The fourth marshal was Robert Stuart, seigneur d'Aubigny, who commanded the oldest and most prestigious guards company in the French royal household, the 100-strong *garde écossaise*, the Scots Guard. He was the head of the Stuart-Darnley dynasty after his elder brother, the earl of Lennox, had been killed at Flodden.[35]

The rest of the French king's guard comprised, firstly, the *Deux-cents gentilshommes de l'hôtel* (Two Hundred Gentlemen of the Household) commanded by Jean de Poitiers, seigneur de Saint-Vallier, and his son-in-law, Louis de Brézé, *Grand Sénéchal* of Normandy. They were elite noble troops, who received annual pensions and fought closely with the king in battle. The *Cent suisses* (One Hundred Swiss) were the king's foot guards, under their captain, the seigneur de Florange, a future marshal of France. There were also three companies of mounted archers, the last of which was a creation of Francis I. The memorandum's reference to '400 archers of the guard, and 4 captains' is somewhat ambiguous, but it suggests that, in addition to the Gentlemen and the Swiss,

Francis was escorted by the three companies of mounted archers together perhaps with the Scots Guard.[36] If this was the case, then the total complement of 700 men in the military household made a significant contribution to the king's retinue.

It is clear that the royal household and guards formed the core of Francis's entourage in 1520 but what proportion of the total numbers on the French side they constituted is hard to say with certainty. Like their English equivalents, each nobleman who held a position in the *chambre* and upper household would have been accompanied by several of his own personal attendants and, if he was married, by his wife and her servants. The total complement of the king's personal retinue might, therefore, easily have been as many as 3,000 people – and this is similar to the final projected figure for Henry's personal entourage.[37] The remaining 3,000 people estimated to have been in the French party comprised those in the households of Queen Claude and Louise de Savoie, together with the retinues of the peers, who attended the king.

Queen Claude, then aged 20, had been married to Francis since May 1514. Like Katherine of Aragon, she had her own entourage based upon her household within the court. This has been estimated to have numbered just over 200 people, of whom twelve were ladies-in-waiting.[38] In June 1520 she was in the seventh month of pregnancy with her fifth child. Her condition had been an important, and at times rather useful, factor in the French refusal to delay the meeting. In mid-May Wingfield had assured Henry that 'you would have had no little compassion if y[e saw] the poor creature with the charge she beareth'.[39] Given her advanced pregnancy and contemporary notions of the confinement of women in its later stages, Queen Claude participated remarkably fully in the various festivities at the Field, including several times watching her husband perform at the tournament. Claude died in July 1524 after a brief illness.

Second only in status to the queen among the women at the event were the king's mother, Louise, and his sister, Marguerite, both of whom took prominent roles in welcoming and entertaining their English guests. Louise de Savoie had her own household within the court (estimated to have numbered 295 in 1531). She continued to advise her son and took some share in negotiations with Wolsey at the meeting. In 1520 Marguerite was married to Charles, duc d'Alençon. Until the birth of the Dauphin François in 1518, he had been heir presumptive and recognised as 'the second person in the kingdom'. After Alençon's death in 1525, Marguerite married Henri d'Albret, King of Navarre, who had also been at the Field. She became an important patron of evangelical religious reform in France and Navarre.[40]

One of the queen's ladies whose presence at the Field of Cloth of Gold is not formally recorded was the king's first official mistress, Françoise de Foix, Madame de Châteaubriant. At some point during the event, Henry gave her a gift of a crucifix worth 2,000 crowns.[41] She is known to have been at court by 1516 and was married to the rather older Jean de Laval, seigneur de Châteaubriant. Her husband and brothers, Odet, Thomas and André de Foix, were all in favour with the king in 1520. Little more is known of her except that she was displaced as Francis's mistress on his return from captivity in Spain in 1526 by Anne de Pisselieu, who became the duchesse d'Etampes.[42]

Antoine, duc de Lorraine, was one of the highest-ranked aristocrats listed to attend the French king at his first meeting with Henry VIII. Like Henri d'Albret, he was an independent sovereign prince, heir to the houses of Anjou and Lorraine. His lands lay within the ill-defined border between French and imperial territory and Antoine remained loyal to France until his death in 1544.[43] His younger brother, Claude de Lorraine, comte de Guise, also attended.[44] Alongside the Constable, the members of the Bourbon family, princes of the blood as the cadet branch of the French royal line, were present in force at the Field of Cloth of Gold. They included his cousin, another Charles, duc de Vendôme, there as governor of Picardy.[45] Vendôme's younger brother, François de Bourbon, comte de Saint-Pol, then governor of the Île-de-France, joined them, as did his uncle, Louis de Bourbon, prince de Roche-sur-Yon.

Many of the great dukes, like Alençon and the Bourbons and several of the marshals, were also provincial governors of France and commissioned captains of the royal *compagnies d'ordonnance* (ordinance companies). These comprised the heavy cavalry of the royal army, known collectively as the *gendarmerie*, in which noblemen served the king in war. They were paid for by national taxes but in practice they tended to be the clients of their captain, with their smaller seigneurial estates lying within his greater orbit. Numbers in such companies were reduced in times of peace, such as in 1520, but they might still have at their heart as many as thirty, sixty or 100 noblemen.[46] The command of ordinance companies was an important way in which territorial magnates protected and demonstrated their status, and the great princes might potentially have brought retinues of several hundred people with them to Ardres. Some restraint on numbers was almost inevitable, but it is still likely that between a third and a half of the French present at the Field of Cloth of Gold would have been there, not as members of the royal household as such, but as the clients or servants of the higher and middle-ranking nobles. In attending on their patrons they also honoured their king, in whose name all had been summoned.

The Courts Converge

While the personal rivalries of Henry, Francis and Charles played out during the spring of 1520, thousands of people in England and in France were being informed that they were required to attend their sovereign at the farther reaches of his realm. There they were to meet and greet people from other parts of their own country, about whom they knew very little, and to encounter a horde of those foreigners who had been their bitterest enemies for centuries. This was surely a daunting prospect for most of the participants. Yet it is clear that virtually all the prominent members of the English political nation and a sizeable part of the French one obeyed their sovereign's command in the summer of 1520. How, then, was this unusual event presented to them and how did individuals react to being summoned to go? Were they compelled out of obedience to their king? And, more prosaically, how did they get there?

In England, the first official notification most people whose names were on the royal lists had of the meeting was Wolsey's proclamation of 12 March 1520.[47] As the contemporaneous English 'Memoriall' prescribed, letters were to be sent out to all those summoned to attend. Of the hundreds sent, only a single complete one survives. It is addressed to Sir Adrian Fortescue (*c.* 1481–1539) of Stonor Park near Henley-on-Thames in Oxfordshire. Knighted in 1503 when Henry became Prince of Wales, Fortescue was a reliable, if relatively minor, 'king's man' in the shire. The long preamble of the letter explains that the personal meeting of the two sovereigns had been agreed in 1518 as part of the Anglo-French peace. It had been postponed from the previous year but now, the French king 'being moche desirous to see and personally to speke with us', Henry had agreed to meet. The letter emphasises the honour done to Henry by Francis 'offering' to meet him on English territory within the Pale of Calais which 'semblable honour of preheminence hath not been yeven by any of the Frenshe kinges to our progenitors or ancestres'. This flatly contradicted the facts since the meeting within the Pale was something Wolsey had more or less forced out of Francis. Now it was trumpeted to Henry's political elite as a triumph over his rival. Henry's 'honour and dignitie royall' required that he, having 'condescended' to meet Francis, should be honourably attended. Fortescue is therefore commanded 'for the honour of us and this our reame' to attend on the queen 'in apparaill as to your degree, the honour of us and this our reame it apperteigneth' together with 'ten tall personnages well and convenienently apparailled for this pourpose'.[48] He and his retinue were to be with the queen by 1 May 1520.

Henry's VIII's reputation among his subjects as a powerful and successful king is at the heart of the letter and it compelled a willing response. In emphasising the king's honour, the need for dress and physical bearing appropriate to station, even among servants, the letter to Fortescue articulates contemporary expectations of all gentry in general and Henry's view of their role at the Field in particular. It made clear to its recipient that he, along with hundreds of others, was part of a deliberately impressive demonstration of royal and national power to the ancient enemy. It was an invitation no gentleman could refuse. It was also rather like a call to arms – and a kind of war it was indeed. Fortescue had participated in the war of 1512–13 in the retinue of Sir

William Sandys and was now summoned once more to join the royal 'host' on this chivalric expedition to France.[49]

Doubtless there were those who baulked at the prospect of being taken away from their pressing commitments at the start of the summer to accompany the king across the Narrow Sea and then being camped for two weeks in the windy Pale of Calais. Not all would have enjoyed the prospect of confronting vast numbers of their French equivalents, whose language was gradually becoming less and less familiar to many English nobles and gentry and whose manners, dress and customs were not infrequently derided by English authors.[50]

The costs associated with such a journey would also be considerable. As in wartime, basic expenses, accommodation and food were provided by the king but, unlike in war, there were no daily wages on this occasion. They were at least spared the enormous expense of providing their retinues with armour and weapons. As was conventional, Henry only paid for wages, livery and material for members of the household, including lengths of sarsenet, damask and satin for coats and linings.[51] As Henry's letter reminded Fortescue, his personal adornment was expected to be of a high standard, according to his degree. Advances on future wages, grants of property and gifts from the crown might, in the longer term, compensate some for expenses incurred by those who travelled with the king, but these were not automatic.

In his play *Henry VIII*, Shakespeare makes the duke of Buckingham chief spokesman for those who allegedly 'have broke their backs with laying manors on 'em for this great journey'. He blames Wolsey for leading the king into such an extravagant event at a time when Buckingham himself had financial troubles. The duke's debts did rise sharply at this time, although there is no suggestion in the play, or in reality, that the expense of attending the Field was crippling. Shakespeare's lines draw on an observation of Polydore Vergil and echo Du Bellay's better-known quip that many on both sides 'carried their mills, their forests and their fields on their shoulders' in attending. Both authors stress the extravagance of the Field, but it is doubtful that anyone was actually impoverished by their attendance.[52] Sir Adrian Fortescue was a wealthy man, due mainly to the estate acquired by his marriage (by 1499) to Anne Stonor, which was worth several hundred pounds a year. A widower since 1518, Fortescue is unlikely to have found too onerous the expense of equipping himself and the required number of servants to attend upon Queen Katherine at the Field.

Whatever its cost, an invitation to a major court event might well have been welcome to most, particularly to someone like Fortescue. His standing as a local man of consequence had suffered since 1515 when he ceased sitting on county commissions. To be again among 'the great and the good' would have been reassuring. He was not a parliamentarian and the Field was an ideal opportunity to be back at the heart of the kingdom's politics, if only briefly. There he might meet others of his rank and above from other localities, renew old acquaintances and make new ones, exchange news and gossip and perhaps have occasion to get himself noticed by the king with the prospect that might entail of a return to front-line duties by which his reputation and family fortunes might be enhanced.[53]

In *Henry VIII*, Norfolk (who was not in fact there) waxes lyrical about the excitement of the event, affirming that it was a wonderful spectacle and a distinct privilege to be in the king's company on such an occasion. His lines evoke what would probably have been the appeal for most members of the elite of England or France summoned to the Field. Seen in this light, it was unlikely that Fortescue would *not* go at the king's command. Most knights and nobles summoned probably reacted in a similar way, seeing it as part of their duty and as fitting with their own honour as gentlemen to attend him to the Field. Their servants would have gone because that is where their masters went.

The French king's entourage was probably summoned in a similar way to Henry's but virtually no documentation of the process survives. Letters, delivered by the messengers of the royal *écurie*, would have begun to reach French noblemen beyond the court during April, at about the same time as their English counterparts were receiving theirs. One significant difference, however, is that whereas the English entourage had to be pre-assembled, as it were, to be shipped across the Narrow

Sea (as the letter to Fortescue makes clear), the French entourage had only to constitute itself by the end of May at or near Ardres. It was not necessary for it to travel en masse. As a good proportion of the high nobles at the Field had lands and houses in the north of France, they would have been able to make the comparatively short journey to the northern border of the realm without too much trouble. Most of those included whose lands lay elsewhere in France, such as René de Savoie, were already with the king as part of their period of service in the royal household and so were away from home anyway. On arrival, they were to be issued with passes by Gabriel de la Chastre, seigneur de Nançay, one of the *maîtres d'hôtel* at the court.[54] Francis came to Montreuil in the last days of May and while he was there, the Chancellor, Antoine Duprat, made an important proclamation about the Field. Possibly this was the first main rendezvous point for the French.[55]

Both courts had officers responsible for the accommodation of the royal household. In France they were the *fourriers*. Working under the supervision of four senior household officials, called the *maréchaux des logis*, the *fourriers* secured lodgings for the French entourage. Their English counterparts were the 'harbingers'. Armed with lists of those attending the Field, both sets of officers arrived in the area in good time, probably by mid-May, as the English entourage began to gather and as the train of carts bearing the tents for the French camp began arriving at Boulogne and Ardres. There, and in the surrounding villages, they sought rooms and whole houses for rent and/or allocated the tents being erected outside the two towns to individual nobles and their retinues.

The officer of the French royal household responsible for policing the court precincts, including on this occasion the camp below the walls of Ardres, was the *Prévôt de l'hôtel*. He had extensive legal powers within five miles of the king's person, including the right to exclude people from the area and to try any offences occurring within it. The equivalent jurisdiction within 'the verge' of the English court was exercised by the Knight Marshal, aided by the Lord Steward. He was empowered to ensure the exclusion of 'boyes and vile persons, and punishment of vagabonds and mighty beggars, not permitting any of them to remaine lie in, about or nere unto the court'.[56] At the Field, the exclusion of such people proved rather harder to ensure, not least because free drink and food were, at different times, offered to all and sundry outside the English king's temporary palace.

Chancellor Duprat's May proclamation also instructed merchants and artisans who wished to supply goods and services to the French court at the Field to obtain permits to trade from the *Prévôt*. Under his supervision, the *fourriers* also seem to have taken some responsibility at least for providing supplies at recognised rates, not just for the royal household itself, but for the entire French and indeed the English entourages as well. Nicolas de Bossu, comte de Longueval, was the royal commissioner responsible for provisioning the court while it was at Ardres. Most of this was arranged through Amiens, the provincial capital of Picardy. The town's council worked with its royal captain, François de Lannoy, seigneur de Morvilliers, and with the regional governor, the duc de Vendôme. The town council's records show that the two men assessed the grain available at Amiens and that sheep were taken (or driven) from there to the royal encampment at Ardres.[57]

On the English side, the Deputy of Calais, Sir John Peche, warned Wolsey at the outset of preparations of the need to provide sufficient food and fuel for the event. Part of an undated set of instructions issued by Wolsey to one 'Waren', presumably a member of his household, seems to have anticipated or responded to these concerns. Waren was to confer with Sir John about a house, possibly 'Mrs Baynam's', for Wolsey at Calais. He was also to 'take his opinion of purveyance', and the relative costs of commodities, especially whether 'beer be as cheap, good and plentiful there as in England' and whether wine and a specified list of types of poultry and game could be had locally. Waren was then to pass on to Guînes and confer with Sir Edward Belknap about ensuring a prime location for Wolsey's tents in a 'dry and convenient place' before returning to inform Wolsey of what progress he had made.[58] Hall's *Chronicle* captures something of the air of urgency, even panic, about the search for adequate supplies in May 1520:

Forests, parks, field, salt seas, rivers, moats and ponds were searched
and sought through countries for the delicacy of viands, well was that
man rewarded that could bring anything of liking or pleasure.[59]

While the English court established itself at Calais and Guînes, the
French court began its journey towards Ardres. At the start of the year
Francis had travelled from Poitiers in south-western France into the
Charente Valley, arriving at his birthplace, Cognac, on 19 February.
There he remained until the end of March before moving north into
the Loire Valley and to Blois, where the tournament which was the
reason for the Field of Cloth of Gold was formally proclaimed on
18 April.[60] Immediately afterwards, the French court moved on to
Chambord. From here it travelled eastwards and slightly south on the
Loire to Gien. River transport was both more secure and more comfort-
able (especially for the heavily pregnant queen) than horseback and
litters. At Gien the king and queen attended the wedding of Odet de
Foix, seigneur de Lautrec, to Charlotte d'Albret, the third daughter of
Jean d'Albret, seigneur d'Orval. From here the royal entourage turned
north and Francis reached the capital on or about 27 April. He spent
about ten days there as the royal household completed its preparations,
before moving north towards Ardres, hunting as he went. The court had
reached Crèvecoeur or Beauvais by Monday 14 May and Francis
intended to be at Montreuil on or about 20 May.[61]

For the next week the records are silent as to the rate of progress, but
Francis and Queen Claude evidently removed from Beauvais, bypassing
Amiens, and came up to the Somme at Picquigny. From here, they and
their courtiers travelled by river to Abbeville, using royal barges and
boats supplied through Amiens. The sight of the royal party on the river
would have been quite a spectacle for those in the several dozen villages
along that stretch of the Somme. Partly enclosed, brightly painted and
manned by liveried boatmen, the royal barges and those of the great
nobles would have made their way at a stately pace, accompanied by
music, with banners and streamers bearing the king's salamander and
queen's heraldic ermine fluttering from the tops of the cabins, and a

large banner with the royal arms at the stern where the master of the vessel stood to the rudder. The barges were accompanied by a fleet of boats for the upper members of the household, while the royal baggage train wound its way along the south bank of the river. Two boat owners from Amiens were paid 40 *sous* over and above what they received from the king's *fourriers* for supplying vessels to the royal party. One Jacques Carpetier, a tapestry-maker, was paid 50 *sous* for refurbishing and hanging tapestries in the boats or barges. One of the aldermen of the town was recompensed for costs in providing forty-four oarsmen and covers of some kind used on these vessels.[62]

The town council of Abbeville prepared for the king's arrival and on 15 May nominated an alderman to present him with the keys of the town. From Abbeville, the king had reached Montreuil on the river Canche by Monday 21 May.[63] While the court was there, Chancellor Duprat made the king's proclamation noted above and Francis called together 'the great personages of the realm' who had by then assembled there. He reminded them of the need to maintain the highest standards of courtesy and friendliness towards the English nobles and gentry whom they were shortly to meet.[64] From Montreuil, on 30 May, Francis moved north to the town of Marquise where he left the queen and his mother.

On Thursday 31 May, the date specified in the treaty, Francis and his immediate entourage arrived at the little town of Ardres.[65] This was his first visit to the town so the king made a formal *joyeuse entrée* welcomed by the council, the trade guilds, the clergy and the people. As part of his formal entry, the king conferred a new coat of arms on the town, which it bears to this day. Its central device is a double-headed eagle taken from the arms of Arnoul II of Ardres, who had died on crusade in Jerusalem in 1099. The eagle is supplemented by the motto *brave et fidèle*. The new arms honoured a town that, since the fall of Calais to the English in 1347, had looked in two directions: out towards enemy territory in the Pale of Calais and back towards France, to which it had remained loyal and for which loyalty it had frequently suffered.[66] Having made his entry, Francis sent François, seigneur de Saint-Marsault, one of his *gentilshommes de la chambre*, to Calais to inform Henry of his arrival.[67]

The king of England had begun his journey to the Field from Greenwich on Sunday 20 May. The same day Charles V sailed from La Coruña. His fleet of sixty ships had crossed the Bay of Biscay and was contacted off Plymouth by 23 May. Three days later it arrived off the coast of Kent where it was met by a squadron of ships under the command of Sir William Fitzwilliam, the Vice-Admiral of England, who had been appointed to 'waste and scowre the sees from tyme to tyme' to ensure the security of the king's fleet as it prepared to cross to Calais.[68] He was on station from late May in command, at least according to the 'Memoriall', of the *Mary Rose*, the *Great Bark*, the *Less Bark* and two other small ships.[69]

Travelling via Leeds Castle in Kent, Henry arrived at Canterbury on Friday 25 May and lodged at St Augustine's Abbey.[70] The next day the court was at Dover to greet Charles V on his arrival. Wolsey met him at the quayside and escorted him to meet Henry at Dover Castle. Charles greeted Katherine and Henry with a demonstrative affection uncharacteristic of him. From Dover they moved to Canterbury where the two sovereigns kept Pentecost Sunday. For the next five days the English court entertained the emperor's large and splendidly arrayed suite. There was, it seems, a last-minute scare that a French war fleet was being equipped. Wolsey demanded that ambassador La Bastie obtain assurances to the contrary from Francis before he would allow Henry to move further, but it was evidently not taken that seriously, because the ambassador would barely have had time to act before the royal entourage set off on the next stage of the journey. On 31 May, Wolsey escorted Charles to Sandwich from where the emperor crossed to Flanders.[71]

Transporting the English entourage to Calais was the responsibility of a team headed by Sir Edward Poynings, Lord Warden of the Cinque Ports. He also provided a number of ships from these harbours for the voyage. Henry VIII is thought to have had about thirty ships of his own in 1520, around half of which were in operational readiness at any one time. The vessels known to have been used by the king's immediate entourage for the crossing were the *Mary and John* (180 tons), the *Great Bark* (250 tons), the *Less Bark* (180 tons) and two rowbarges, the *Sweepstake* and *Swallow* (each 80 tons).[72] Despite the claims once made on the strength of the Hampton Court painting called *The Embarkation at Dover*, Henry did not cross to Calais in 1520 on board his flagship, the *Henri Grâce à Dieu*, usually called the *Great Harry*. At 1,500 tons, it was then the largest English warship. Its immense carrying capacity would certainly have been useful on this occasion, but it was so large that it could not be accommodated in either Dover or Calais harbour and it is not mentioned in the records of expenses for the royal voyages in May or July.[73] The king and queen sailed to Calais aboard Henry's newest vessel, the *Katherine Plesaunce* (100 tons) built the previous autumn at a cost of £323 13s. 9d.[74] Described by one commentator as 'like a very early royal yacht', it was fitted out with particular luxury, having 'cabins and chambers' of wainscot for the king and queen, the windows of which were glazed with 112 feet of glass, including panes with their respective arms.[75]

Ferrying around 6,000 people and their baggage and horses across to Calais and back was a major operation by any standards. Together with the king's ships and those Poynings obtained from the Cinque Ports, Miles Gerard, Thomas Partridge and Sir Wistan Browne were charged with securing some forty hoys to help with the task.[76] These were small, sloop-rigged, coastal ships or heavy barges used for freight and passengers, usually displacing about 60 tons. Some indication of the cost of hiring ships and hoys is given in the accounts Sir Edward Guilford, Master of the Armoury, submitted later in 1520. Early in the year he had hired vessels to bring horses purchased in the Netherlands back to England and in May and July paid for transporting armour, horses and equipment over to Calais and back. Two hoys were hired to carry horses to England for a total of £6. Another ship of 44 tons was hired from Greenwich to transport the mill of the royal armoury's forge to Calais for just over £7. A total of thirty-eight wagonloads of 'armory' stuff was brought back from the site of the tournament field and Guînes to Calais at a cost of £7 18s. 8d. Most of this was presumably then shipped back to England.[77]

The personal bedding, furniture and clothes of the king and queen were transported by the officers of the wardrobes of the Robes and Beds, sub-departments of the Chamber, using a range of packing materials, cases and coffers. The king's plate, for example, was trussed in cotton and packed into baskets. Carts and sumpter horses were used to move these possessions to the docksides, to Guînes and back, supplemented by carts hired in Calais.[78] The king's jewels were transported in the *Christopher of Hyde*, presumably one of Poynings's ships, whose master was paid 20s. for the task.[79] For the crossing to Calais, or for the return, part of the king's armour, his 'headpieces and mantlets', were stuffed with 13lbs of wool at a cost of 5d. Three short standard chests were made by, or purchased from, one Philip Sewaker at a cost £3 each, and a longer one at £6 to transport items used by the king in the tournament. The Revels Office paid the master of another ship, the *Clement*, £5 for shipping 'the King's stuff' to, or from, Calais.[80]

Some proportion of the people, baggage and horses would have been shipped ahead of, or after, the main party which set out with the king himself as happened in war – the nearest analogous operation. The entourage required careful organising and marshalling by officers of the royal household to ensure that people were where they needed to be on time for an early-morning departure. The captains of Dover and Calais, the municipal authorities and their officers were occupied in ensuring that both towns were ready for the thousands of people who briefly thronged the streets, taverns and docksides. The port authorities needed to ensure that sufficient labour and equipment was on hand for loading and unloading of ships. All of this was, of course, well within their capacities, as had been demonstrated seven years earlier when Henry had passed through the same ports with similar numbers on his way to war in France. Then, the quartermaster-general and presiding intelligence over the operation had been the industrious, up-and-coming, royal almoner Thomas Wolsey. Now, Cardinal-Archbishop and Lord

Chancellor Wolsey played a similar role but from a more elevated perspective and certainly with a much higher profile. It is known that Wolsey did not travel with the king because he was escorting the emperor to Sandwich when Henry took ship and he may himself have sailed from Sandwich or Deal.

Finally, preparations complete, early on the morning of Thursday 31 May, Henry and Katherine boarded the *Katherine Plesaunce* to cross the Narrow Sea. The painting *The Embarkation at Dover*, at Hampton Court Palace, was once thought to document Henry's actual crossing that morning but art and naval historians are now more inclined to accept it as a general evocation of the strength and power of Henry's navy, albeit one with a possible allegorical reference to the 1520 meeting in the cloth of gold sails which are a prominent feature of the vessel upon which the king is shown standing. This depiction of Henry's principal ships in or around 1520 certainly gives a lively impression of what the scene might have been like. The painting presents the viewer with a veritable forest of masts, of sails and rigging. When set alongside contemporary pictures of the king's ships, it suggests how the vessels used might have been decorated for the occasion. Their decks are depicted flying standards and flags with the royal arms and king's beasts supplemented by deck shields (pavises) showing the royal arms, the Tudor livery colours of white and green and Tudor roses. From the mastheads fly streamers with the cross of St George.

The painting also shows the frenzied activity surrounding the king's departure, with boats ferrying people and last-minute supplies out to join the ships. Sailors are shown climbing the rigging and one almost hears the shouted orders of masters and boatswains as sails are hoisted to billow out in the strong breeze. Guns fire in salute as each captain turns his fully laden vessel before the wind and the flotilla gets under way. The sailing conditions the painting shows, with clear skies, a fair wind and sea swell, were not just artistic licence or intimations of good fortune either. The English ships made good sail and had a quick crossing of some few hours or so, in sunny weather. The king and queen arrived in Calais around 11a.m.

Wolsey's Final Negotations

According to the treaty arranging the Anglo-French meeting, Henry was due to have been at Guînes by 31 May, but took advantage of a respite of four days conceded by Francis earlier in the spring, and now reiterated on his arrival at Calais, to take a few days' rest. As the baggage, equipment and horses of the English entourage were brought across from England, the king and queen were accommodated at the Exchequer in Calais and Wolsey completed the final negotiations prior to the personal encounter between the two sovereigns.

On Friday 1 June Wolsey set out from Calais to meet the king of France for the first time. He went in some style, escorted by the fifty gentlemen of his household. Wolsey wore scarlet silk and velvet robes and a clerical hat and rode a mule richly caparisoned in gold and red, preceded by another caparisoned mule. Carried before him was his *galero*, the broad-brimmed, multi-tasseled hat of a Renaissance cardinal. In front of Wolsey rode six of the eight English bishops who had come to France. These ecclesiastical grandees were joined by Thomas Docwra, Prior of the Order of St John. The whole procession was escorted by 100 archers of the king's guard, fifty riding before and fifty after it. It made its way under two crosses. One signified Wolsey's status as Archbishop of York and was not carried beyond the confines of the lordship of Guînes. The second, a double cross, signified his episcopal and legatine status and, together with Docwra's presence, reminded all who saw it that the Anglo-French peace of 1518 under which the two kings would meet was part of a Europe-wide peace orchestrated by Wolsey, ostensibly under papal auspices, as the prelude to military action against the Ottomans.[81]

Francis sent the Admiral Bonnivet and Marshal Lescun to Calais to meet Wolsey. Once the cardinal was on French territory, not too far from Ardres, he was met by the dukes of Alençon, Bourbon and Vendôme, by Marshal Châtillon, the seigneur de La Trémoïlle and other gentlemen together with fifty archers of the royal guard. As he arrived at Ardres, the recently installed artillery boomed in salute from the renovated battlements. The archers of the cardinal's guard stopped outside the town and through its gate came Francis, escorted by more of his archers, to meet Wolsey. The two men embraced and Wolsey removed his hat as a mark of respect for Francis but, as he stood in place of the pope himself, Wolsey made no other deferential gesture, nor did he dismount. They rode together to the king's lodging in the town, escorted on foot on each side by the Swiss Guard. After dismounting, the king and cardinal embraced again.

Wolsey's splendid procession and his assurance in meeting the king of France in the way he did seems at first sight to have been character-istic of that lordly arrogance which his critics scorned in him. Doubtless Wolsey did enjoy the grandeur of ceremony inherent in his high offices and of this occasion in particular. But his behaviour on 1 June 1520 should be seen in its proper context. His journey to Ardres that day was the first time Wolsey had left English soil and appeared in a foreign country as Cardinal Legate *a latere* and Lord Chancellor of England. According to Hall, the French record of the procession was notable for 'shewyng the triumphant dooynges of the Cardinalles royaltie'.[82] Its emphasis on his 'royalty' is important. Wolsey came as no ordinary ambassador to the French king, however exalted. He came, in effect, as the pope himself and, just as importantly for him, as the personal repre-sentative of a king whose international status he was charged with maintaining at the meeting.

On a more personal level Wolsey wanted to impress and persuade Francis with his power, dignity and personal charm. Since 1514 he had been receiving and negotiating with French ambassadors who had sent reports of him back to their master. Foreign envoys, especially the Venetians, had given the king of France detailed, and not always entirely favourable, accounts of the English cardinal. Francis knew that Wolsey was 'ipse rex' in English foreign as well as domestic affairs, but Wolsey still wanted to emphasise his importance in the recent past and for the immediate future of Anglo-French relations. Moreover, as Hall reminds us, Wolsey knew that his audience was not just the king of France and his entourage of nobles but the whole French political nation and European observers beyond it. The meeting was being written up for immediate publication in France and elsewhere. His entry to Ardres was in fact first described in *L'Ordonnance et ordre*. It is likely that Hall used this pamphlet when constructing his narrative of Wolsey's ride to Ardres. In short, Wolsey was acutely aware of the eyes of the world upon him during such an event. Today the French would describe him as 'médiatique', knowing instinctively how to play his part before this audience.

That Wolsey's effort to impress Francis with his ecclesiastical status and legal authority in England was not merely cosmetic was made clear in the negotiations with the French that followed. Hall says that Wolsey remained at Ardres negotiating for two days before going to Guînes where he found Henry. That Henry did not in fact move from Calais until 5 June matters less for Hall's account than his emphasis on Wolsey's request for plenipotentiary power from Henry when they met. This being granted, Wolsey then went back to Ardres and demanded the same from Francis in order to dispense with French and English councils and negotiate directly between the two kings. A man sent from the pope's side would hardly have expected less. Apparently anxious to close a deal, Francis was effectively bounced into granting Wosley equivalent plenipotentiary power. Then, having demanded this power, Wolsey scrupulously refused to accept it unless and until he had Henry's express permission to do so. To do otherwise would have contravened his duty to Henry, but in the circumstances Wolsey's action allowed Henry effectively to arbitrate on Francis's decision to delegate his own sovereign power to Wolsey. Thus, Henry assumed a subtly superior position as the one whose final consent was required for Wolsey to exercise both royal and papal power. As Hall smugly put it, 'It was highly esteemed & taken for great love that the Frenche Kyng had geven so greate power to the Kyng of England's subject'.[83] Wolsey did this as yet another way of reassuring Henry of his fidelity and publicly exalting the king upon whose favour his own career entirely depended.

No record has survived of the negotiations Wolsey conducted at Ardres with this ample power. They evidently dealt with Anglo-Scottish disputes and may have touched on the disputes between Francis I and

Charles V. Wolsey may have soothed the French council over Henry's recent meeting with the emperor and the one shortly to follow. The resultant treaty of 6 June was essentially diplomatic housekeeping, which ratified the agreements of the previous six years, taking into account financial and other obligations now met, such as the return of Tournai. It confirmed a total French debt to Henry of one million crowns, to be paid in six-monthly instalments of 50,000 crowns; some of this had already been paid by the French. The annual 'pension', as the French referred to these payments, was to continue beyond the payment of the debt for the remainder of Henry's life should Princess Mary's marriage to the Dauphin François go ahead. It would then continue into their reigns as well. If the marriage did not happen, then only the main debt of one million to Henry was to be paid.[84] Charles V had recently suggested his own marriage to Princess Mary despite the difference in their ages – something Wolsey was sure to have brought to the attention of the French. That would have been a worrying development for them, and the generous terms to which they soon agreed and the visit to the princess directly from the Field by a delegation of French gentlemen were very pointed demonstrations of their commitment to keeping Henry and Charles as distant from each other as possible. The 1520 treaty also provided that Wolsey and Louise de Savoie would work together to resolve outstanding issues between England and Scotland. A price Henry was prepared to pay for securing the other more attractive terms of the treaty, this mediation began in rather dilatory fashion and was overtaken by events the following year when war broke out between Francis and Charles V.

While Wolsey talked at Ardres, the lords and ladies of France and England began to introduce themselves to each other. Doubtless to reciprocate Wolsey's going to Ardres, on Saturday 2 June his counterpart as Lord Chancellor, Antoine Duprat, together with the Admiral Bonnivet, went to Calais and were graciously received by Henry and Katherine. Observing the same strict reciprocity that was the hallmark and safeguard for the whole event, a number of English gentlemen came simultaneously to Ardres to meet Francis. The talks concluded that day and Francis went to Marquise where he remained until Monday evening, then returned to Ardres. On Tuesday 5 June, Queen Claude and Louise de Savoie brought their retinues and the rest of the principal members of the French entourage to join the king. The same day, Henry and Katherine moved from Calais and took up residence in the castle at Guînes. The Hampton Court painting apparently shows Henry's train entering the town that day, making its way into the castle as its cannons fire in salute, frightening the swans in the moat. As we shall see, however, it does not represent that event, which was relatively low-key. On Wednesday 6 June there were further exchanges of visitors. The Chancellor and the Admiral called on Henry once more. So did Francis's *premier chambellan*, Louis II de La Trémoïlle. Received by Sir John Peche and the earl of Shrewsbury as Lord Steward, the three French nobles and their retinues were feasted by the English 'as if they were brothers'.[85] Then, nothing remained but the first, great and most difficult set-piece of the whole encounter – the personal meeting the following day for the first time in their lives of Henry of England and Francis of France.

CHAPTER 4

Right Chivalrous in Arms

Item, as the said serene princes of Englande and Fraunce, be like in force corporall, beautie, and gift of nature, right experte and having knowlege in the arte militant, right chevalrous in armes, and in the flower and vigour of youth, whereby seemed to us a right assembly, that for to decore and illustre the same assembly, and to shewe their forces in armes, they shall take counsaill & dispose themselfes to do some faire feate of armes, aswell on fote as on horsebacke, against all commers.

Cardinal Wolsey[1]

As CARDINAL WOLSEY's declaration in March 1520 made clear, the Field of Cloth of Gold was, first and foremost, a tournament held to inaugurate a state of peace and alliance between England and France. As signatories to the treaties of 1518, as the chief military officers of their kingdoms and as sovereigns of their respective national orders of chivalry, Henry VIII and Francis I led these celebrations and jointly hosted the tournament as allies. As the necessary prelude, they met each other for the first time on Thursday 7 June 1520, the Feast of Corpus Christi.

Dubois assures us that, in the best Homeric tradition, the day dawned clear and bright: 'The sun had risen and with his rays had revealed the world with full brilliance, and quit the red-hued sea.' Like any other great state occasion in the history of either kingdom, the morning would have been occupied with final preparations of all those invited, or commanded, to attend. From the lists of the participants drawn up months beforehand, it is clear that this meeting was to be largely, although not exclusively, a male-only event. As they awoke that morning, each of the hundreds of men who were to be involved, from the kings themselves to the great dukes of Bourbon and Buckingham down to esquires like the young Nicholas Carew and the archers of the royal guards, would have had a palpable sense of the importance of the day ahead and the role he was to play in it. Bringing together as it would the social and military elites of both kingdoms, just as in battle, the day was imbued from its start with a competitive spirit of honour as much within as between the two national entourages. Each man was there, in whatever capacity, to support and defend his sovereign lord who was 'on parade' as the supreme commander of the nation before his keenest rival. Although fraught with anxiety, the event may also have had something of the pride that the members of the modern Household Division might feel about Trooping the Colour on the sovereign's official birthday or the troops of the Republican Guard might about the Bastille Day parade down the Champs-Elysées.

One can imagine the nervous energy and activity in and around the royal quarters in Ardres and Guînes and in the vast tented encampments outside each town as the day got into its stride. Hundreds of grooms and pages were up early, brushing and readying coats, jackets, cloaks and boots for their masters, whether they served one of the officers of the royal guards or the king himself. The grooms and ushers of the royal wardrobes brought carefully chosen and prepared garments to the gentlemen attendants in the kings' chambers. Meanwhile, in the stables and yards in both towns and in the camps beyond, hundreds of horses were groomed, saddled and dressed for the day's work, bridles and bits glinting in the morning sun.

While these preparations went on, Wolsey, whose own servants would have been among the first awake and at work, rode forth once more to Ardres to meet Francis. He dined with the French king as a final gesture of reassurance and goodwill, for tension remained very high. Some sort of dispute, probably about the relative numbers on both sides, had to be settled before the legate returned to Guînes at about 3p.m. Then, personal preparations completed, the core of Henry's procession to the meeting began forming.

At about 5p.m. three cannon salvos sounded from the castle at Guînes, answered by three from the walls of Ardres. This was the signal that the two kings had set off towards the appointed meeting place, about a mile east of Guînes in a place called the Val d'Or or golden valley which Hall also calls the vale of Andern. There are many descriptions of the two kings' processions towards the Val d'Or. They provide much corroborative detail on some points, but on others there is significant variation between them. So far as can be ascertained, as the English procession left Guînes castle it was headed by some 100 or more mounted archers of the royal guard and of Wolsey's guard. They were followed by his household gentlemen, by knights and by gentlemen of the royal household. Then came the members of the nobility charged with escorting the king. There followed twelve mace-bearers and twelve trumpeters in the Tudor livery colours of green and white, then twelve heralds. Thomas Grey, Marquess of Dorset, preceded the king, bearing the sword of state upright. Then came Henry, who rode with Wolsey on his left. The legate was dressed in crimson satin and was preceded by his two crosses. Also with the king was Sir Henry Guildford, Master of the Horse, leading the king's spare courser. Behind Henry and Wolsey rode the king's young pages or 'henchmen'. The sources put their number variously as eight, nine or twelve but all agree that they rode handsome coursers. More noblemen and gentlemen followed behind the king, escorting the bishops and a number of ambassadors.[2]

As it moved a little way beyond the castle towards the meeting point, this central core of the procession was augmented by a large force of infantry troops led by the royal guard dressed in the Tudor livery chequered with golden Tudor roses on their short coats. Hall says that the guard, together with many servants of the lords attending Henry, constituted so large a force that it had to assemble in 'a plain felde directly before the castle' at Guînes. Its total number was estimated to be as high as 4,000. The Venetians observed that as it joined the royal procession, the infantry 'placed the king in their centre'. This suggests that some proportion of the force marched in front, led by a company of the king's guard carrying halberds. Another section of infantry brought up the rear, armed only with swords (and bucklers, according to one source).

It is likely that the infantry also marched alongside, flanking the central procession as some are shown doing in the Hampton Court painting *The Field of Cloth of Gold*.[3] The consensus among art historians is that this painting does indeed show Henry's procession to meet Francis on 7 June rather than, as it appears to show, Henry's entry two days earlier through the town of Guînes to his lodgings in its castle. Professor Anglo, who has written on the painting in greatest depth, points out that the initial order in the depicted procession accords in a general way with that on 7 June as described in the written accounts. Thereafter, however, there are significant variations between these descriptions and the painting. The numbers in the middle of the procession are much smaller than those given in the written descriptions. Instead of twelve heralds there is only Sir Thomas Wriothesley, Garter King of Arms. Thomas Grey, Marquess of Dorset, is shown bearing the king's sword immediately before him, as in the descriptions. Wolsey rides alongside the king but is a darkly dressed and insignificant figure who appears more like a humble priest than the satin-clad cardinal found in the written sources. The number and nature of attendants following the king are also rather at odds with published descriptions. The king's henchmen are conspicuous by their absence. Behind the king rides a group of four noblemen which includes Charles Brandon, Duke of Suffolk. To his left rides Henry Bourchier, Earl of Essex. Other figures identifiable from their portraits include John Russell, first Earl of Bedford, George Talbot, fourth Earl of Shrewsbury, and Sir Henry Guildford as Master of the Horse, although he is not leading the king's spare courser as he was described doing in the written accounts.

Like *The Embarkation at Dover*, *The Field of Cloth of Gold* was painted some twenty or more years after the events it portrays. Based on the style of the composition and the depiction of clothing, the consensus among authorities is that the painting was commissioned by the king, who appears three times in it, as a recollection of the event and probably intended as part of the decoration of Whitehall Palace. The painting is likely to have been set within a custom-made recess on the walls of a room or gallery in the palace. It may be for this reason that it does not appear among the king's pictures inventoried at his death in 1547. Certainly, Henry and many of his courtiers are depicted as they looked in the early 1540s, rather than as they would have been two decades earlier. The depiction of the king's head owes much to Holbein's several portraits of him in the 1530s. Either by design or as a result of damage, the original version was evidently cut out and replaced with the present one some time after the painting's completion.[4] Like the *Embarkation*, *The Field of Cloth of Gold* is not, therefore, a reliable document of any one episode it purports to show, or even of the event as a whole, but it does present an array of details about the Field, some remarkably accurate, but all embellished and altered with artistic and curatorial licence, to evoke its spirit to a later generation of observers.

A much more dynamic and near-contemporary depiction of the meeting between the two kings can be found on the walls of the courtyard of the Hôtel de Bourgtheroulde in Rouen, Normandy. The building was constructed during the first two decades of the sixteenth century and in 1520 was the property of Guillaume III Le Roux, abbé d'Aumale. During his occupancy in the 1530s the celebrated Aumale gallery was constructed and decorated with a series of bas-reliefs at ground floor level.[5] The first in the series shows the start of the English procession leaving Guînes, with figures in a gallery in the wall of the town observing it. Carved roses decorate the turrets of the walls and the gateway through which the procession passes. The figures move from left to right across the panel. The second panel shows a priest on a tall mule, bearing a bishop's cross. Behind is an ecclesiastical figure, dressed as a cardinal, between two unidentified gentlemen. The panels are now much eroded and damaged by the elements, but on the collar of the gentleman who rides to the right of the cleric and in the foreground can be seen the letters HO and NCE. The antiquarian Abbé Noel first suggested that

these letters originally spelt out the English royal motto HONI SOIT QUI
MAL Y PENSE and that the cleric depicted is therefore Wolsey as
Cardinal-Archbishop of York. There is, however, no visual reference
whatsoever in this panel to his legatine status.

The third panel shows the two kings on horseback riding towards
each other and almost about to embrace, Henry on the left and Francis
on the right. The bards of their horses bear the arms of England and
France respectively. Henry is accompanied by running gentlemen and
guards on either side of him, wearing the Tudor rose on their breasts
and carrying bows. Francis is accompanied by his guards wearing the
salamander emblem and carrying lances. Behind them, ranks of
gentleman on horseback and more guards on foot watch the scene
intently. Each king holds his hat in his right hand, his arm extended in
a flourish of greeting. Their horses, whose head pieces, or chaffrons, are
decorated with huge ostrich feathers, canter and prance towards each
other spiritedly and there is a vibrant sense of movement and drama
here that is rather lacking in the Hampton Court painting.

The fourth panel depicts another cardinal who approaches from the
right, so from the French side in the overall scheme. He is preceded by
a priest on a mule bearing a legatine double cross. A dove, representing
the Holy Spirit, flies towards him. Montfaucon identified him as Adrien
de Gouffier, Cardinal de Boisy, who was nominated at Francis's meeting
with Leo X at Bologna in December 1515 and was made legate *a latere*
for the Universal Peace in 1519.[6] Like 'Wolsey' in the second panel, this
figure is accompanied by two gentlemen. They wear what appear to be
collars of the Order of St Michael. Other members of the group also
wear this collar and there is another cardinal behind the central figure.

This French depiction of the procession to the Field locates the most
senior papal representative there on the French side and in effect
'demotes' Wolsey to no more than Cardinal-Archbishop of York. This,
despite the fact that Wolsey had a much greater role in organising the
event and communicating with Leo X about it than Boisy ever had. At
the High Mass that formally concluded the event on 23 June, both
Wolsey and Boisy sat to the right of the high altar under canopies as

cardinal-legates, but Boisy's was placed a little lower than Wolsey's and it was Wolsey alone who pronounced the plenary indulgence and absolution for all those in attendance. The final panel depicts the end of Francis's procession from Ardres, marching, again from right to left, matching and balancing the first panel and keeping the left–right, right–left processions with the one featuring the two kings in the middle. Ardres's walls also have galleries with people watching the cavalcade.

The composition of Francis's procession was broadly similar to Henry's save that he was not apparently accompanied by any large force of infantry. It was led by between 100 and 200 mounted archers of the royal guard dressed in their short coats of goldsmith's work. There followed some or all of the Two Hundred Gentlemen of the royal household, then the Hundred Swiss on foot. Twelve trumpeters preceded the great nobles who accompanied Francis. These nobles included Bourbon who, as Constable, bore the king's sword upright and Bonnivet the Admiral. Galeazzo da San Severino, the Master of the Horse, held the sword of state clothed in its sheath of blue velvet, strewn with *fleurs-de-lis*. King Francis followed on a bay courser closely escorted by his *enfants d'honneur*. Riding with him was the king of Navarre and the dukes of Lorraine, Alençon and Vendôme, each of whom also escorted an ambassador. The cardinals of France and other ecclesiastics, together with the knights of the Order of St Michael, followed and then, in turn, came several dozen other gentlemen and another contingent of mounted halberdiers (possibly the Scots Guard) who brought up the rear of the procession.[7]

As the two parties drew closer, it became evident that each side was larger than the other had expected. The English infantry were evidently spotted by French scouting parties and Francis objected to the large number of troops. Assuming most estimates of 3–4,000 are accurate, his anxiety is understandable. As we have seen, from the outset of the planning the French were worried about the safety of the king and the nobles at this encounter. Some Venetian sources say that the French had troops in reserve, available at short notice. Henry's leading military men had also been keeping an eye on the French whose total numbers, the absence of infantry notwithstanding, exceeded the English. Both sides panicked briefly. According to Hall, the two kings halted their processions, hesitating about continuing until urged by advisors, the earl of Shrewsbury in Henry's case, the seigneur de Morette in Francis's, that the other side was more in awe of them than they were of it, or that the overall numbers were still more or less equivalent and that therefore they should continue.[8]

Slowly, still hesitantly at first, the two columns set off once more towards what Hall describes as 'the vale of Andern', named after the village of Andres a short distance east of Guînes. The Mantuan ambassador Soardino specified that the meeting place was in a valley 'about one and a half miles from the French borders, where two mounds were raised expressly for this occasion, distant a bow shot from the other'.[9] These two mounds of packed earth had been thrown up so that the two sides could assemble at an equal height and get a clear view of each other in the minutes before the two kings were due to meet. The need for such an artificial platform shows how suspicious each side remained of the other and how fearful it was for its own sovereign's safety. A special pavilion dressed with cloth of gold, furnished with chairs and cushions and decorated with large tapestries and hangings had been pitched in the vale the day before. Richard Gibson had set four green and white pennants to mark the place where the two kings would meet but these, according to Hall, had been 'in rigorous and cruel maner' thrown down by Châtillon. Henry and his entourage eventually arrived first at the appointed place 'on the bank [i.e. side] of Andern' and stopped with 'their regard or faces towards the vale of Andern', that is, with the village of Andres somewhere to the left and facing eastwards towards Ardres. To this point also came the French king and his entourage. They stopped, having Andres to their right and looking westwards towards Guînes.

The precise location of this meeting place is not easy to identify with any certainty in the modern landscape. The terms 'Val d'Or' or 'goulden dale' may refer to the whole area between the two towns which is prime wheat-growing country, but Soardino's precise description indicates that the event took place in one of several shallow valleys which run southwards from the village of Andres, 'in the midwaie betwixt Guisnes and Ardre', as another source puts it.[10] Local settlement and land usage over the past 500 years has obviously affected the topography considerably. Nevertheless, the general area of the meeting lies south of the village of Andres, in open country along the modern D231 road which runs between Guînes and Ardres. As it leaves Guînes, the road climbs reasonably steeply to the top of a hill on which stand the remains of an ancient windmill known as 'Les Trois Frères'. From here the landscape falls away to a shallow gully which runs south from Andres towards the Forêt Domaniale de Guînes. It is quite narrow at its base and could not accommodate any sizeable assembly. About half a kilometre further east, however, there is another somewhat shallower and broader vale partly identified on modern maps as 'les terres Labat' near where the modern D231 is met by the D248 as it rises from the village of Campagne-lès-Guînes. It has somewhat shallower sides and its floor is rather broader than the one to its west. It is about 500 metres at its widest point, consistent with Soardino's description of the 'width of a bow shot'. On modern appearances at least, this looks the most likely location of the 7 June meeting between the two kings.[11]

The music of trumpets, sackbuts, flutes and drums, which had accompanied the marches to this point, was stilled. A tense silence reigned, broken only, it is pleasant to imagine, by the whinnying of horses and the twittering of swifts in the late-afternoon sky above. After a short time Francis moved his horse a few steps forward. His three attendants, the Admiral, the Master of the Horse and the duc de Bourbon, still bearing the king's sword upright, moved with him and descended from the low ridge. Henry saw at once that the French king's sword was uncovered and commanded Dorset to unsheathe the state sword of England. That done, Henry, too, moved forward and down to the floor of the vale with his three attendants: Wolsey, Dorset and Sir Henry Guildford. Sir Richard Wingfield, still the accredited ambassador to Francis's court, also rode forward with Henry, wearing a brocade garment given to him by the French king and doubtless there as one final gesture of reassurance to the French.

The dress of the two kings on this occasion was minutely described by many observers. Over his shirt and hose, Henry wore a doublet of silver brocade and over this a thickly pleated mantle of cloth of silver, ribbed or slashed with cloth of gold. It had jewels pendant from silver cords at the slashes. Henry wore the great collar of the Order of the Garter with a large St George pendant. He also wore a gold belt. His hat was of black velvet with a black plume. His horse, a bay courser (rather than the grey shown in the Hampton Court painting), was trapped in fine gold with classical decoration or motifs. Bells, 'as large as eggs' according to one source, hung from the trapping of the king's horse.

Francis wore a somewhat more elaborate outfit. Hall describes him as wearing over his shirt what was then a newly fashionable garment called a 'chemew' or chammer, first seen in England in 1518 when worn by the younger Frenchmen who accompanied Admiral Bonnivet on embassy. It has most recently been described as 'a type of jerkin constructed from a lattice of strips of fabric or passementerie'. A contrasting fabric was placed behind the strips to highlight the effect.[12] Francis's chammer was of cloth of silver, ribbed or laid on cloth of gold. It was slashed, with the material of his shirt pulled out through the cuts, each of which was tied with a gold aglet and the whole embroidered with jewels. Over this he wore a cloak of cloth of gold which itself had 'a certain bit of cloth of gold, slashed, looking like a half-cape or well nigh a half mantle, fastened over the left shoulder', which was richly ornamented with jewels. Francis's riding boots were white and, like Henry, he wore a black velvet cap with jewels and a black plume.[13] Like those for Henry, the materials and adornments of Francis's clothing would have been chosen primarily for their cost and visual splendour, proof in themselves of his wealth and sophisticated fashion sense. The particular colour combination would indeed have been quite striking and might even be seen as a luxurious version of the king's own livery colours of white, black and tawny or, in this case, gold.[14]

The trumpets and sackbuts sounded again. The two kings detached themselves from their attendants and now faced each other alone with only a short distance between them. A spear about 100 paces in front of the tent marked the point where the kings were due to meet. At a given signal or instinctively, simultaneously, the two kings spurred their horses forward. To the orchestrated cheers of their respective sides, each man reached for his bonnet and doffed it to the other in salute. They gained a little speed and then, closing together, they embraced (or at least attempted to embrace: the sources vary) three times on horseback, their bonnets still in hand, just as they are shown in the Rouen bas-reliefs. The two kings then dismounted and embraced once more. By now they were joined by pairs of running footmen and their respective attendants. Henry placed Francis on his right, the place of honour, in recognition that the French king was now his guest on English territory. Arm in arm, they entered the tent and began talking together for the first time.

The best clues we have to the attitudes of the two kings towards each other and towards their meeting are in the conversation that now ensued. Hall's account of their words inside the tent is admittedly second hand, but it is corroborated in its essentials by French and Italian sources. Francis apparently told Henry that he had crossed his vast kingdom and that this betokened his sincerity and desire to meet. To which Henry is said to have replied a touch brusquely:

> Sir, neither your realmes nor other the places of your power, is the matter of my regard, but the steadfastnes and loyal kepyng of promesse, comprised in charters between you and me; *that observed and kepte*, I never sawe prince with my iyen, that might of my harte be more loved.[15]

Whether or not Henry actually spoke those particular words, they constitute an accurate summary of the English king's attitude to the meeting. Friendship with Francis was welcome, but only for so long as the French king acknowledged Henry's high status in Europe by abiding by the agreement which they were affirming. Henry's words stressed the importance of honouring agreements and princely fidelity. In this respect they recalled Richard Pace's oration to the French ambassadors in St Paul's Cathedral in October 1518 at the signing of the treaty which

had ultimately led to the meeting. To Henry's mind, it was in Francis's
own best interest to have made his long journey across France and even
to have left his realm in order to meet him. His presence that day
acknowledged his need for Henry if he was to have any importance in
Christendom under the new dispensation of the treaty of London. Why
else, after all, had he come? Henry and Wolsey were there to reinforce
the achievements of 1518. In this conversation, and in the iconography
shortly afterwards deployed on his elaborate tournament costumes,
Henry was portrayed as the master of the political moment.

Francis's view of the Field is somewhat more enigmatic but no less
assertive. In his conversations with Henry and in the displays he would
make through his tournament gear, Francis presented himself as a
philosopher king, whose heart and mind were set on the highest ideals
of chivalric monarchy. Du Bellay notes that at their meeting, Francis
said that he and Henry should leave the business to their clerks
and officials while they dedicated themselves to princely pleasure. Its
effect was to undercut or set at a discount Henry's apparent wish that
they personally settle the final details of their agreement.[16] One Italian
account of the kings' first meeting notes that as they prepared to affirm
their alliance personally in the tent, Henry's title as 'King of France' was
read out. An awkward silence followed from which a clearly embarrassed Henry sought to extricate them by saying 'expunge that title' and
that it was 'good for nothing'. Francis's counter-intuitive reaction was
first to insist on the value and honour of the title 'King of France' by
ordering that the reading continue. Then he said:

> My brother, now that you are my friend you are the King of France,
> king of all my possessions, and of me myself: but without friendship
> I acknowledge no other king of France than myself, and thus, with
> the aid of our Lord God, do I hope to be able to defend and preserve
> this kingdom for myself and my successors.

Whereupon Henry is said to have risen, embraced Francis and promised fidelity, saying that a breach of his promise would render him 'the

most base and sorry prince and gentlemen in the world'.[17] He clearly felt obliged to make some demonstration in response to Francis's offer of friendship, implicit in his having Henry's title as king of France recognised and explicit in his qualifying remarks. All of this just emphasised the gulf that stood between Henry's claim to France and the reality of Francis's kingship over it. Francis was really saying that Henry could call himself whatever he liked, the fact remained that he depended upon Francis's goodwill and active support if he was to have the kind of significant role in Europe envisaged by the treaty of London. As far as Francis was concerned, the status quo had not been changed by Henry's recent diplomatic triumph, nor had his own freedom of movement been curtailed by it. In the tent that afternoon, Francis welcomed Henry's presence and proffered friendship as an acknowledgement of *his* own power over France and his importance beyond it. Why else, after all, was Henry there? The Bastille banquet of December 1518 had proclaimed exactly the same message. Some days later, Francis would emphasise this point even more dramatically with a very personal impromptu visit to the king of England. After talking further, the kings ate and drank together and the mood became more convivial.

Meanwhile, outside the tent guarded jointly by the Constable of France and the marquess of Dorset, things remained initially rather awkward and tense. As hosts of the meeting, the English household officers offered wine in tall silver jugs and drinking bowls, together with spiced cake, to the French. Nevertheless, as Hall rather proudly notes, none of Henry's entourage broke ranks from where they had stood on the brow of the vale at the moment the kings entered their tent. The French did likewise at first but then broke ranks and 'came into the English partie speaking faire'. Even then, apparently, the English 'kept still their arraie'. The contrast between English reserve and French spontaneity has become something of a modern cultural cliché, but it was often remarked upon, not only by Hall in his *Chronicle*, but by several of Henry's ambassadors at the French court. The kings emerged after an hour or so and each received and embraced the higher-ranked members of the other's entourage. Towards sunset, Wolsey became

concerned and urged an end to the meeting. The two kings embraced
once more and amidst much talk of not wanting to do so, they finally
parted from each other and so rode back to their own towns.[18]

The Field of Cloth of Gold: Tournament

It becomes evident that in bringing the two kings together that June
afternoon in 1520, Wolsey had enabled both Henry and Francis to
indulge what was, in the end, an illusion but a very important illusion.
Namely, that each met the other entirely on his own terms. The possibility of peace between them could therefore be celebrated, not for its
own sake, whatever the rhetoric, but as a token of each king's ostensible
victory over the other. In Wolsey's mind, the treaty of London operated
as a metaphorical tournament. The elaborate rules and regulations and
the blunted weapons used at tournaments gave the participants scope
for aggression while protecting them from serious harm. So it was with
the alliance under the treaty of London and it was particularly appropriate that it should be inaugurated with an actual tournament. It was
customary to hold a tournament to celebrate an alliance treaty. As on
this occasion, peace was thereby invigorated, rejuvenated, heroicised and
thus made acceptable to the chivalric elite of both nations, who were
being asked to enter into it.

The 1520 'deed of arms' was the second Anglo-French peace
tournament of Henry's reign. The first had been in Paris in 1514 for
the celebration of Mary Tudor's marriage to Louis XII. The 1520 tournament was also the second to be held on the border between English
and French territory near Ardres. The first had occured 143 years earlier,
in 1377.[19] There were two other famous fourteenth-century tournaments that, between them, provide precedents for the Field. One
took place in the spring of 1390 at Saint-Inglevert which is about six
miles (10 km) east of Guînes between Calais and Boulogne. Three
French knights, the seigneurs de Boucicaut, de Roye and de Sempy,
challenged all comers for thirty days. In October the same year, King
Richard II hosted a 'deed of arms' over four days at Smithfield in

London.[20] Both tournaments were held during a truce in the Hundred Years War and at a time when Richard II was certainly pressing for peace between himself and Charles VI.

The three challengers at Saint-Inglevert offered to joust either with 'rebated', that is, blunted, weapons as was appropriate for peace, or with sharp ones, reflecting the fact that they expected the majority of responders to be English, with whom the French were still technically at war, albeit under a truce. In practice, all knights who came to answer the challenge at Saint-Inglevert chose steel-tipped lances. At Smithfield, by contrast, and as in 1520, the competition was definitely a 'deed of arms of peace', and so only rebated weapons were allowed. At Saint-Inglevert, the shields of the three challengers were hung up on an artificial tree so that they could be touched by the challengers to show with whom they wanted to fight and on what terms. At both events the deed of arms consisted entirely of jousting at the tilt. At Saint-Inglevert, about 100 knights took part, each entitled to five runs or 'courses' against his chosen challenger. Froissart's account of it emphasises the strength of competition, the clash of weapons and the particular competence of the three French challengers. They were said to be motivated by the love of ladies and their desire to use their youthful energy in honourable pursuits. At Smithfield, the combats at the tilts were followed each evening by banquets and entertainments at which the noble ladies of the king's court played a prominent part and at which prizes were given out.[21]

Grand tournaments became increasingly popular courtly entertainments in the fifteenth century. By the mid-1400s, the dukes of Anjou and Burgundy led a trend towards making such events, called *pas d'armes*, as much artistic and dramatic entertainments as paramilitary competitions. René d'Anjou organised a number of them with elaborately allegorical titles and conceits such as the 'Chasteau de la Joyeuse Garde' and the 'Emprise de la Gueule du Dragon' held near Chinon in 1447.[22] René also wrote a number of treatises on tournaments including the *Traicté de la forme et devis d'ung tournoy*, which described how one should be arranged 'at the court or elsewhere in some region of France when princes wish to hold one'. As practised in these courts, tournaments became fantastical events combining elements of disguising and theatre, feasting, music and speeches with the actual combats fought in the lists. The high point of these events was probably the deed of arms held at Sandricourt near Pontoise in 1493 in which the ten defenders set themselves to await challengers as self-conscious imitators of the knights of the Round Table.[23]

The *pas d'armes* was influential in late-fifteenth-century England and culminated in the elaborate allegorical, and often specifically Arthurian, tournaments staged under Edward IV, Henry VII and especially Henry VIII. Knights dressed up as hermits, angels or figures from allegorical romance and as knights of the Round Table. They entered the lists, which resembled stage sets with elaborate scenery, and acted out their parts before a long gallery which housed an elite audience for the spectacle. All these elements were, for example, present in the tournament held at Westminster in February 1511 to celebrate the birth of Henry's first-born and short-lived son, Prince Henry.[24]

The 1520 event mixed elements from both fourteenth- and fifteenth-century types of tournaments just outlined. There was, for example, no elaborate staging or artificial settings in or around the lists, apart from the 'Tree of Honour'. There was no overall theatrical theme or conceit, such as by then were common at the English court, nor were there speeches made by the participants as supporting 'characters' in stories or romances. There were, however, elaborate allegorical costumes which were worn over several days and which spelt out (literally in Francis's case) claims to chivalric and royal virtue, to which we will return.

The ostensible reason for the 1520 event reflected contemporary practice with its emphasis on the tournament as military training in peacetime. William Caxton's translation of Ramon Lull's *Book of the Order of Chivalry*, which appeared in 1484, presented the tournament as the antidote to idleness among young gentlemen in peacetime. The English proclamation of the 1520 tournament stated explicitly that it was held to recognise God's gift of peace to England and France and for the prevention of 'idleness and sedition'. The same message was proclaimed more emphatically in Lescaille's *L'Ordonnance et ordre du tournoy.*

> Since chivalrous Mars has left behind delightful means of avoiding
> idleness in time of peace: by joyous tournaments jousts and combats
> (all enmity set aside), so there are sixteen gentlemen of renown and
> noble blood (eight of France and eight of England) desirous of
> honour, not trying to outdo one another, but to continue in good
> deeds, for the honour of God and Our Lady and all the company of
> heaven, and for the love of their ladies, having the permission of their
> prince and intending to maintain the articles of the challenge.[25]

The two kings were joint leaders of this team of challengers or *tenans*
who would answer all comers, the *venans*. The feat of arms consisted of
three competitions. These were jousting at the barrier or tilt, a tourney
(a freer form of mounted combat in the arena or 'field') and foot combat
over barriers. Those answering the challenge were to enter the contest
by touching three shields hung on the artificial tree (which was ready
only at the last minute), each representing one of the different competitions: a grey and black shield for the tilt, gold and tawny for the field
tourney and silver for the foot combat. The challenge also prescribed
the various weapons to be used, the defensive equipment and armour
permitted, the number of 'courses' or charges down the tilt allowed to
each man, the number of strokes in the foot combats and the penalties
for improper or incompetent participation. There was to be no competition on Sundays or on feast days of the English and French churches.
The regulations of the 1520 tournament are similar at many points to
the famous 1466 ordinances issued for 'jousts of peace royal' by John
Tiptoft, Earl of Worcester.[26]

The terms of the challenge also reflected several months of discussion between the two kings mediated by Wingfield, in which Francis
strove to have the final say about the form of the tournament, which he
had been assured by the English would be the quid pro quo for his
having agreed in May to its being staged on English territory. Much of

the evidence for this comes from a 'Memorial' sent to Henry by Sir Richard Wingfield in mid-May. The king, or those around him, would almost certainly have known René d'Anjou's tournament book, and the arrangements made in 1520 certainly echoed its emphasis on the use of rebated weapons and appropriate armour which enhanced the safety of participants and allowed them to put on a good show. For example, René specifies that the sword for the field tourney must be wide enough not to penetrate the opponent's visor, 'and so that it should not be too heavy, it must be very much hollowed out in the centre'. In 1520, Francis insisted that lighter swords be used in the tourney as these would enable the participants to deliver 'more strokes and more gorgeously than with the pesaunt [heavy] sword'.[27]

Francis and Wingfield were also concerned about the sheer number of respondents that a tournament starring two kings as challengers might attract. Wingfield advised that at least 200 answerers were expected from France alone. Francis therefore wanted to limit the number of individual runs at the tilt to six (in the end, eight was the agreed number). Wingfield warned Henry against allowing 'vainglorious' knights to run too often each day and so spoil the opportunities for others. Francis worried about the possibilities of injury with so many men participating in the tourney. He wanted to avoid at all costs anything untoward happening at such a high-profile and politically significant occasion.

Henry also cared about the safety of the participants, not least his own, and wanted to take the opportunity to show off a new suit of foot combat armour made for him by the royal armoury at Greenwich. This suit, the earliest surviving armour made there, was revolutionary in the protection it afforded the wearer. It incorporated sets of narrow, articulating steel plates (or lames) joined together over leather strips which allowed great freedom of movement at all the joints in the body. The shoulders were protected with symmetrical pauldrons and the head by a bascinet that locked on to the pauldrons. The armour also incorporated cuisses: a pair of laminated steel breeches shaped to the buttocks which locked over the top of the thigh protections. The result was that from head to foot the wearer was completely enclosed by articulating steel plates of varying sizes without any gaps between them. Because the weight of the armour was more evenly distributed over the body, it is likely to have been easier to wear than a more conventional suit.[28]

Either because he was ignorant of Henry's snazzy new armour or, more likely perhaps, because he was aware of it, Francis decided that, in accordance with contemporary practice in Germany and France, the foot combatants should wear an armoured skirt or 'tonlet' designed to protect the lower body and groin against injury. He also specified the wearing of the great bascinet, incorporating a reinforced visor, to minimise the possibility of facial injury. In mid-March, within two months of the event, Wingfield reported that a final 'memorial' of the terms of the tournament was being drawn up by Francis in consultation with Marshal Châtillon, several other high-ranking nobles and 'two other personages of his privy chamber'. Francis thought 'some little changes necessary' to preliminary terms agreed with Henry. The wearing of the tonlet seems to have been one of them. Henry's acceptance of this stipulation, despite the inconvenience (and perhaps disappointment) it entailed, indicates that he did in fact respect Francis's right to determine the form of the tournament and equipment to be used.[29] Accordingly, the Greenwich armoury hurriedly prepared a somewhat more conventional suit of foot combat armour made from existing pieces but incorporating newly made symmetrical pauldrons and a tonlet. The neck of the bascinet was etched with a collar of the Order of the Garter and the top of the headpiece was etched with roses and figures of St George and the Virgin and Child. The armour gives a precise indication of Henry's stature that year. Film footage made by the Royal Armouries of a man wearing this armour and using a long two-handed sword demonstrates the remarkable ease of movement this suit afforded the wearer and the flexibility of the tonlet.[30]

Henry's personal armour for the jousts and the foot combat were doubtless the *pièces de résistance* of the Greenwich armoury that year, but a vast amount of other equipment was also required for the Field. As hosts, the English were responsible for acquiring the greater proportion of this equipment and it was obtained in the spring of 1520 in England, in the Low Countries and in Germany. According to the accounts submitted in December by Sir Edward Guildford, Master of the Armoury, some 1,500 spear staves were sent to Guînes from the Tower of London. About 1,700 swords of various types and weights used for the different competitions were made or purchased on the Continent. These included 600 two-handed swords at 7s. 6d each. As many as 500 of the 1,000 Milanese swords purchased were then shortened, blunted, given new pommels and hand guards, and in other ways reconditioned to make them suitable for use in the tournament.[31] Two thousand steel 'mornes' (fittings to rebate the point of a jousting lance) were purchased at 18d each, together with 1,000 'vamplets' or vamplates (funnel-shaped guards on the staff of jousting lances to protect the user's hand) at 5s. 10d each. According to an anonymous mid-fifteenth-century French description of the equipment used in tournaments, the inner sides of the vamplates, towards the hand, had to be lined with flock stuffed between two pieces of leather.[32] Leather was also used to cover the hand grips of staves, fighting axes and casting spears used in foot combats. Guildford's account also records the purchase of leather hides at a total cost of £8 together with '20,000 nails to nail the leather onto the staves, counter rowndells, and "bawrres" or "burres"' (the metal ring around the staff of a lance just behind the vamplate). A 'great woolhouse' at Calais was hired for a year as an armoury. Four forges were set up in or near Guînes so that armaments could be refined and repaired as the tournament went on. Ten loads of charcoal for the forges were also brought across from Dover. The mill of the Greenwich armoury was dismantled, transported across to Calais and then set up again at or near Guînes. Two mill horses were brought across together with fifty-four wagonloads of equipment and armaments. A team of twenty-four armourers were on site to attend to the inevitable adjustments and repairs needed in the course of each competition. Guildford paid five men, presumably armourers, 4s. 7¾d between them for 'working a whole night at the beginning of the jousts'.[33]

Records of the purchase and preparation of armour for the French king and his nobles do not survive. Nevertheless, such limited evidence as we have suggests that Henry's armourers did not have a monopoly on technological innovation at the time. Francis's armourer was Louis de Lacque, 'dit Merveilles', a Milanese-born master armourer who had worked for Charles VIII and Louis XII. He had also worked for Henry. In November 1514 the English king had paid 100 marks in gold 'to the Frenche kynges armourer upon a prest by indentur towarde the making of divers complete harness for the kinges grace'.[34] The armourer was also to be rewarded with £40 in gold. In February 1515, the duke of Suffolk, who was then in Paris to congratulate Francis on his accession, assured Henry in two separate letters that while he was not able to obtain any more suits of armour for himself or for the king as the latter had evidently suggested, 'the harness that Master ... had promessed shalt be redde [ready]'.[35] These are the earliest and only surviving references to Henry purchasing armour from Milanese armourers working in France. Doubtless the receipt of these items helped him to keep abreast of the latest trends and led him to demand work of the same or higher standards from his own Milanese and German armourers at Greenwich.

All this armour and weaponry would have been pretty useless but for the presence at the Field in vast numbers of the animal which gives | its name to chivalry. In December 1519 and the early months of the following year, Sir Edward Guildford, Master of the Armoury, with several assistants and grooms, made an extensive tour of the Netherlands and northern France to buy horses to be used for transport and in the tournament. No total numbers are indicated but many of the horses bought were for the king, who gave some of them to men participating in the tournament. These horses were generally ridden to Calais and then shipped to England. One individual shipment was of some twenty-seven animals. Prices ranged from £79 for a horse bought near Ghent to £50 for 'a white horse of Nassau' and £41 for two young bay horses bought at Delft. The total cost of Guildford's expedition was just over £1,450.[36]

In the early sixteenth century the term used for a tournament horse was a 'courser'. This referred not to a specific breed but to a type of large horse used at the tilt. Many of these animals were bred in the kingdom of Naples. They were strong, well proportioned, tractable and brave animals, physically and temperamentally suited to the demands of cavalry warfare and the tournament. A shortage of such horses in England led Henry to make considerable efforts during the years prior to 1520 to acquire, by gift or purchase, a stock of Neapolitan horses. In the summer of 1519, Henry had paid £500 for eighteen Neapolitan coursers. Francis looked more readily to Mantua where coursers were also bred, but they were lighter than the Neapolitan ones, being cross-bred on the Gonzaga stud with Barbary and Turcoman breeds. On 7 May Sir Richard Wingfield wrote from Paris that one 'Parker' was on his way to Calais from Italy 'with seven goodly coursers', among the best to be found there.[37] The other main type of horse used in display at the Field was the jennet or ginete, a smaller, lighter Andalusian breed renowned for its agility and speed. On 20 June, San Severino demon-strated his skills on a ginete before the two kings, both of whom owned numbers of the breed imported from the Habsburg stables at Cordoba and from Mantua.[38]

On Saturday 9 June the two sovereigns met for a second time at the tournament lists to hang up their shields on the artificial 'Tree of Honour' as the two chief challengers and so inaugurate the competition. Each was escorted by sixty of his noblemen and sixty guards. The question of precedence arose once again over whose shield was to be placed where. Once more, Francis was accorded the place of honour, in recognition of the fact that the tournament was on English soil. His shield, bearing his arms within a collar of the Order of St Michael and surmounted by a closed crown imperial, was hung on the right. Henry's shield, displaying his arms within a Garter collar below a closed crown imperial, was hung to the left but at the same height as the French king's. Below them were the shields of the fourteen remaining chal-lengers and below these, the three shields for each of the three competi-tions within the tournament. Those of the *venans* were hung on the railings that surrounded the *perron* on which the tree stood.

Estimates of the total number of participants come to rather less than Wingfield's prediction of 200 on the French side alone. The assumption seems to have been that, as in past tournaments, a large number of knights from Germany and the Netherlands would attend. In April 1520, Henry sent Norroy King of Arms to Marguerite de Savoie's court at Ghent in the expectation of attracting champion jousters to the tournament. These lands were, however, now those of Charles V. As his regent there, Marguerite initially refused to allow the proclamation of the tournament, or at least stipulated a delay. As she explained in undated instructions to the imperial ambassadors about to leave for England, the intended proclamation of the tournament coincided with the emperor's own announcement that he would shortly travel from Spain to the Netherlands to meet his subjects there. The proclamation was, she believed, a deliberate attempt by Francis to dishonour Charles by luring the emperor's people away from him in order to sow dissension between a loving prince and his subjects. She would not suffer them to be put in this position and told the ambassadors in England to convey to Wolsey her disappointment that he had not understood the implications of the tournament's proclamation and her surprise that the king of England should allow himself to be associated with the French king in this way. Henry rejected this reasoning out of hand and insisted that it meant no dishonour to Charles – as Marguerite perfectly well knew.[39] The tournament was eventually proclaimed, by 12 May, but the delay and the construction put upon it had their intended effect. As Hall noted ruefully:

> From the court of the Emperor, nor of the Lady Margaretes court, nor of Flanders, Brabant, nor Borgoyn came never a persone to answere to the challenge: By that it semed that there was small love betwene the Emperor and the Frenche kyng.[40]

Lescaille's *L'Ordonnance et ordre du tournoy* indicates that for the jousts, fourteen 'bands' or teams, each of between ten and twelve answerers, responded to the challenge. These 145 men, together with the sixteen challengers, make up a total of 161 recorded participants in the first competition. No similarly precise records survive of the numbers for the tourney, nor for the foot combats. Individuals were free to enter as many or as few competitions as they wished, and there may well have been more participants in the second and third competitions than in the first, which required the highest degree of technical skill. The total number is likely to have been somewhere between the figure of 220 given by the Venetians and the 300 given by Florange.

As challengers, the two kings were assisted by the duc de Vendôme, the comte de Saint-Pol, the duke of Suffolk and the marquess of Dorset, together with Anne de Montmorency, seigneur de La Rochepot, Sir William Kingston, Philippe Chabot, seigneur de Brion, Sir Richard Jerningham, Jean de Tavannes, seigneur de Dalle, *dit* Tonavis, and Sir Giles Cappel. Among their younger team-mates were Pierre de Laval, seigneur de Montafilant, Anthony Knyvet, Nicholas Carew and Charles de Refuge, seigneur de Boucal who was an *écuyer d'écurie* in the royal household.[41] On Monday 18 June and Tuesday 19 June this core team was supplemented by a number of 'aides'. These included one of the English king's favourites, Francis Brian, and Sir John Neville, later Baron Latimer, who fought only on the last day of the jousts. Michele-Antonio, Marquess of Saluzzo, an ally of Francis, had led a team of answerers on Friday 15 June, then fought as a challenger the following Monday.[42]

The core team's membership comprised equal numbers of French and Englishmen and notionally encompassed the whole elite hierarchy, from kings to squires. Its members were not merely token representatives, however, but among the foremost jousters of their respective courts. The early careers of Suffolk and Thomas Grey of Dorset had virtually been built upon their capacity to provide skilled competition for the king in the lists. Grey had been 'chief answerer' at the tournament celebrating the wedding of Prince Arthur to Katherine of Aragon in November 1501. He and Suffolk distinguished themselves at the 1514 Paris tournament for Louis XII's marriage. Sir Giles Cappel had also participated in that contest, as had the duc de Vendôme and his brother the comte de Saint-Pol. On the same occasion La Rochepot and Chabot had fought well as companions to the host, Francis of

Brittany, and did so again at a tournament in February 1515 to celebrate his accession as king. At a tournament to honour visiting Flemish ambassadors in July 1517, Suffolk and Dorset again triumphed. Nicholas Carew made an extraordinary debut as one of the king's new young favourites, 'the minions', by competing in the jousts and then running 'a very long way' with a 24-foot beam on his head 'to the marvel of everybody'.[43]

One surprising absentee from this list of tournament luminaries was Galeazzo da San Severino, the French Master of the Horse, who was a renowned jouster, praised for his martial skills by Castiglione. He had been taught by Pietro Monte, who credited him with developing new and more useful pieces of armour. Monte's *Collectanea* was dedicated to him.[44] San Severino accepted a number of horses from Henry on Francis I's behalf at the Field but took no recorded part in the fighting. Neither did Bourbon, the Constable, despite being listed as the leader of one team of *venans*. The reasons for this are unclear, but both men shared responsibility for the king's security. It may have been decided that the risk of injury or distraction caused by their own participation might have compromised their capacity to protect the king and so they refrained from entering the competition.

The principal team leaders of the *venans* were the ducs d'Alençon, Vendôme and Bourbon and the comte de Guise. Like Bourbon, Vendôme did not actually joust with his team but, as noted above, fought on the side of the *tenans*. Most of the *venans* were French, but there were a couple of Italians and about fifteen Englishmen as well. The Admiral Bonnivet, Marshal Lescun, the seigneur de La Trémoïlle and Robert de La Marck, seigneur de Florange, were prominent royal officers who led teams. Two somewhat younger team leaders, both from Picardy, were Jean III, seigneur de Rambures, who was then an *échanson* [cupbearer] in the royal household, and Antoine de Hallewin, seigneur de Piennes. In 1520 he was of the king's *enfants d'honneur* and led a team of six on Monday 18 June.[45]

Henry Courtenay, second Earl of Devon (later Marquess of Exeter) and second cousin to the king, was the most prominent English answerer at the tournament. Brought up with the king, the earl had been called to Henry's council in May and became a gentleman of his Privy Chamber immediately after the Field. In 1520, he led a mixed team of English and French contestants including two of Francis's *gentilshommes de la chambre*. The first was Antoine de Lettes, *dit* Des Prés, seigneur de Montpezat. He had been one of the original hostages held in England under the treaty of London and in 1521 served briefly as ambassador. The other was Charles du Mouy, seigneur de Mailleraye, identified as 'Moye' on the earl's team. Like De Lettes, he had been one of the original hostages in England in 1519.[46] The 'Memorancy' on the team list was François de Montmorency, the younger brother of the seigneur de La Rochepot.

The earl's team included a number of the younger nobles and gentry who held various positions in the King's Chamber and Privy Chamber. These included Henry Pole, Lord Montagu, and his younger brother Arthur, the sons of Margaret, Countess of Salisbury, and thus cousins to the king. Henry Somerset, Lord Herbert, the son of the earl of Worcester, also fought on Devon's team. Lord Edmund Howard, the younger son of Thomas Howard, second Duke of Norfolk, led a team which joined Richard and John Grey, the younger brothers of the marquess of Dorset, with William Coffin, then a gentleman usher in the king's Privy Chamber. Other team members drawn from the king's immediate circle were Sir William Sidney, a cousin of the duke of Suffolk, Henry Norris and William Carey.[47]

The jousts began on Monday 11 June. The queens of France and England met for the first time around the middle of the day when they arrived for the tournament accompanied by their ladies. They entered the specially built and now richly furnished pavilion to the side of the lists, greeted each other with all courtesy of honour and talked together for a time. Queen Katherine had made no secret to her court that she would have preferred that the Anglo-French meeting had not gone ahead. Intelligent politician and dutiful wife that she was, though, she seems to have made the best of it. Doubtless she congratulated Queen Claude on her advanced pregnancy. Claude was known throughout

1 Henry VIII in about 1520, at the time of the Field of Cloth of Gold.

2 Francis I by Jean Clouet. The portrait was made at the time of his return from captivity in Spain in 1526. The hopes of peace expressed at the Field could not prevent a war between the king of France and the Holy Roman Emperor.

3 Cardinal Wolsey, the architect of the Universal Peace inaugurated at the Field of Cloth of Gold and the chief organiser of the event.

4 Pope Leo wanted peace throughout Europe in order that its rulers might together check the power of the Ottomans. His plans were hijacked by Wolsey and made to serve the interests of Henry VIII.

5 One of a series of tapestries which may have belonged to Cardinal Wolsey and of the kind that decorated his apartments in the temporary palace at Guînes.

6 A painting from the 1540s that celebrates Henry VIII's naval power. It evokes the scene in Dover harbour as Henry crossed to Calais in 1520, but is not an accurate portrayal of that event.

7 This painting represents a number of different aspects of the Field including Henry's procession to meet Francis I on 7 June 1520, the meeting of the two kings that day and the jousts and the feasting that followed. Note the fountain flowing with wine in the lower right-hand corner.

8 The designs for tents depicted in this large painting are generally accepted to be ones for the Field. They feature gold decorative work on the rich red velvet which covered the canvas structure. The roofs feature 'king's beasts' of various kinds.

9 Another set of designs for tents for the Field. These feature the Tudor livery colours of white and green. The roofs are set with stands to hold 'king's beasts'.

10 This bas-relief shows the moment when Francis I and Henry VIII first encountered each other on horseback on the evening of 7 June 1520, closely watched by the leading members of their entourages and attendants.

11 This armour was adapted by the Greenwich armouries from the original set intended for use at the Field after Francis I insisted on the use of the tonlet, the protective skirt, and a reinforced visor. Note the two-handed heavy tournament sword that Henry favoured in the foot combats.

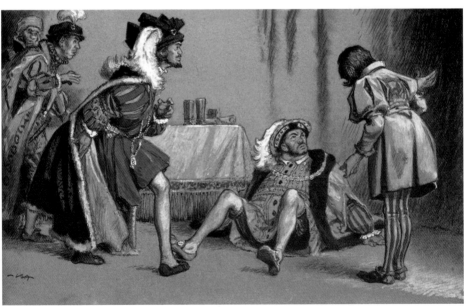

12 This humorous depiction of the episode of the wrestling match between Francis and Henry VIII is very much at Henry's expense. The match is mentioned by one French commentator but English sources are, perhaps unsurprisingly, silent on the subject.

France for her amiable personality and was genuinely loved by her courtiers. She would have responded to Katherine instinctively with all the *politesse* at her command as a noblewoman of the age. The two then sat to await the arrival of their husbands and the other knights. Henry and Francis duly entered 'armed at all pieces', leading the *tenans* against two teams of challengers, ten men led by the duc d'Alençon and twelve by the Admiral Bonnivet. As the ladies of the tournament, Katherine and Claude were the focus of its elaborate chivalric ceremony. Led by the two kings, all the competitors presented themselves to the ladies in the royal pavilion and were presumably greeted with varying degrees of enthusiasm and encouragement.

Henry's first run of the day was against Charles de Vendôme, seigneur de Graville. Hall says that the king shattered his lance to the vamplate. On his second run, the king hit Graville's helmet so hard with his lance that its hinge was damaged enough to put him out of action for the rest of the day. The French score check does not in fact record any broken lances on the first day but both Hall and the author of Ashmole 1116 affirm that many were broken.[48]

On Tuesday neither king appeared in the lists but they may have watched the competition from the galleries with the queens, as they are shown doing in the top right-hand corner of the Hampton Court painting. The following day the kings reappeared but the wind and rain storm that did so much damage to the tents struck on the Wednesday and prevented any jousting. Instead, there were wrestling competitions between the English guards and Breton wrestlers, reputedly the best in France. Twenty-four members of Henry's guard also gave a demonstration of their archery skills. Francis made 'but small countenance at that pastyme'. The sight of English archers in action might not have been an unalloyed pleasure for a king of France. Henry and Francis appeared in the lists again on Thursday 14 June. Henry ran against the Marshal Lescun and had good sport from him and his team-mates, but in the end the two kings did best. Once again the weather disrupted jousting on the Friday, but although it continued, neither king participated in it, nor did the queens attend the tournament that day. The two kings gave their best performances on Saturday the 16th. Hall's description of Thursday's competition actually relates to this day, when Henry is recorded as breaking a total of eighteen lances and Francis fourteen in fighting against teams led by the earl of Devonshire and Lord Edmund Howard. Francis was slightly injured on the side of his head, in the region of the temple and the eye. In keeping with the rules, there was no fighting on Sunday. On Monday 18 June their supporters jousted, but the kings did not, owing to continuing adverse weather conditions. Tuesday the 19th was the last day of the jousting competition and the two kings once more led their teams. They first ran against the team of the seigneur de Bonneval and saw them all off before the duc de Bourbon's team of thirteen ran against them. Once more the kings excelled themselves, Henry winning all his runs against all comers. Francis also performed valiantly enough to wring approval out of Hall, who says that he 'so well ended his challenge of Justes, that he ought ever to be spoken of'.

In full classicising mode, Dubois has the two kings, like all the knights, performing wonders at the tilt:

> They bend forward upon their horses, and are poised for the blow . . .
> they collide and exerting themselves with all their might, crash into
> each other with a noise like thunder, that resounds to the very stars.
> So great is the bulk with which they press upon each other! Dashed
> against a shield, the lance is broken in pieces, and bucklers glitter
> with the sparks struck out of them.[49]

Sparks did indeed fly in such encounters and very spectacular they could be, but, as the score checks show, the general standard of tilting was not high. On Thursday 14 June, Francis broke only four lances and Henry five and none of their team-mates did any better. The high scores on the Saturday were achieved partly because both kings were allowed more runs than the prescribed number of eight in order to afford more challengers the opportunity of running against them and to give them both every opportunity to display their skills. The relatively poor competition

in the jousts was due mainly to the windy and occasionally rainy conditions which persisted all week and the removal of the counter-lists.
These were low rails or timber walls which ran parallel on either side of
the tilt, creating corridors down which the horses charged and keeping
the horses closer to the central barrier. Removing them allowed the
horses to swerve out from the tilt wall, making it harder for their riders
to score winning strikes.

The standard of tilting may have been disappointing, but the appearance of the competitors evidently was not. Although, as noted above,
there was no complex allegorical setting or overall theme for the 1520
tournament, the participants still wore an array of colourful, allegorical
costumes as they fought. As Anglo, Kipling and Mattingly among
others have noted, by the early sixteenth century this was as important
an ingredient in the successful staging of a tournament as the actual
paramilitary competition. The meaning of the various colour schemes
and combinations, badges, symbols and motifs on the participants'
clothing and the bards of their horses not only identified them to spectators and to other participants but were used to make complex and
often deliberately obscure allusions to, or claims about, the wearer's
personal valour, bearing, ancestry, rank and ambitions. The detailed
descriptions of the costumes in the accounts of the tournament by
Hall and the Venetian ambassadors demonstrate their centrality to the
spectacle.

Henry's costumes proclaimed his chivalric prowess and nationalistic
fervour. On the first of the four days on which he jousted the king's
garments and his horse's bard were of russet velvet decorated with 'water
work', or waves made of damask gold. These decorations were interpreted by Hall and others as signifying mastery over the waters of the
Narrow Sea. On Thursday 14 June, Henry's clothes were embroidered
with lozenged eglantine flowers of gold. The eglantine is the native rose
of England and according to Hall it was 'swete plesant and grene if it be
kyndely and friendly handled, and [but] if it be rudely delt with it will
pricke and he that will pull up the whole tree by the top, his handes will
be hurte'.[50]

On Saturday 16 June Henry wore a garment, the border of which was decorated with the phrase 'God willing, my realm and I ...', left pointedly unfinished.

In contrast to the presentation of Henry as the English national hero, Francis seems to have been presented as a slightly more abstract and elusive figure, a philosopher king, whose heart and mind were centred on the highest ideals of chivalric love and monarchy. On each of the four days he jousted, Francis's costumes progressively spelt out in words and symbols, of book, chains, feathers and the like, the phrase 'heart fastened in pain endless/when she/delivereth me not of bonds'.[51] This meaning was carefully explained by Hall to his readers and was evidently discussed by the *savants* present. It simultaneously indicated the king's passionate nature and his ability, through learning and wisdom, to endure the pains of love while himself triumphing through loving purely. If this was indeed the intended meaning, it has a striking resonance with the allegorical significance usually ascribed to the king's personal badge of the salamander amidst flames and his motto 'Nutrisco et extinguo'.

The various costumes worn by the *venans* were no less intricate than those of the two kings, but they do not receive as much interpretative comment. They seem, for the most part, to have been relatively conventional allusions to the wearers' supposed chivalric virtues and prowess in the fields of battle and romantic love. The earl of Devon's team on Saturday 16 June was dressed in blue and white costumes, the colours divided vertically. On the blue side was the image of a man's heart burning in a woman's hand while her other hand poured water on the heart from a watering can. On the white side were the words 'pour reveiller' (to awake), a fairly straightforward allusion to the condition of courtly love.

On Wednesday 20 June the tourneying began. The tourney was a freer form of group combat where opponents faced each other in pairs rather than individually, as in tilting. They fought on horseback with swords, staves and clubs rather than couched lances but, as in the jousts, spectacular display and numbers of strokes delivered determined the

scores. Horsemanship was also an aspect of the tourney and contemporary treatises indicate that the skill lay in the rider keeping his horse
moving, using its impetus to lend force to his own blows against his
opponent. Quick thinking, improvisation and daring were essential in
tourneying, as they were in real mounted combat, for which it was seen
as training. The tourneying knight had to keep on the move and,
according to one authority at least, ensure that he went through the
whole field (of opponents) 'seeking the places of the most important
onlookers', a reminder that it was primarily a sport of court spectacle.
Hall notes that during the tourney the judges and heralds were on hand
'to marke and write the dedes of noblemen'.[52]

The motifs on Henry's accoutrements became more conventional,
but the nationalistic boasts remained. On Thursday 21 June the royal
costume displayed little mountains planted with branches of golden
basil. On the borders were the words: 'Breake not these swete herbes
of the richemounte, doute for damage'. This image of an enriched
mountain, damage to whose flora would provoke retaliation, was an
allegory already familiar to the Tudor court. It referred to the earldom
of Richmond held by Henry VII and, by extension, to England's power
against France under its Tudor king. It had first been deployed as part
of the Twelfth Night celebrations of 1512–13 prior to Henry's attack on
France the following summer. It is ironic that the French (and other)
onlookers seem to have completely ignored the literal and figurative
point of the design of this royal costume. Richard Gibson's Revels
accounts for the Field make clear that the 'basil' leaves made of gold
were actually broken off by the French at the end of the day and were
presumably kept or traded as souvenirs or for their value. This was
customary practice at the English court and doubtless Henry reacted
with typically grandiose largess.[53]

The final two days of the tournament were taken up with the foot
combats, the ones in which Henry had been so eager to appear in his
new suit of Greenwich armour, using the mighty double-handed sword.
The 'Memorial' Wingfield had sent to Henry in mid-May had expressed
Francis's objection, explaining that were competitors able to use such

swords, few opponents' gauntlets would sustain the force of the strokes which they would have to withstand. If they had to be used at the barriers, then they were better made optional. In the end, they do appear to have been used alongside the customary rebated thrusting spears or pikes and specially shortened single- and double-handed swords. As Francis reminded Henry, shorter weapons were also more manoeuvrable and thus helped to provide a more spectacular show.[54] Like the tilt in jousting, the barrier was essentially designed to reduce the risk of serious injury in hand-to-hand fighting. The barrier prevented the competitors from grappling, lessened the area of the body to be defended and reduced the number of blows that counted for points to those delivered above it. In 1520 it was still a relatively new competition and the rules were not always obeyed, or even understood, by knights. As the century progressed, however, fighting at the barrier became an increasingly effete courtier's game rather than a serious military exercise.[55] No sources give a clear indication of the standard of competition at the barriers at the Field but, as ever, Hall gives the impression of no quarter being asked or given and ends his description of the 1520 tournament by noting that 'this [these] same two kings safe in body and lymmes ended battail for that day at the barriers with great honor'.[56] The prizes for the tournament were given out on the Saturday evening during one of several spectacular banquets and entertainments hosted by both sides.

Although Henry and Francis always fought on the same side in the tournament, one of the most famous episodes of the Field was a wrestling match between them, apparently initiated by Henry. It was reported by the seigneur de Florange, but no mention is made of it in any English source. One day while they were drinking together, Henry suddenly challenged Francis to a match and shaped up to him. They grappled briefly before Francis overthrew the Englishman with a move called the 'tour de Bretayne', a sort of rapidly executed hip throw, not unlike what the Italian masters called a *gambarola*. The Bretons were regarded as the best wrestlers in France and Henry does not seem to have appreciated just how well Francis, as their duke, had mastered their skills. So decisive was Francis's win that, according to the conventions governing these things, he was not obliged to offer Henry a second go when asked to, and chose not to do so.[57] Henry seems to have recovered his dignity somehow, but it must have been a rather embarrassing moment for a man so confident of his own masculine strength and dexterity.

The wrestling match is about the only thing most people seem to know about the Field of Cloth of Gold. The incident was depicted humorously several times in the nineteenth century and Henry is always made to look a bumptious fool. It is, nevertheless, characteristic of the spontaneity of which both men were at times capable and probably of Henry's immense frustration at the formalities of protocol that hedged every encounter between them. This may have been his way, finally, and literally, of getting to grips with the man with whom he had felt the most acute personal rivalry for the last five years. That he would dare to do such a thing to a fellow sovereign must also, however, betoken a certain confidence, not only in his own ability to win, but in Francis's ability to respond in a robust but reasonable way. Doubtless he expected to triumph and it must have been a terrible shock to him to discover that he had underestimated Francis and would have to be reasonable and magnanimous in defeat.

These two kings could demonstrate masculine prowess more easily than most of their fellow sovereigns, and in the mentality of the sixteenth-century elite the physical beauty of princes was equated to, even taken as proof in itself of, their legitimacy and virtue as princes.[58] Dubois's description of Francis waiting to meet Henry on 7 June is strongly in this tradition and perhaps even responds directly to Richard Pace's description of Henry VIII in his 1518 St Paul's oration before the French ambassadors:

> ... his neck bears the chain in the form of shells; his neck bears the chain, magnificent with gold and gems; there is nothing more sumptuous in the whole wide world. His milk-white neck receives his flowing locks and a golden band clasps them together with marvellous art: through his face and shoulders Francis is like to a god, with the nobility of his head of hair and beard; he was like to a god in all other ways. Ablaze in his eyes, like the lamp of Phoebus, twin flames

pour out from his joyous brows. Francis, through his whole body, his valour, his triumphs, his lineage, his counsels, his religion, mighty: Francis, the most just sovereign that we have ever seen, the greatest in war, and the greatest in piety ... For us, under the reign of Francis, the age of gold rises up once more, such as they say existed when Saturn was king.[59]

Dubois is also complimentary to Henry. Though less effusive than he is about Francis, he still avers that 'nature exhausted her phials of beauty' when she fashioned the English king. All early-modern male rulers were expected by their fellow nobles to demonstrate in some way their physical strength, agility and virility. Clement Marot wrote a poem about the Field in which, like Dubois, he praised Francis's handsomeness and charm for engendering peace with Henry. Yet, as Phyllis Mack has noted, the poem may also be read as a rather more ironic comment on how Francis's extravagance and charisma were also provocative and actually made conflict with Henry VIII more likely. As she observes:

On the one hand beauty is somehow related to goodness; it inspires love and a sense of serenity which are good things. But beautiful clothes also intimidate people and make them subservient ... in the political arena, beauty is a sign of power.[60]

Both kings were keen to display their physical qualities during the tournament. Henry also did so through displays of archery and doubtless in the wrestling match he began with Francis. The tussle is, at the very least, an apt demonstration of what lay below the surface in relations between most early-modern male monarchs. Competition, of all kinds, at the Field of Cloth of Gold was not an unwelcome intrusion on expressions of peaceful goodwill, as it has usually been characterised, but actually the way the two kings and their supporters validated their claims to be able to offer genuine friendship between equals and also demonstrated their potential in war. After all, one needs to know the strength of a friend just as surely as that of an enemy.

CHAPTER 5

Generous to a fault

At one door [of the English temporary palace] were two gilt pillars, bearing statues of Cupid and Bacchus, from which flowed streams of malmsey and claret into silver cups, for any to drink who wished.

L'Ordonnance et ordre du tournoy, fo. C ii

THE HOSPITALITY STAGED by Henry VIII and Francis I at the Field of Cloth of Gold was on a truly monumental scale. It was an absolutely central feature of the meeting. The feeding and watering of some 12,000 people for just over two weeks, together with several prodigious banquets, required serious expenditure by both kings and were vital aspects of the awe-inducing spectacle of royal power at the 1520 event.

Divided into the various service departments of the household, the accounts drawn up by the English court after the Field show the enormous quantities of food and drink consumed during the six weeks it was on the Continent, including during Charles V's visit to Calais. The final accounts of the expenses of the English royal household on food and drink from 31 May to 16 July survive and they total £8,839 2s. 4d. An estimate of the expenses drawn up, probably in the early spring of 1520, came to £7,409 13s. 4d. The relatively minor discrepancy between estimated and actual costs demonstrates how expert the Tudor household officers were in calculating the expense of large-scale events. As might be expected, the highest expenditure on both the estimate and the actual records was for beer and wine, red meat, poultry of all kinds and spices.[1]

The bulk of supplies were obtained through commercial contracts with merchants, but the English monarch and his French counterpart also had rights of 'purveyance', to which Wolsey had alluded in his instructions to Waren. When the court travelled or when a royal army was in the field, supplies could be raised locally at advantageous prices set by the crown. This practice minimised the problem of storage and transport of supplies over long distances, but it did not always work easily because it relied on there being sufficient resources in the localities into which the royal entourage travelled. This partly explains the sense of panic when it was realised that the English court could not be supplied from the Pale of Calais or surrounding territories alone. The usual incentive to traders was that they would be offered 'reasonable' prices, usually slightly below market rates. A seller could generally expect to make a modest profit based on high volume. Henry had used purveyance to supply the army of 1513 (not without problems) and did so again for the 'army' of 1520, but there is also ample evidence of direct sales from English, French and Flemish suppliers.

The English royal household accounts indicate that, as in the war of 1513, a good proportion of the equipment and provender needed was purchased or hired in the city of London and the south-east of England. Venison, for example, was brought from royal parks at Walden, at Eltham and Leeds Castle in Kent, from a number of private estates in these counties including that of the earl of Arundel, in Sussex. One of the king's purveyors, John Copeland, received 11s. for 'riding into Flanders for poultry'. Stephen Cope was paid 4s. for the carriage of 40 dozen quails from Antwerp to Calais. One Julian Loder brought poultry from 'The Haven' to Calais and £12 14s. 8d was paid for poultry brought from 'Brydges' (Bruges). The names of certain suppliers, such as James Anderpoden, Julian Palyard and Basteau Albright, suggest that they were of Flemish or French origin. The search for food in the area went on even after Henry had arrived at Calais. On 5 June, he sent Thomas Palmer, one of the ushers of the chamber, to the mayor and aldermen of the town of Saint-Omer in Artois requesting their urgent assistance in obtaining provisions. Explaining that he was entertaining the king of

France at nearby Guînes, the king promised that if they would encourage the food merchants of the town to come to Guînes with their wares, he would ensure that they were well received and recompensed. What sort of response this message received we do not know, but one John Byrling of Saint-Omer provided 160 quails at 2s. per dozen.[2]

The French authorities may have helped their English counterparts to some extent in securing supplies of grain and red meat at least. In April, Châtillon had assured the earl of Worcester that food, wine and fodder for horses would be available at a 'staple' or supply base to be set up at nearby 'Merguyson' (Marquise). The English could purchase what they needed at reasonable prices. Wolsey was informed of this and the French seemed to have honoured their undertaking.[3] On 10 May, while he was at Amiens, the duc de Vendôme issued a proclamation that all merchants able to supply the king's camp with meat, fish, wine, wheat and other necessities were to convey them to the towns of Marquise and Fiennes in the Boulonnais (the latter about ten miles south of Calais). All those who did so would be provided with letters from the commissioners exempting them from all local taxes and tolls and declaring them to be under the king's special protection. A number of sellers were later reimbursed for costs incurred in conveying wheat and other commodities to Ardres. Merchants from other towns, such as Péronne and Boulogne, were also involved in providing supplies to the royal camp.[4]

Some 3,406 sheep and lambs were accounted for together with 842 veal calves, 373 oxen and sixty-nine whole pigs of various kinds. Most of these animals were transported near to Guînes and pastured there before slaughter. There are references in the accounts to water, cages, fodder and pasture for the animals and the thousands of birds also purchased by the Poultry department of the royal kitchen.[5] Two houses, one at Guînes and one at Newnham Bridge, were rented for use as abattoirs. Indeed, each of the various departments of the English royal kitchens hired one or more houses at Calais, Guînes or other villages nearby. Here, and in other locations close by, were gathered the one and a quarter million 'billets' or planks of firewood consumed by the ovens of the English royal kitchens.[6]

Drink was required in vast quantities for the event. Wine and hippocras were enjoyed by the higher echelons of the royal party, but ale was the principal daily drink of the entire English entourage. An Italian observer in 1500 remarked on English drinking preferences:

> The deficiency of wine is, however, amply supplied by the abundance of ale and beer, to the use of which these people are become so habituated, that at an entertainment where there is plenty of wine, they will drink them in preference to it, and in great quantities.[7]

Made from malt and water, without hops for flavouring, ale was partly supplied through London. The physician Andrew Boorde called it the 'natural drink' for Englishmen and no fewer than 48 tuns of ale were purchased through the capital. Brewing was also an important business in Calais, not least because of the large garrison there. In the south-west corner of the town was Bullen Well, a conduit whose water was used chiefly in brewing ale and beer, and more supplies would doubtless have come from the town. Beers were brewed in different strengths and the malt would be used several times. 'Best beer' was brewed with the first use of the malt, 'small beer' with the third. The latter is what servants (and children) commonly drank. It was very weak and not infrequently rather bitter – but safer than water. Ale did not keep well and had to be brewed fairly shortly before drinking.

With about 6,000 people to supply, a special brewing house was also established in a rented property at 'Medelweye' for thirteen weeks at 40s. rent. This hamlet is shown as 'the medelve' or 'middle way' on a survey map of the Pale of Calais made by a German surveyor in 1540 who labelled its features phonetically. It lay just east of the town along the road to Guînes and, together with the nearby hamlet of St Peter's, served as a storage and preparation area for a number of household departments. It is likely that 'Middle Way' is also the 'Medelham' noted in the accounts where one Jane Whitefield had a mill where wheat was ground for use by the bakery and perhaps for the buttery as well. The stream flowing through the hamlet powered the mill, supplied water for brewing and for the livestock and poultry penned nearby.[8]

At the highest social level of sixteenth-century society, that of the great nobles and the monarch, hospitality was a vital aspect of the noble virtue of 'liberality' or 'magnificence'. Both these terms were used very precisely in the period, to encapsulate a range of qualities also summed up as 'good lordship'. A monarch was expected to show 'largesse', which implied the giving of rewards without apparent expectation of return, immediate or otherwise. In England in particular, but in France too, hospitality was very consciously linked to the maintenance of the social hierarchy and order. Hence the elaborate concern for precedence in seating arrangements for dining at court feasts or public festivals.[9]

The kings offered hospitality mutually and reciprocally, according to a strict protocol of visits, in order to maintain a careful balance of honour between them. Neither king could be allowed to offer, or receive, from the other greater or lesser hospitality than he himself provided. It also meant that one could not directly upstage the other by the standard of feasting he offered, nor was there any intimation that in accepting food from each other, either acknowledged the other's 'good lordship' over him.[10] This was particularly important because Henry's formal title still made a claim for him as 'king of France'.

It was for this reason that, counter-intuitively perhaps to modern sensibilities, at none of the three splendid banquets did the two kings actually dine in each other's company. They did make relatively simple repasts together on four occasions. The first was after their meeting on 7 June. The second and third were after the respective early-morning visits to each other and the last was after High Mass on Saturday 23 June. Otherwise, Henry was entertained at Ardres by Queen Claude, Louise de Savoie and the other principal members of the French party while Francis was entertained at Guînes by Queen Katherine. Being received by each other's wife meant that each king was undeniably the highest-status person at the banquet and could accept food as a gift without danger to his reputation as at least equal to the other sovereign. Compare this with the meeting of Henry III of England and Louis IX of France for the confirmation of the treaty of Paris in 1259. There the two kings *did* eat together at a grand feast given by Henry at Saint-Germain-des Prés on 6 December, but two days earlier Henry had done homage to Louis for Gascony. Acknowledging Louis's lordship over him for these lands was the basis of peace between them and this was celebrated at the feast. The situation in 1520 was totally different; Henry and Francis only agreed to meet as allies and equals.[11]

The first banquet was held on Sunday 10 June and set the pattern for the two that followed on succeeding Sundays. Hall does not mention it at all but descriptions by French, Venetian and Mantuan observers survive. The two kings left their respective quarters at the same time in the early afternoon, cannons signalling their departure. They met each other briefly at the lists. On arriving at Guînes, Francis was formally received by Katherine and the English court at the temporary palace and dined under a cloth of estate in what, judging from Soardino's description of it as hung with tapestries 'worth 15,000 ducats representing foliage', was the queen's Presence Chamber. Beyond this, the long hall was divided to create two dining chambers. In the first there dined 134 ladies of the court, attended formally by about twenty young Englishmen of rank, who, as at the banquet for the emperor at Canterbury, stood behind or near the ladies, but did not themselves eat. Beyond them, in a second chamber the duc de Bourbon and the Admiral Bonnivet dined with about 200 gentlemen. Meanwhile, in his apartments on the other side of the palace, Cardinal Wolsey entertained Etienne Poncher, the Bishop of Paris, and attendant prelates and priests.

Francis was served on gold plate and each course consisted of fifty dishes. There would have been at least three, and perhaps more, courses for the banquet proper. These had little in common with the courses in a modern extended meal apart from a sense of progression through a display of different kinds of food and cooking techniques as the banquet went on. Savoury and sweet elements were often combined in dishes served alongside each other in a course. John Russell's *Book of Nurture* describes alternative dinners of flesh and fish. One description of the former, which may have been a Christmastide feast, has the first course consisting of dishes of pork brawn and mustard, potage, beef, mutton, stewed pheasant, swan, capon, suckling pig and venison pie or pasty. The course ended with the serving of 'subtlety' or table decoration made from a variety of materials such as spun sugar or marzipan. Russell describes one such decoration showing the Annunciation. The second course mixed a similar number and range of dishes as the first and concluded with a 'device' of an angel appearing to the shepherds on a hillside. The third course followed in similar manner and concluded with a 'subtlety' of the kings of Cologne being presented to the mother of Christ. The meal ended with apples, wafers and hippocras – the cele-bratory spiced wine drink.[12] Such a meal could easily encompass fifty individual dishes as a whole, so the scale of the banquet for Francis on 10 June becomes readily apparent when we recall that each individual course alone consisted of fifty dishes.

Game, birds and fish, served in a variety of ways, were the principal dishes of both the English and the French royal banquets. The finest and rarest of these were reserved for the royal tables and those of the highest nobility. More mundane types of farmed meat, such as lamb, mutton and beef, together with geese, capons and pigeons and the like were served to the middling nobles, who accompanied the magnates and ate at the tables within the dining halls. Salt and freshwater fish figured largely on the English tables, judging by the amount and expense of that purchased. For example, two sturgeon were bought by the English kitchen officers in Antwerp for £3 18s. 8d. One of the fish was evidently presented whole to Francis as a gift from Henry. Total purchases for the English camp come to a staggering 29,518 fish including, among much else, plaice, flounder, conger eels, crayfish and turbot. There was also one dolphin. Perhaps it was used in some form of tribute to Princess Mary's betrothed, the dauphin of France? Although fish was a staple of the Tudor diet a fair way down the social scale, not least due to the necessity of eating it on Fridays, for the middling ranks this more usually meant salted, dried and smoked fish rather than fresh. A significant proportion of the fish accounted for in June 1520 would have been consumed on the three Fridays of the meeting, not just at the feasts.[13]

Large exotic birds were usually presented with great style by royal cooks, none more so than swans and especially peacocks. The feathers, skin and head removed in one operation, the bird would be cooked whole. Once cooled, its head would be reconnected and the bird re-dressed in its own plumage, its beak painted with gold, and it would be arrayed on a serving dish amidst foliage and other decorative touches.[14] Storks, bitterns and egrets were sometimes served in similarly theatrical ways. Some 6,475 birds of various species were presented on the tables at the Field. The English kitchen accounts also record payments for no fewer than 98,050 eggs! Venison was of course the principal game meat of the royal table, and we have already noted how herds of deer, sheep and pigs were shipped from England and penned near Guînes before slaughter.[15]

The range, amount and expense of food on these occasions was astounding, even by royal standards, and quite out of proportion to that of the middling ranks of Tudor society. Compare the £3 18s. 8d spent on the two sturgeons from Antwerp in 1520 with 15s. 1d for the cost of the 'chapter feast' for ten senior members of Merton College, Oxford, on 11 July 1504. This sum furnished none of the kinds of food and spices served at the 'top tables' at the Field, but was enough for a good dinner of veal, goose, capons, beef, mutton and lamb together with some sort of dessert after the meat and poultry dishes.[16]

Soardino states that after the meal on 10 June, dancing began in the main hall with the music of tabor, pipe and viols. The duchess of Suffolk led the revels, dancing with a French nobleman. After this Francis, who had brought with him a band of fifers and trombones, had a dance 'performed in the Italian manner'. Francis was as passionately committed to the dance as his English counterpart. It was he who took the initiative in the development of the masque in the Italian fashion north of the Alps. In 1515, after his conquest of the duchy of Milan, he spent approximately four months in his newly acquired territory, making himself known to his Milanese subjects and other Italian notables. Federico Gonzaga, the son of Francesco, Marquess of Mantua, and Isabella d'Este, lived at the French court between October

1515 and March 1517. Federico's correspondence with his parents, and that of his secretary, relate how Milanese and Mantuan music and dress (especially for women) were favoured by the king. According to the young Gonzaga prince, Francis held almost nightly entertainments featuring *moresques* and *mascarades* during the time he was in Italy and after his return to France in January 1516.[17]

The masque 'in the Italian fashion' was already known at the English court. It was at the Twelfth Night celebrations in January 1512 that this form of disguising was first performed there. Hall records the event thus:

On the daie of Epiphanie at night, the king with xi other were disguised, after the maner of Italie, called a maske, a thyng not seen afore in Englande, thei were appareled in garmentes long and brode, wrought all with gold, with visers and cappes of gold & after the banket doen, these Maskers came in, with sixe gentlemen disguised in silke bearyng staffe torches, and desired the ladies to daunce, some were content, and some that knewe the fashion of it refused, because it was not a thyng commonly seen. And after thei daunced and commoned together, as the fashion of the Maske is, thei tooke their leave and departed, and so did the Quene, and all the ladies.[18]

There has been much debate about the precise nature of the masque, but it is reasonably clear from Hall's account that, apart from the long robes as costumes, the crucial difference between this 'Italian' masque and the disguisings until then practised at the Tudor court was that the dancers invited members of the audience to join them in the dances that followed.[19] Until then, men and women would dance in separate companies for the disguising – although they might dance together more informally later. Sydney Anglo has observed that the custom of masquers dancing with members of the audience added only one further element to the 'multiform spectacle combining music, poetry *débat*, combat scenic display and dance' common at the court since the last years of Henry VII's reign. He noted that its introduction to the English court in 1512 was 'more noteworthy as an illustration of Henry's desire to increase the brilliance of his own court by introducing fashionable continental revels into England'.[20] Soardino says nothing about the masquing costumes being worn on 10 June 1520, but he does specify that some twenty couples danced together and that Francis danced with the girlfriend of the seigneur de Montepezat, one of his younger courtiers who was then a hostage in England.[21]

Meanwhile Henry, accompanied by his senior nobles, had ridden over to Ardres on the bay charger that Francis had given him the previous day. He was received outside the town by the roi de Navarre, the duc d'Alençon and the cardinals of Bourbon, Lorraine and Albret. Chancellor Duprat escorted him through the town to the royal lodgings where he was greeted by Queen Claude, Louise de Savoie and the duchesse d'Alençon. Henry was led to a chamber 'where he was to repose' before entering the hall, covered in pink brocade for the occasion. He was served by noblemen of the French household supervised by the *Grand Maître* with twenty-four trumpeters playing the whole time that the courses were brought up from the kitchen in gold dishes with gold covers. There was also vocal and other music throughout the meal. Heraldic table decorations, called *entremets*, rather like the 'subtleties' described by Russell, were displayed on this occasion. The duc de Bourbon's painter received 25 *livres tournois* for preparing them for this banquet and they included salamanders, leopards and ermines bearing the arms of the French king and queen. We are told that there were so many courses at this banquet that the diners remained at table four hours and there followed dancing until the evening of that summer day. The time of Henry's departure from the banquet, one source says at 5p.m., was once again co-ordinated with Francis's departure, signalled by a cannon salvo. After bidding farewell to the principal ladies of the court, Henry left Ardres and met Francis again at the lists as he made his way back to Guînes.[22]

Much more is known about the second set of banquets, which took place a week later on Sunday 17 June. As on the previous occasion, Francis came to Guînes castle, but did so unexpectedly, very early in the day and with only a few companions.[23] Having greeted Francis, the king of England escorted him to Mass and thence from the castle to the temporary palace, possibly via the covered gallery that connected the two buildings. While the household officials busied themselves preparing a banquet, Francis evidently remained at the palace as the guest of Queen Katherine and later in the day he was joined by his mother. When the meal was ready, Francis was served in Henry's Presence Chamber, dining off gold plate while noblemen were served on plate of silver gilt 'and all other in silver vessell', as Hall puts it. Soardino reports that the two queens dined together while Wolsey entertained the French princes who had accompanied the king. Another source maintains that Katherine and Wolsey entertained Louise de Savoie in Wolsey's apartments.[24]

At this and the other two banquets, the wine and other drinks flowed freely. Wine was bought in prodigious quantities. Purchases by the department of the Buttery in the English kitchens totalled not less than £744. Wine from the German lands, from the Balkans, Greece and the Ionian islands was served alongside that of France. Apart from Burgundy the precise types of these wines were not specified in the accounts. What was called 'Gascon wine' in 1520 is now, if red, 'claret', usually referred to as Bordeaux; and, if white, the Graves or Entre-Deux-Mers wines grown on estates immediately to the south and east of Bordeaux itself. The 'French wine' in the accounts is most likely to refer to that produced along the banks of the Loire, such as Sancerre, Touraine, Anjou, Saumur and the Pays Nantais. The total recorded cost of alcoholic drink (including beer and ale) for June–July 1520 was £1,568 1s. 11¾d.[25]

On 17 June the hall of the temporary palace was once again divided into two dining spaces, the men in one and women in the other. Afterwards, the tables having been cleared away, there was dancing in which Francis participated, first 'in the French fashion'. In the formal dances, usually the *basse-danse* and the *pavane*, dignified balance and control, elegance and ease of movement were demanded of the man. The *pavane* was often followed by the *galliard*, a pairing brought from France to England and known there as the *double dance of France*. In her recent book on Renaissance dance Margaret McGowan has described the *galliard* as essentially a dance devised to display the choreographic powers of the male dancer who, having circled the room with his partner at least once, left her at the end of the hall while he executed difficult passages for her admiration, returning to her from time to time to ensure that she understood that his display of skills were for her particular pleasure.[26]

Then followed the entrance of ten masquers, including Francis, 'dressed in long gowns of velvet and satin, with plumes and hoods' and they danced in what was reputedly the 'Ferrarese fahion'.[27] Throughout his reign, Francis danced very athletically and with great speed and precision. Cardinal Ippolito d'Este praised his dancing of a *galliard* in January 1541 and in July 1546, at 51, the king distinguished himself at a masquerade held to celebrate the baptism of his granddaughter. Francis also danced in a variety of sometimes rather unexpected costumes designed by Francesco Primaticcio, such as a 'man-beast', a centaur, a tree, a bear and even as a lobster.[28]

On 17 June, Henry once again went to Ardres, this time accompanied by his sister, Mary, and her husband, Charles Brandon, Duke of Suffolk. Arriving at the French royal lodgings, he was greeted by Queen Claude and the French court. Queen Claude sat with the duchess of Suffolk on her left hand and nearly under the queen's canopy. As at Guînes, after dinner the women of the court readied themselves to dance. Hall then tells us that 'the king the more to glad the quene and the sayd ladies, departed secretly and put himself with xxix persones more in maskers apparell'.[29] This 'secret' disappearance was typical of Henry's participation in masques or disguisings.

As in the tournament, the king's role in masques was always carefully choreographed to focus maximum attention on his presence, both disguised and then at the moment of dramatic self-revelation.[30] The following description from Hall's account of Twelfth Night 1511 is typical:

And in the moste of this pastyme, when all persones were most attentyve to beholde the daunsyng, the king was sodenly gone

unknowen to the moste parte of the people there, onles it were of the
Queen and of certayne other. Within a littel while after his departing,
the trompettes at thende of the Hall began to blow.[31]

The king then entered, visored, dressed identically with his partners and
apparently as anonymous as anyone else on the floor, but in fact by his
physique, manner and movement recognisable to most people in the
court. At Ardres on 17 June, Henry had three companies of masquers
with him. They evidently prepared themselves in another house in the
town because they were then escorted back to the royal *hôtel* by drum-
mers. The first group comprised ten young noblemen dressed as visitors
from 'Ruseland or farre Estland' whose costumes included 'purses of
seals skins and girdles of the same'.

Dressing as exotic foreigners was common at the Tudor court. The
foreground of the Hampton Court painting *The Field of Cloth of Gold*
depicts two characters dressed in what appear to be masquing costumes
of yellow or gold, who are perhaps meant to be 'Turks'. Evocations of the
'great enemy' of Christendom had appeared at several masques in 1518
in the celebration for the treaty of Universal Peace. The calf-length coats
emblazoned with some sort of heraldic design worn by the figures in the
painting, their high caps adorned with crescent-shaped feathers and the
fact that they carry horns and have scimitars at their side are all sugges-
tive of a westernised view of the dress of Ottoman janissaries.

The members of the second group of ten masquers were dressed in
the theme of 'adieu jeunesse' – farewell youth – and wore gowns over
their costumes of black velvet which, as Soardino observed, were 'such
as were worn of old by doctors in England' and which were embroidered
'with mottoes in English unintelligible to us'. The masks made them
look like old men. The third company comprised the king and nine
others in gowns which Soardino describes as in Milanese fashion and
which Hall specifies further were lined with green taffeta. Their faces
were visored with beards made of fine wired gold. In the Italian–English
masquing custom, 'these revelers toke ladies and daunced in passyng the
tyme right honourably'.[32]

Once these formal dances were concluded and the masquers unmasked themselves, a sweet refreshment was served. Hall informs us that 'spices, fruites, jellies, and banket viands wer brought'. Here he uses the word 'banquet' in its secondary sense, as a synonym for the older French word 'void' or 'voidee' used at both the Valois and Tudor courts to refer to a sweet course originally taken after the main meal. The highest-ranked guests left (or 'avoided') the hall while the trestle tables used for the majority of dinners were cleared away, often to make room for dancing or theatrical entertainments. By 1520 the 'void' had become a separate event in itself, which might well immediately follow the main meal, or be served, as at Ardres on this occasion, after the dancing, or even at another time altogether, without reference to a main meal. It became yet another form of status-enhancing entertainment offered by the royal host. At the Tudor court it might signal the formal end of the main banquet and its entertainments, but often it might also be followed by more informal dancing that continued sometimes for a short while and sometimes, apparently, for hours afterwards.

The young Henry was a noted and enthusiastic dancer. In September 1513, Paulo da Laude, the Mantuan ambassador at Henry's court, reported to his master that at a banquet given at Lille by Emperor Maximilian and his daughter, the king danced with Marguerite de Savoie, 'from the time the banquet finished until nearly day, in his shirt and without shoes'. Dancing without a doublet was the Tudor equivalent of being stripped to the waist; the king's physique could not have been more overtly displayed without breaking the bounds of propriety. The same ambassador reported that a few days later, the king broke off a discussion with him, 'as he was in a hurry to go and dine and dance afterwards. In this he does wonders and leaps like a stag.'[33] At a banquet on 18 September the ambassador reported the king as having spent 'almost the whole night in dancing with the damsels'. In October, in celebration of the conquest of Tournai from France, another banquet was held. The same ambassador wrote that he had seen Henry dance 'magnificently in the French style, in his doublet and play the virginals and the flute in company most creditably, affording great pleasure to all those present'.[34] On 17 June 1520, however, the banquet did end with the 'void' and then, once again at about 5p.m., the king bade farewell to his hosts. He and his companions replaced their visors. Horses were led into the courtyard and the English company rode out of the town and back to Guînes.[35]

We are relatively well informed about Francis I's personal expenditure on these banquets, thanks to one financial account not previously referred to. Now preserved in the Archives Nationales in Paris, this is the account prepared by Sebastian de Mareau, Master of the King's *Chambre-aux-deniers*, the officer who was responsible for regulating royal household expenditure. The account records payments made during the month of June 1520 while the king was at Boulogne and Ardres for the meeting with his 'most dear and most loved good brother and ally, the king of England'. The preamble to the account, drawn up in September 1520, specifies that it records ordinary expenses for the whole month, together with

> great and sumptuous expenditure for the feasts and banquets which were made at the order and command of the said lord [Francis] to the king of England, the queen his wife and to the princes, princesses, lords and ladies of the said country of England who had come to the said place of Ardres to accompany the king of England.[36]

It evidently covers some, though probably not all, the expenditure on entertaining the English at Ardres, certain ancillary expenses, those incurred during the king's journey back to Paris afterwards and the wages of the officers of the *Chambre aux deniers*. Some items of expenditure are specified to be for the king's privy kitchen and related departments (*bouche*) and others for what in England were called the 'great' kitchens (*cuisine du commun*). Total expenditure for the month comes to 30,484 *livres*, 10 *sous*, 5 *deniers tournois* (*c.* £3,048), for which the king authorised payment in September 1520.[37]

The largest individual items of expenditure were, as for the English, on meat and fish. Some 12,146 *livres* (*c.* £1,214), 19 *sous* and 3 *deniers tournois* was spent over the month on various kinds of meat, but principally venison, for the banquets, the king's privy kitchen and the great kitchens.[38] The king's *poissonniers* supplied him with freshwater and saltwater fish to the total value of 4,986 *livres*, 1 *sou*, 11 *deniers tournois* (*c.* £498).[39] His *pâtissier* provided delicacies which cost 741 *livres*, 9 *sous tournois* (*c.* £75). Purchases of various spices, condiments, other additives and fruit came to a total value of 3,210 *livres tournois* (*c.* £321).[40]

There are surprisingly few references to the cost of wine consumed at the banquets in Mareau's account. One total is given of 1,927 *livres*, 10 *sous* (*c.* £193) for various kinds of claret brought from Boulogne to Ardres and accounted for by the household stewards at the end of the month. A further amount of 400 *livres*, 1 *sou* (£40) was paid for wine consumed between 25 June, the day after the meeting concluded, and the end of the month. Some white wine was purchased, but nearly all of it is specified as 'claret', although it was evidently not from Bordeaux as we might expect; some was 'claret beaune', what we might call Burgundy, and the rest 'claret auxerre' or 'auxerrois'.[41] In the absence of further evidence, we might reasonably assume that something like three or four times as much would have been purchased for the previous fortnight.

A few items in the account allow us a glimpse behind the glamorous scenes. There were regular deliveries of wood, charcoal, candles and lights for use in the kitchens (and chapel) at Ardres. Around 700 *livres* (£70) was spent on table linen, pots, spoons, glasses and various dishes for both the privy and great kitchens, along with several lengths of canvas to cover or extend the area of the kitchens at the royal lodgings in Ardres. One Monsieur de Balanzac was reimbursed the 40 *sous* (4s.) he had paid for having an Englishman who had been wounded at Ardres taken back to Guînes. There is also an entry for 14 *sous*, 6 *deniers* (*c.* 1s. 1d sterling) paid for 'tree stocks and leafy boughs' supplied to the 'maison de la ville', probably the king's house or possibly the town hall, 'where the gentleman of the chamber of the king of England dined'. None of the contemporary written descriptions record any kind of royal or civic reception for Henry's closest courtiers as a group but this item indicates that some such hospitality was offered during, or independent of, Henry's several visits to the town.[42] Louis Lemaire, one of the sommeliers of the king's private service, was reimbursed the 4 *livres* (*c.* 8s.) he paid to one of the English heralds to act as a translator for the domestic officers who went with the king to Guînes.[43] This item confirms the observation of one of the Venetian ambassadors that language was an issue at times during the meeting. The king and his immediate entourage may have spoken French, but clearly many of the gentry and their servants did not, or at least not sufficiently well to be able to socialise or work easily together.

On Sunday 24 June, the meeting concluded with a final round of banquets and masques. Whereas on the two previous occasions the assembled companies dined together and changed into masquing apparel afterwards, on this Sunday both the English and French kings were accompanied by their principal lords and ladies all in masquing costumes from the outset. Henry left Guînes for Ardres with his sister Mary, each accompanied by nineteen masquers, making a total company of forty, the whole divided into four groups. Hall describes only two of the four companies. The first was led by Hercules, presumably Henry himself, who was equipped with a club covered with green damask and a lion's pelt made of cloth of gold of damask and ears of flat gold. He led the Nine Worthies: three pagan heroes, three Hebrew kings and three Christian warriors. They were Hector, Alexander, Caesar, King David, Joshua and Judas Maccabeus, together with Charlemagne, King Arthur and Godfrey de Bouillon. By 1520 these figures were recognised representations of heroic chivalry throughout sixteenth-century Europe. They had preceded King Henry VI in his triumphal entry to Paris in 1431. In 1520 Lucas van Leyden produced a series of engravings of the nine, and a rather comical set of them appear in Shakespeare's *Love's Labour's Lost*. In France they were known as 'les neuf preux' or 'valiants', and Godefroy le Batave illustrated one volume of François Demoulins's *Commentaires de la guerre gallique* with depictions of Francis's generals at Marignano as 'les neuf preux'.[44]

It is reasonably clear (without need of elaborate over-analysis) that the deployment of these well-known figures of royal soldierly courage and generalship at the concluding masque was intended to authenticate the meeting's overtly chivalric nature and to honour the ancient heritage of England and France as Christian nations led by chivalric warrior kings. Mary, Duchess of Suffolk, led nineteen of her fellow country-women, half of them dressed in Genoese fashion, half in Milanese. Riding side by side, these English nobles arrived at Guînes and were met at Ardres by Queen Claude. They removed their visors for the banquet that followed and afterwards danced until the end of the festiv-ities, in the course of which those who had triumphed at the tourna-ment were awarded their prizes.[45] Meanwhile the French king and twenty-eight nobles passed in the other direction towards Guînes and were there welcomed by Queen Katherine. The dinner and dancing followed, after which Francis changed into his usual dress to take leave of the queen. Those English and French men present who had won the prizes in tournaments were named and they received jewels, rings, collars and similar gifts. After parting from Queen Katherine and the court, Francis set out for Ardres, escorted on his way by Wolsey and the duke of Buckingham as far as the lists where he and Henry met briefly and bade each other a final farewell.[46]

So the great feasts and banquets of the princes for which the Field is now famous came to an end. The accounts for food and drink show that beyond the banqueting halls, hospitality of a more basic but sustaining kind was extended to all members of the French and English entou-rages, but very little specific information about this more general 'catering' for the event survives. Meals were provided on a daily basis throughout the two weeks for both the high lords and the servants, gentry and commoners, who were part of the royal household – as was usual. Some meals at least may also have been provided communally for those in the entourage not there specifically as members of the house-hold, men like Sir Adrian Fortescue, for example. Nevertheless, the establishment of 'staples' at Marquise and other places also suggests that there was an element of 'self-catering' among such nobles and gentry not directly attached to the royal household who had to pay for their own supplies. By the Eltham Ordinances of 1526, the Clerk of the

Market was charged with ensuring when the court was on progress, as it was effectively in the summer of 1520, that there were sufficient supplies at

> convenient and reasonable prices . . . soe as the noblemen and others attending on the court, and also the sewtors [suitors] and others following the same be not compelled in default of the said clerk to be put unto excessive charge for their expenses as they now be . . .[47]

We have already noted the practice of purveyance, by which both the French and English monarchs sought to provide supplies for their courts in the ordinary run of the year and while on progress. Nevertheless, Hall and the author of *L'Ordonnance* also indicate that hospitality was, at certain times, extended to anyone who came to the English temporary palace – and that people did so in significant numbers. As Hall puts it:

> Duryng this triumph so much people of Picardie and west Flanders drew to Guysnes to see the kyng of England and his honor, to whom vitailes of the court were in plentie . . . there were vacaboundes, plowmen, laborers and of the bragery [rabble], wagoners and beggers that for drunkennes lay in routes and heapes, so great resort thether came . . .[48]

Hall and the Venetian observer, Donado, describe a fountain built outside the temporary palace surmounted by a figure of Bacchus, which 'by the conduyctes in therth ranne to all the people' red and white wine. Gioan Joachino described two fountains. Such a fountain is depicted in the Hampton Court Palace painting of the Field. Hall's description suggests that wine flowed under pressure along pipes and could be had in silver cups either throughout the event, at significant moments during it such as the banquets, or whenever a royal party arrived or departed from the palace – according to the various sources. The right-hand foreground of the painting shows people willingly accepting what was on offer and drinking at the fountain, from wooden or earthenware vessels rather than silver cups. They do not stint themselves and several are shown as much the worse for wear. Two men brawl and another leans unsteadily against the side of the temporary palace as he vomits against its walls. Hall's observation suggests that the sort of characters depicted in the painting were not alone![49]

Gift-giving

When Henry and Francis jointly inaugurated the tournament at the Field on Saturday 9 June, each rode to the tiltyard on one of his finest horses. Henry was mounted on a Neapolitan courser and Francis on a horse named Dappled Duke from the stud of Francesco Gonzaga, Marquess of Mantua. Henry admired the Mantuan horse. Francis immediately offered it to him. Henry reciprocated with his own mount. Reporting this, Soardino, the Mantuan ambassador, tactfully told his master that Henry's horse was 'far inferior to Dappled Duke'.[50] Gift-giving was an important aspect of the Field. One monarch's gift to another was both a token of friendly affection and a gift of liberality intended to declare the suffi-ciency of his own material and human resources. It could also express an expectation of continued association and co-operation even as it demon-strated the giver's apparently spontaneous generosity and his gentlemanly prowess and honour as a prince. Gift-giving of this sort had the essential feature of reciprocity. A gift had freely to be given in order to be a gift, but it also carried obligations to its recipient. Assurances of gratitude and an affirmation of mutuality, or even the assurance of future help to the donor, were the appropriate responses to a neighbourly gift.[51] Many of these kinds of exchange have been noted in recent studies of nobles' patronage networks in sixteenth-century France.[52] The two kings gave each other more horses on Monday 18 June. Francis gave Henry six coursers, four of which were from the Gonzaga stables at Mantua. Galeazzo da San Severino rode them around the lists and Henry rode three of them after their presentation to him.[53] In the course of the tourney, Charles, duc de Bourbon, and Marshal Lescun gave Henry their horses.

The Field of Cloth of Gold may have been the first occasion on which the two kings personally gave each other presents, but a pattern of extravagant gift-giving between them had been established in late 1518 with the initial celebrations for the signing of the treaty of London. Henry presented fifty-two large silver drinking cups to the members of the French embassy that came to London to agree the treaty. He gave his own cloak to its leader, Guillaume Gouffier, seigneur de Bonnivet.[54] The French ambassadors left London on 11 October, Bonnivet laden with a further twenty-four items of gilt or pure gold and silver plate including 'a standing cup of gold garnished with great pearl'. He and his fellow ambassadors also received richly lined and furred cloaks, plate, gold chains and horses with rich trappings.[55] To Francis himself, Henry sent several horse bards of cloth of gold set with precious stones. He also sent a gold chaffron, which the French king liked very much. As Hall reports, 'all this liberality the strangers much enjoyed'.[56] The reciprocal English embassy was treated to similarly distinguished hospitality in Paris during the winter and returned with gifts of an equivalent kind and value.[57]

A few months later gifts were sent to the French court for the christening of Francis's second son, Henry, duc d'Orléans, in June 1519. Sir Thomas Boleyn presented the queen with a gold salt cellar, cup and dish of gold. Henry gave these presents as one of the child's invited godfathers. Cardinal Wolsey also sent £100 to be given to the child's nurse, his cradle-rocker and the gentlewomen of the Queen's Chamber. Francis's reaction to these gifts neatly encapsulates the ritual elements of gift exchange. Sir Thomas Boleyn reported him as saying that:

> Whensoever it shall fortune the king's highness to have a Prince, he shall be [honoured] to do for him the like manner and that he is minded after his said son shall come to age and be able to ... he purposeth to send to him to the king's grace into England to do him service.[58]

The focus on reciprocity and on the personal bonds between the giver and recipient and the honour accruing to the giver is instructive – as is

Francis's dig at Henry's lack of a son to compare with the dauphin of France and his new younger brother. The notion of one day entrusting their sons to each other's care draws on the tradition common to England and France, of nobles placing their sons and daughters in the households of a near kinsman or important patron and indeed in the royal household itself, for service and training (or *nourriture*, as the French called it). Young noble men and women practised their genteel accomplishments and became part of the wider familial-client network of their host. Because of their vulnerability and impressionability, there is a sense in which these young people were both offered and received as gifts between the families concerned as well as investments in the future of good relations.[59] Francis did not in fact send any of his three sons to England, but Henry eventually met them at Boulogne in 1532.[60] The young French noblemen sent to England in 1519 as hostages for Francis's performance of the terms of the treaty of London were treated with particular generosity during the royal summer progress into Essex and Kent. Hall assures us, 'the king did shote, hunte and ronne daily with the hostages to their great joy'.[61]

On or about 16 March, barely a week after his arrival as Henry's ambassador in France, Sir Richard Wingfield had presented Francis with a new kind of double-handed sword, a gift from his master. As it was much heavier than anything the king was used to, Francis was unable to handle it properly. Perplexed, he turned to the Admiral Bonnivet who explained that during his embassy in England in 1518, he had seen Henry using an even heavier sword 'as delverly [dexterously] as could be devised'. The Admiral had been sworn to secrecy by Henry and would reveal only that this was done 'by meane of a gauntlet'. Wingfield reported to Henry that Francis had immediately offered to swap one of these new gauntlets for a pair of cuirasses 'such as your highness hath not seen', to be ready at their forthcoming meeting. He would only say that their design enabled the weight of 'such peces as reste upon the cuurasse' to be taken off the shoulders. Henry should, as soon as possible, send one of his 'arming dobletts' so that his measurements could be taken. On the same day that Francis finally authorised

Wolsey to prepare the meeting, Wingfield wrote from the French court reminding the king and Wolsey about the gauntlet and doublet.[62]

Although there is no direct evidence, an exchange of this kind may well have taken place at the Field of Cloth of Gold. Something very like the English gauntlet and the design of the French cuirass were later incorporated into several suits made by the Greenwich royal armoury.[63] In April 1527, Henry entertained another large French embassy in London. He presented the leader of the delegation, François de La Tour d'Auvergne, the vicomte de Turenne, with a suit of Greenwich armour. It incorporated an inner ventral plate whose function is consistent with a 'device ... for the easy bearing and sustaining of the weight of such pieces as rest upon the cuirass'.[64] This feature sounds very much like the cuirasses Francis had promised to give Henry in 1520. This suit is a superb example of the high standards of workmanship of the royal armouries.[65] The 'device' on the Turenne armour consisted of a single trapezoidal stomach plate which sat behind the principal breastplate and was attached to it by a 1½ inch bolt. It was also attached to the back plate by four leather straps, which could be tightened around the wearer, rather like a corset. The weight of the reinforcements used in tournaments – the manifer, pasguard and granguard – could thereby be more evenly distributed over the body. Exactly the same device is featured on a suit of Greenwich armour made for Henry himself in 1540.[66]

The most expensive individual gifts exchanged by the French and English parties were of jewellery and plate. From Francis, Wolsey received gold basins and ewers decorated with Francis's initials and one of his badges, of friars' knots. Soardino estimated them to be worth 20,000 crowns.[67] From Louise de Savoie the cardinal received a jewelled crucifix said to be worth 6,000 crowns. Wolsey gave the king's mother, in return, a small cross of precious stones apparently containing a piece of the true cross.[68] Wolsey's possessions, seized at his fall in 1529, were inventoried but none appear that are readily identifiable as the gifts from the French royal family in 1520. Nevertheless, an inventory of the royal Jewel House in April 1533 includes 'two basins and ewers with friars girdles by the French king' which *may* be those given to Wolsey in

1520 although they might have been given to Henry himself at his second meeting with Francis in 1532.[69] An inventory of Louise de Savoie's personal possessions taken at her death in 1531 does not indicate that she still possessed the cross given to her by Wolsey.[70] The cardinal gave the Admiral Bonnivet a large jewelled salt cellar with a figure of St George at the top. This figure may have looked something like the one that adorns the finial of the lid of the Howard Grace Cup which was made in 1525.[71] From Henry, the Admiral received a jewel which the king had worn in his cap, worth 4,000 crowns, and cups worth 10,000 crowns. The French Master of the Horse was given a jewel and gold vessels to the value of 1,800 crowns. Bourbon was presented with a gold cup studded with jewels, worth about 6,000 crowns. Henry gave Francis's mistress, Françoise de Foix, a crucifix worth 2,000 crowns. He gave her brother, the Marshal Lescun, a gown of cloth of gold lined with sables.

These gifts were only part of an ostentatious display of gold and silver and other precious metals and jewels at the Field intended to demonstrate the high standards of royal artistic patronage.[72] Henry's principal goldsmiths in 1520 were John Twisleton, William Holland and Robert Amadas, who between them are likely to have contributed the bulk of items which adorned the king and which he gave as gifts to the French. Amadas also worked for Cardinal Wolsey. In May 1520 Amadas received £414 for 'mending and making gold stuff' for Henry and he regularly received orders from the king and the cardinal for as much as £2,000 a time.[73] Pierre Mangot and Jean Hotman were the two principal goldsmiths in French royal service in the 1520s. In 1532–3 Mangot made his most famous piece, a coffer which eventually became part of the earl of Chesterfield's collection.[74] Jean Hotman made cups, plates and other vessels and gold chains used as diplomatic gifts for Francis to present to ambassadors during the 1530s.[75]

Each king also gave demonstrations of 'largess' to the other's entourage in the course of the tournaments and banqueting. A total of 2,500 crowns was given in general reward to the French royal household. Francis reciprocated. The amount he gave to the English household is unknown but is likely to have been very precisely calibrated to match what his own officers received. Several of the more prominent members of the French king's *chambre* were given cash and jewelled collars. The seigneurs de Morette, de Brosse and de Pecalvary, all *gentilshommes de la chambre* and former hostages in England, were among those who received no fewer than nine gold chains between them, most taken from members of Wolsey's household.[76] We should also recall the golden 'basil' branches ripped off bards and bases of cloth of silver worn by Henry and his band in the field tourney on 21 June. Gibson's accounts record that, presumably on Henry's orders, Francis was given another eight horses' bards and bases of cloth of gold by 'Assamus the king's armourer'.[77] In the decade before 1520, the practice of giving away tournament and revel costumes at the conclusion of festive events was common at the English court. On Sunday 24 June the two kings met together at the lists for the last time and exchanged what Hall calls 'gifts of remembrance'. Henry gave Francis a collar of jewels called 'balastes', diamonds and pearls. Francis gave Henry 'a bracelet of precious stones, riche jewels and fayre'.[78]

The two sovereign ladies also made presents to each other. Queen Katherine presented Queen Claude with several hobbies and palfries with all necessary accoutrements, or 'well trapped' as Hall puts it. The hobby, an Irish or English horse of about fourteen hands, was favoured for long-distance travel by men and women because of its longer and smoother, ambling gait. These qualities meant that hobbies were exported to France and Italy even quite early in the sixteenth century where they were known as 'haquenées' or 'hackneys'. 'Palfreys' were also amblers and thought particularly suitable for women to ride but the word fell out of use in the course of the sixteenth century.[79] Louise de Savoie received a saddle and harness from Queen Katherine. Queen Claude gave Katherine a litter of cloth of gold, as well as mules and pages.[80] At some stage in the proceedings, Katherine presented bonnets, which she and her ladies seem to have made, to Francis's youngest noble attendants, the *enfants d'honneur*.[81]

The 'best' gifts were given and received as spontaneous acts of generosity. On one occasion during the Field, Francis acted in so unexpectedly a spontaneous manner that he may be understood to have presented himself as a sort of gift to Henry. On the morning of Sunday 17 June, the French king rose early and, accompanied by a few courtiers, rode to Guînes castle. Met by the astonished governor of the castle and the archers of the royal guard, Francis demanded to be taken to Henry's chamber and was duly escorted there. According to the account by the seigneur de Florange, Francis first banged on the door, then opened it and entered the king's chamber unannounced. Henry had not long been out of bed. Francis grandly declared himself to be Henry's prisoner, while assuring him of his good faith. Francis was then asked, or allowed, to help Henry on with his shirt. The kings embraced and Henry gave Francis a collar of great value. The sources vary on this point but Francis apparently returned the compliment either with his own collar or with jewelled bracelets. As we have seen, Francis had wanted a mutual exchange of membership of chivalric orders at the meeting, something Henry had absolutely refused, so the giving and receiving of collars carried undertones of that debate.

The seigneur de Florange, one of Francis's childhood friends, who relates the story, was furious that anyone should have advised the king to do as he had done. Francis told him that he had acted entirely on his own initiative.[82] That may well have been the case but Francis, consciously or otherwise, was playing upon the recent traditions of Anglo-French relations and on more remote traditions of medieval diplomacy and the law of arms. His gesture was redolent with paradox and double meaning. Francis deliberately characterised himself as a prisoner, actually a hostage, to Henry as an apparent demonstration of his own good faith. Florange noted that Francis was increasingly frustrated by the atmosphere of suspicion which had dominated the encounters of the previous ten days. This led him to upset the delicate balance of protocol and was in fact a considerable imposition on Henry, who was charged with Francis's protection and honourable treatment while he was on his lands. Francis's leaving his own territory and entering Henry's, apparently without agreement and even ostensibly as a 'prisoner', was a direct challenge to Henry's authority over his own realm – an extraordinarily provocative gesture. Helping to dress the English king, though apparently an act of great humility in Francis, was also a bold assertion of his right as one sovereign to behave familiarly towards another.

By 1520, Francis had something of a record in disregarding conventions just because he could. Hall disapprovingly recorded how, in late 1518, he had ridden through the streets of Paris with some young English courtiers there on embassy, 'throwing eggs, stones and other foolish trifles at the people, which light demeanour of a king was much discommended at'.[83] Nor was his visit to Henry that Sunday morning in June 1520 the last occasion on which Francis would upset carefully staged protocol in order to get what he wanted by a compelling display of his superiority over an erstwhile rival and putative friend and ally.

In July 1538, Francis met Charles V for the first time in twelve years at Aigues-Mortes on the south coast of France. The protocol for the meeting was as strict and as balanced as that for the Field of Cloth of Gold had been and for very similar reasons. Neither sovereign was, strictly speaking, the guest of the other in this encounter and there was little real trust between them.[84] When the imperial fleet dropped anchor in the harbour at Aigues-Mortes, Francis commanded that he be rowed out with only a few great noblemen and no guard, to greet the emperor personally. They were not due to meet until Charles came ashore. The emperor was highly disconcerted by Francis's coming out to meet him, but, like Henry before him, was forced to respond. Charles took Francis's hand and helped the French king to board his own vessel. Francis's gesture simultaneously shocked and pleased contemporaries, just as his behaviour at Guînes had eighteen years earlier.[85]

The following day Charles landed and, after dining, retired for a siesta. Learning that the emperor had reawoken, Francis went to Charles's lodgings unannounced and burst in, greeting him effusively. Divested of the usual trappings of majesty and, in that sense at least, undressed, Charles leapt out of bed to be on terms with Francis. The king of France, who was splendidly dressed, gave him a diamond ring worth 30,000 *écus*, an obvious token of good faith.[86] Charles 'counter-attacked' as best he could by placing a collar of the Order of the Golden Fleece around the

French king's neck. Now Francis completed the rout by placing his own collar of the Order of St Michael upon the shoulders of the emperor. Charles had to accept the collar as he and Francis had each been members of the other's chivalric order since 1516. Yet Francis's gesture was, in effect, a renewed demand that Charles should recognise him as an honourable prince and treat him accordingly.

The 1538 episode is a useful retrospective comment on that of 1520. Francis was, on both occasions, apparently trying to demonstrate good faith and a willingness to trust an erstwhile enemy. Henry wanted Francis to accept that getting what he wanted depended upon keeping the terms of agreements they were making. Francis knew that, but in appearing at Guînes as he did, he also wanted to personalise peace between himself and the other man. Placing himself in an apparently vulnerable position, he broke through the physical and metaphorical boundaries of protocol. Once there, he made gestures of trustworthiness in expectation of the same from the other. His visit was intended simultaneously to impress and intimidate.

Whether in the longer term Francis's very confrontational approach to gift-giving worked quite as well as he hoped may be doubted. But in the short term, it paid off handsomely. The Mantuan ambassador reported from the Field that, two days later, the English king duly responded with a somewhat ponderous early-morning visit to Ardres, where there was another round of gift exchanges. Soardino's report neatly captures how competitive gift-giving between them worked. He observed:

> The whole court of France rejoices, for until now, no mark of confidence had been displayed by the English king; nay in all matters he invariably evinced small trust; but the Most Christian King has *compelled* him to make this demonstration, having set the example by placing himself with such assurance in his hands last Sunday in the Castle of Guînes.[87]

Evidently aware of the way Francis was gaining esteem among the nobles for his visit, Henry had little choice but to reciprocate and simultaneously try to outflank Francis publicly by giving full weight to the latter's claim to have visited in order to do him honour. This seems to have been the message circulated throughout the English entourage, picked up by the royal council in England and fed back to the king in a letter to him of 23 June. The councillors praise Henry for the general success of the meeting as reported in his letters to them:

> also of the speciall truste and confidence that the said Frenshe king haith in your highnes manifestly declared by his subdain repaire and commyng unto your grace into your said castell of Guysnes, and putting hymselfe hooly into your handes, which approveth his desirous and affectuous mynde to attaine your favour and amitie, and the moor specially because he canne not be satisfied till he have visited and seen your grace within this your realme.[88]

Even before the Field of Cloth of Gold had ended, similar efforts to explain and memorialise the two kings' actions were being made. The first of these came during the ceremonial climax of the Field, a High Mass sung on Saturday 23 June, the eve of St John's and Midsummer Day. The Mass solemnised the event and invested it with spiritual significance. As cardinal legate *a latere* and the most senior churchman present, Wolsey presided over the Mass and thus, to the end, he remained a powerful presence at the Field of Cloth of Gold.

On the night of Friday 22 June, the tiltyard between Guînes and Ardres was transformed into a public stage for the Mass. A temporary open timber chapel was built on wooden posts, opposite the viewing galleries from which the queens and their entourages had watched the tilting only days before. The galleries were turned for the occasion into temporary oratories for members of the royal parties, senior nobles from both nations and the many ambassadors of other realms present at the meeting. The chapel, which was erected at Henry's expense, was hung with rich hangings and tapestries and the altar was adorned with ten large silver-gilt images of religious subjects. It had two golden candlesticks and a large jewelled crucifix, probably all taken from the chapel of the temporary palace at Guînes.[89]

The Mass of the Trinity began at noon. Dressed in full vestments and with jewelled slippers on his feet, Wolsey sat enthroned as papal representative under a canopy to the right of the high altar. The legate to France, Cardinal de Boisy, sat opposite him under a canopy to the left of the altar but one step down from Wolsey. A further step down under a canopy on the same side were the three remaining French cardinals, Albret, Bourbon and Lorraine. Some twelve prelates of France sat near these cardinals and the eight or nine prelates of England sat on the opposite side below Wolsey. The bishops of Armagh and Durham assisted him directly at the Mass.

Below and in front of the altar was an area which corresponded to the choir stalls of a conventional sixteenth-century church, and here assembled the choirs of the Chapels Royal of France and England, probably supplemented by singers from Wolsey's own chapel. The two groups of singers and musicians performed alternately, 'which was a heavenly hearing' according to one witness, each accompanied by the organist of the other choir. The Mass began with Introits from each choir. The English choir sang the *Gloria* and *Sanctus* and the French sang the *Credo* and the *Agnus Dei*. The *Kyrie* was played by the French organist Pierre Mouton on the instrument brought from the chapel in the temporary palace, augmented with sackbuts (early trombones) and cornets.[90]

In 1520, as far as can be determined given the complete loss of its records for that year, the French *Chapelle de Musique*, as it was known, was directed by Antoine de Longueval. A minor composer in his own right and now overlooked, Longueval came from a powerful noble family whose members served the king in a variety of offices. Antoine had first joined the chapel under Charles VIII and later was made a *valet de chambre* to Anne Bretagne, then to Louis XII, and held the same office under Francis I. Longueval's staff comprised about twenty-three adult singers and six boys although these forces may well have been augmented at the Field by singers and musicians from the chapels of other nobles present.[91]

The English Chapel Royal in 1520 was formally headed by its Dean, John Taylor, assisted by the sub-dean Roger Norton, and had a total staff of about thirty-eight. A list of the staff who attended the Field of Cloth of Gold survives. It includes chaplains who were ordained clergy, some of whom assisted in the singing of services; gentlemen, choristers and boys who performed the choral polyphony that added to the aural magnificence of the great liturgical feasts and public occasions such as the Mass on 23 June. The identity of Pierre Mouton's counterpart as organist from the English court is not known precisely. Most commentators suggest that it was probably Benedictus de Opiciis (also known as Opitiis) who came to England from Antwerp and was in Henry's service from 1516. The most recent account of Henry's musical establishment disputes this, however, asserting that Opiciis served in the king's Privy Chamber only, and ordinarily had little connection with the Chapel Royal.[92]

During the Mass, and as was customary, both kings and queens kissed the Gospel carried to them by Cardinal de Bourbon. As a courtesy, Francis invited Henry to kiss the Gospel first. Henry declined and so Francis did. The same thing happened when they were presented with the 'Pax'. The two queens also kissed the Gospel but declined the Pax and instead embraced clerically; arm in arm but with no other physical contact. Wolsey ritually washed his hands at three points in the Mass, assisted successively by three barons, three earls and finally by the earl of Northumberland and the dukes of Suffolk and Buckingham.[93]

At the moment of the elevation of the Host, the most sacred moment of the Mass (or just afterwards, according to one source) there occurred perhaps the most curious and certainly one of the most celebrated incidents of the Field of Cloth of Gold. This was the appearance in the sky above the tiltyard chapel, at a height of a crossbow bolt shot, of a 'dragon'. A fanciful version of this creature is depicted in the Hampton Court painting. Dubois's poetical description of its appearance and movement is the fullest and is partly quoted as follows:

Lo! flying in great loops, a splendid and hollow monster stretched out in the sky, over the earth, a dreadful monster, of immoderate size, thanks to the cunning art of English constructed on the inside from hoops and on the outside woven from cloth. This shapeless monster is a dragon. From the skies of Ardres it flies to Guînes, this artificial dragon fashioned by the great skill of the English ... Its eyes blaze, and with quivering tongue it licks its mouth, which opens wide; the dragon hisses through its gaping jowls ... It makes a sound as it advances over the earth with rustling wings while with its grey body it cleaves a path through the air ... Whether by means of the wind stirring in the hollow recess of its belly, wind which the dragon draws in through its gaping mouth, or by means of a wagon pulling from afar a thin cable, it already occupies the space next to Guînes.[94]

The full and surprisingly technical description of its construction and operation suggests very strongly that the object was a kite rather than, as has generally been thought until recently, a firework or line rocket of some kind which perhaps broke away from its moorings and drifted accidentally over the site of the tiltyard. Dubois's description also contradicts the prevailing assumption, probably derived from the Hampton Court painting, that the object was launched inadvertently or otherwise from Guînes. His observation that it was made of timber hoops within and covered with material and that it dipped and rose on the air currents but – most importantly – also followed a clear direction across the sky from Ardres to Guînes, and that it may have been drawn on a thin cable behind a wagon strongly suggests that it was a kite flown deliberately over the site of the Mass. Nevertheless, the blazing eyes and hissing mouth indicate pyrotechnics of some kind. Stephen Bamforth has suggested that there was indeed a fire inside, generating hot air and lift. Given its large size, at nearly four yards long, some sort of hot air principle might well have been required to keep it aloft and give it its dramatic appearance. As he notes, such kite devices, called 'flying dragons', were known in Italy at the time and evidently in England too where, as Anglo reminds us, fireworks and associated aerial pageantry were much used in celebrating the eve of St John's Day.[95]

The author of *L'Ordonnance* describes the object as 'une grande salemandre ou dragon faicte artifciellement'. The salamander amidst flames was the principal emblem of Francis. While it was often depicted spitting water, fire-breathing salamander decorations featured at the 1518 Bastille banquet referred to above and on the illuminated frontispiece of another Anglo-French peace treaty signed in 1527.[96] The description in *L'Ordonnance* raises the possibility that it was intended as a tribute either to Francis, or to Henry if it represented the Welsh-Tudor dragon. That it was made by the English is clear, both from Dubois's comment and the 20s. 4d paid to one Thomas Wright for 'canvas for the dragon', for which Robert Fowler accounted.[97]

Whatever it symbolised, given that it was an English creation, why was it launched from the French town of Ardres? If it was a salamander it may have been intended to evoke the journeys to Guînes, and to English territory, taken by Francis himself in pursuit of the peace with Henry being celebrated at the Mass. Such symbolic meaning is a possibility. More likely, however, is that simple aerodynamics determined its direction of travel. In the summer in northern France, as in southern England, the prevailing winds tend to come from a south-south-westerly direction. If the kite was launched from Ardres and pulled towards Guînes, it is likely to have been heading into the prevailing wind and thereby obtaining lift, just as an aircraft does as it takes off. Heading westward towards Guînes into the wind enabled it not only to gain height but to dive and weave in the currents in the manner of any kite and in exactly the way Dubois describes.

More puzzling still than the kite's identity, or even its direction of travel, is the timing of its journey. The appearance of 'a dreadful monster, of immoderate size' with its flames, blazing eyes and hissing noises, would surely have been at the very least a distraction from the ceremony on the high altar if not a cause of alarm among some spectators. Dubois asserts this with his customary poetic licence: 'At first, their faces pale at the sight, and unaware of the trick involved, the crowd, terrified, scatters, seized with panic'.[98] No other source confirms a terrified stampede from the galleries and the chapel, but the effect upon the congregation of the dragon's appearance was surely inconsistent with the reverential decorum usually expected at the high point of the celebration of the Eucharist. Being upstaged by a kite at such a moment surely cannot have amused Cardinal Wolsey!

Thus ended the extraordinary meeting of June 1520. What, then, did it all cost? Unfortunately, there can never be a full and final reckoning of the bill for all the labour, provisions and building of the Field. The ultimate financial cost for each side defies exact quantification because complete records of the many dozen heads of expenditure simply do not survive. What can be offered, however, is a general estimate based on ordinary expenditure of the royal households, estimates of expenditure drawn up by the royal councils at the time and of course the evidence of accounts already relied upon for information here.

On this basis, Francis is estimated to have spent around 400,000 *livres tournois*, or about £40,000, on the Field. He is known to have borrowed 200,000 *livres* from the bankers of Lyon, and this was spent on preparations including the costs of tents and rich cloths recorded in the artillery accounts. Their final costs may have been as much as 300,000 *livres*, and it took until 1543 for Francis's officials to get into the royal coffers the whole of the 124,099 *livres* made from the sale of those materials after the Field. We have seen that the surviving account for the king's banquet costs in June–July 1520 comes to 30,290 *livres* and the Estates of Normandy are known to have contributed 99,000 *livres* to the costs. Other regions and towns in Picardy may also have contributed proportionately to the total cost.[99]

Francis certainly knew how to entertain. The costs associated with the birth and baptism of the Dauphin François in 1518 (including a celebratory tournament) came to 18,647 *livres*. He spent 2,740 *livres* on a single banquet given at Cognac in February 1520. He gave three banquets for the English court in the course of the Field. Given the numbers of diners involved, the exceptional number of courses and the emphasis on the highest-quality food and entertainment on these occasions, each banquet is likely to have cost at least half as much again as the one at Cognac, giving a total of between 14,000 and 16,000 *livres*.

This seems a reasonable proportion of the 30,000 accounted for by the *chambre aux deniers* for the king's expenditure on food and drink during his time in northern France in the summer of 1520.

If the estimate of 400,000 *livres* is reasonably accurate, it is quite an extraordinary amount to have spent, given the brevity of the event. In broad terms, it cost Francis almost as much to host the Field of Cloth of Gold for two weeks as it did to run the entire French court for a year. From surviving household records and estimates David Potter has shown that this cost around 500,000 *livres* a year by 1490, that it rose a little after Francis's accession and by 1523 stood at 543,800 *livres tournois*.[100] This figure includes the costs of materials and wages in the king's and queen's separate households, those of the royal children and of Louise de Savoie. The figure compares, for instance, with just under 572,000 *livres* for the king's non-cavalry-related military expenses, the *extraordinaire des guerres*, for the whole of 1520 – admittedly a year when he was at peace and one of the lowest annual totals of the whole reign.[101] Unfortunately the annual budgets drawn up for the king for the early 1520s do not survive so we have no way of knowing what proportions these amounts represent of his total projected expenditure for 1520.

Things are not much clearer on the income side of the ledger. During the first five years of his reign, the king's annual income is likely to have been about 3–4 million *livres* based on returns from the hearth tax or *taille* of about 2.4 million per year in 1515, the salt tax or *gabelle* of 400,000 *livres* and indirect taxes of various kinds which brought in about 1.5 million a year in the early part of the reign.[102] On that basis, the Field cost the same amount as the king earned from the salt tax in a year or, in other words, approximately one-eighth to one-tenth of his notional annual income for 1520.

The amount Henry spent seems to have been of an equivalent order. In April, May and June 1520, the Treasurer of the Chamber disbursed a total of £41,614 on purchases, wages and other items. That sum approaches almost half the total expenditure of the Chamber for 1520 of £86,030.[103] When items evidently unconnected to the Field are subtracted and £600 for shipping the king from Calais to Dover in July are added, we reach a total of about £36,000 expended through the Chamber for the Field during these months. Some of this expenditure was later accounted for through various household departments, such as over £8,000 laid out for victuals, but at least £1,452 was accounted for separately by Sir Edward Guildford on his horse-buying expedition. Ship-building and shipping costs, including those for the construction of the *Katherine Pleasaunce*, also accounted for elsewhere, come to at least £1,401.

The sums Henry spent on the Field represented a considerable proportion of his annual expenditure for 1520. It has long been acknowledged that Henry had ample liquid assets to pay for what he wanted, but that accurate figures on his income and expenditure in his first two decades as king are very hard to establish. It has been estimated from allocations made by the Exchequer that the wages and provisions of the royal household came to about £16,000 per annum at Henry's accession. By 1520 this assignment was no longer sufficient. The size of the court had grown significantly and the Treasurer of the Chamber began adding money to make up the deficit from the Exchequer assignments. Thereafter the annual cost of wages and provisions seems to have stabilised and inflation was low for the rest of the decade. Subjected to a major overhaul in 1523, direct household expenses were calculated at £25,000 as late as 1538. To the cost of wages and provisions must be added the expenditure of the Great Wardrobe which, in 1513, accounted separately to the Exchequer for about £4,000, a figure likely to have been exceeded in 1520. There were also the king's Privy Purse expenses, which could include those for household and other costs although records do not survive for 1520. On these figures, therefore, an overall basic estimate for the household and wardrobe expenditure of £22,000 per annum in 1520 seems reasonable.[104]

Henry had spent the great bulk of the wealth he had inherited from his father on his first war against Francis in 1512–13, which cost him around £1 million. Finances were tight in the early 1520s, and he is estimated to have had no more than £80–90,000 a year from his own resources (his ordinary income from the royal demesne). Estimates of his customs and other revenues in 1520 vary from about £42,000 to at least £50,000. Parliamentary subsidies and clerical tenths averaged about £30–40,000 a year in the mid-1520s but these were not collected in peacetime. From 1519, Henry also had £10,000 a year from Francis in part payment of a total French debt by that time of £257,300, including £105,000 for the resale of Tournai in February that year.[105] If these estimates are relied upon, then the £36–£38,000 Henry spent on the Field would represent substantially more than an entire year's costs of the royal household. They amounted to a higher proportion of Henry's income than Francis had paid out of his, much larger, revenues.

CHAPTER 6

The Cold Light of Day

Tho[ugh] the Prynces of whom we spake of before, were nat so/but
they had dyvers wylls, dyvers councels, and no perdurable amyty, as
after that dyd well appere. These Prynces were mortall and mutable,
and so theyr wylles dyd chaunge and nat abyde.

Bishop Fisher of Rochester[1]

BISHOP FISHER HAS spoken for many down the centuries in expressing
a certain disappointment in the apparent outcome of the Field of Cloth
of Gold. The words quoted above come from a sermon he preached not
long after the event. As he observed, the immediate circumstances of
the Field certainly 'did not abide' for very long after, and all its extravagant gestures of friendship and promises of peace seemed rapidly to
come to nothing. The fact that Henry and Francis were at war with each
other within two years of the event invites an understandable scepticism
about their expressed desire for peace in the first place. As a reformist
prelate, and for Erasmus the ideal bishop, Fisher saw all before him as a
poor counterfeit of the true joys of heaven and his sermon reflected
vividly on the emptiness of the display. In his sermon, Fisher summoned
again the winds that had filled the air with dust, torn down the French
king's tents and 'shaked sore the houses that were builded for pleasure'.

Like the Du Bellay account of the event, Fisher observed that 'many
great men's' coffers were emptied and many were brought to 'a great ebb
and poverty' and that some even died as a result. He reflected, a touch
sourly, that all the splendid fabrics displayed were 'borrowed of other

THE COLD LIGHT OF DAY 179

creatures', from the backs of sheep or other beasts and, in the case of silk, 'out of the entrails of worms', having no time at all for the human skills and ingenuity required to fashion them. All the glory could not avail against the mortality and fallibility of the greatest participants. Bishop Fisher also made a connection between magnificence and competitiveness:

> Never was seen in England such excess of apparelment before, as has been used ever since. and thereof also must needs arise much heart burning and secret envy amongst many for the apparel ... Thus many for these pleasures were the worse, both in their bodies and in their souls.[2]

His disparaging comment largely stands as the accepted English historiographical view of the event to this day: 'these Princes were mortal and mutable, and so their wills did change and [did] not abide'.[3] Bishop Fisher and those historians who have commented on the Field to date in like vein do have a point. Yet the real consequences were not immediately obvious to Fisher and appearances were somewhat deceptive.

It is easy to assume that Henry VIII's relations with Francis I were always essentially bad and those with Emperor Charles V were good, or at least neutral, until the issue of the king's marriage arose in the mid-1520s. It is also easy to infer from that assumption that it was *always* Henry's intention to deceive Francis and that he met Charles before the Field and immediately afterwards in order to stitch up a deal with the emperor that would nullify the commitments made to Francis. Yet, as we have seen, despite a family connection, Henry and Charles were more strangers to each other in early 1520 than were Henry and Francis. It was Charles, not Henry, who assiduously sought the May meeting at Dover, although Henry agreed to it readily enough. Charles did so out of a genuine anxiety about the 1518 Anglo-French rapprochement and upon this Wolsey had played to bring his plans for the Universal Peace to fruition.

While Henry had been at the Field, the emperor had been on progress through his Flemish dominions, visiting his native city of

Ghent and then Brussels. In May it had been agreed that the two were to meet at Gravelines on Wednesday 4 July. They were due to remain there for three days and then the emperor was to return with Henry to Calais on 7 July. Festivities would take place and Henry would leave Calais on 10 July.[4] Henry arrived back in Calais from Guînes on 25 June and began to oversee final preparations for the emperor's visit. It was therefore something of a surprise when, on 27 June, the English agent at the imperial court reported a suggestion that the meeting between the two sovereigns might now take place at Bruges. 'They had proposed Bruges as more commodious; Gravelines is not sufficient for the company.'[5] While there does not seem to have been any suggestion that Charles would not eventually come to Calais, he was then busy receiving a large number of his Flemish and German magnates. As the English agent in the Netherlands, Thomas Spinelly, reported, Charles had just publicly welcomed the Archbishop of Cologne. Asking Henry to come to Bruges was, in effect, asking for a delay to the meeting. Intentionally or otherwise, however, it was also a statement that the emperor considered his current business to be more important than the meeting with Henry at Gravelines, agreed months earlier. It was intolerable to the English.

Wolsey rejected the suggestion out of hand the same day. Through Spinelly, he informed the emperor's leading official, the Imperial Grand Chancellor Mercurino Gattinara, that if Charles persisted in this demand, Henry would not delay his departure for England beyond Monday 2 July. Neither Wolsey nor Henry was content that the king of England should trot meekly up to meet Charles, given the considerable preparations that had been made to welcome him to Calais and the expense of keeping the English entourage assembled there. It also risked creating the impression that Henry met the emperor as a client, just in the manner of the many territorial princes then flocking to the imperial court.

Status brinkmanship was once again the game. Wolsey insisted, as he had done with Francis, that the king having gone on to imperial territory at Gravelines, the emperor must immediately reciprocate and be received on English territory by Henry. The following day, 28 June, Spinelly reported:

> The Chancellor suggests that while the Emperor is on the way, the t[wo] might commune with Wolsey. They blame the Bishop for not informing him of the reasons for the King's hasty return to England. They have delayed their provisions hitherto, in order to keep secret the meeting with Wolsey.

The two men to whom Spinelly referred were the Chancellor himself and Guillaume de Croy, the marquis d'Arschot. Gattinara reminded Wolsey how hard he had himself worked 'for the anticipation of the day appointed by the last treaty and sworn of both parties'.[6] The idea of Henry going to Bruges had been hastily dropped. On 30 June, Charles advised Wolsey that he was now preparing to come to Gravelines and Calais as agreed, but that he would be a little delayed, and was sending Gattinara and Arschot with a request for credence for them.[7] Spinelly anticipated that they would be with Wolsey by Tuesday 3 July.

It becomes clear that the emperor's delaying tactics were really designed to create an opportunity for his two most senior officials to have a 'secret' meeting with Wolsey before he arrived. But what was there to talk about; and why the need for secrecy? The subject of these proposed talks was almost certainly an idea that Wolsey had canvassed a few weeks earlier at the Field, of a new tripartite alliance. According to a report from the imperial ambassador at the papal court, Juan Manuel, sent to Charles V on 13 June, Wolsey had boasted to a papal official with the court at Guînes of his power to 'conclude an alliance between the King of England, him [the emperor] and the King of France'.[8] That the emperor wanted something rather different is clear from Gattinara's note in the margin of Juan Manuel's letter to the effect that the ambassador in Rome was not to worry about Wolsey's boast because 'we are about to conclude a treaty with the King of England'. Other correspondence from the papal court indicates that this was to be an offensive alliance between Leo X, Henry and Charles against Francis in support of Charles's attempt to wrest Milan from French hands: exactly the sort of alliance that Francis feared.

Talk of a triple alliance was certainly around in the French king's entourage at the Field, and Wolsey's most recent pronouncement on the significance of the event had rung alarmingly in the imperial ears. Shortly after the Field, Wolsey declared he knew that the pope did not trust him and was deceived by others, but that in striving for peace between three sovereigns, he, Wolsey, was acting in the true interests of the papacy and Christendom.[9] It becomes clear why Charles was playing for time. He was unsure what to expect from Henry and Wolsey and what, in English hands, an imperial visit to Calais might be made to betoken internationally. Knowing how influential Wolsey was with Henry, he wanted his ministers to dissuade Wolsey from his idea of a triple alliance in favour of an Anglo-Imperial one instead.

No record of the discussions between Wolsey and the imperial representatives survives, but further news from Rome at the time shows that Wolsey had long since been identified as the key to Henry. Juan Manuel reported that the pope so much wanted an anti-French alliance that, notwithstanding Wolsey's insufferable arrogance, if he could bring one about, then the pope would 'make the Cardinal his legate in England' (actually to renew his existing, and at that stage temporary, legateship). Ten days later, Leo also conferred the see of Badajoz on Wolsey. Charles had first asked the pope to give Wolsey this plum sinecure in May as he journeyed to England. Wolsey soon afterwards resigned the benefice in favour of an annual pension of 2,000 ducats out of the revenues of the see of Palencia. He received news of these preferments from Spinelly in early June. The confirmation of them was clearly a bargaining chip in Gattinara's hands and an inducement to Wolsey to join the proposed anti-French league.[10]

Henry and Charles did meet finally on 10 July at Gravelines. The following day, they came to Calais where the emperor was lodged at the Staple and entertained over the next three days. There was no tournament this time, but another temporary banqueting house was made. On a very much smaller scale than that at Guînes, the 'house of solace', as Hall describes it, was still innovative in the English context, but it had obvious affinities with the Bastille banqueting house of 1518, referred to above. Unfortunately the weather was again so inclement that the wind tore the roof loose from its moorings and the banqueting house could not be used. Henry's guests were entertained instead at his residence of the Exchequer to which the temporary house was connected.[11]

The request for an Anglo-Imperial alliance failed. Nothing in the treaty that was eventually signed that July between Henry and Charles contradicted the pre-existing Anglo-French agreement for Mary's marriage to the dauphin. Resident ambassadors were to be exchanged for the first time, eighteen months, it should be noted, after the first resident English and French ambassadors had been exchanged. The two rulers agreed to send special representatives to Calais *within two years* to work towards increased co-operation between them. Evidently there was to be no urgent conferring about an attack on France. Finally, the two sovereigns were to maintain all existing agreements between them.[12]

This was surely not the grand alliance against France to which Henry was already supposedly committed by May 1520, as has so often been argued. It looks rather more like the emperor's best face-saving effort finally to get himself into serious political relations with Henry VIII. The suggestion that Henry should abandon all his preparations at Calais to go to Bruges for Charles's convenience was inept and was made to a king who had just confidently outfaced his great rival – a king to whom Charles had hitherto paid little attention, despite a family connection. Imperial envoys in Rome had openly derided Henry before the pope as insignificant until the spring of 1520 when it was clear that he would meet Francis I. Henry had just spent more than two weeks asserting his international status and military potential in front of the French and ambassadors from half a dozen European rulers, and his own nobility. Was he now to do less before Charles, his junior by some six years, who needed his help against Francis more than Henry currently needed his? Henry and Wolsey held all the cards. As we have seen, Charles had suddenly found room in his schedule to visit England in May as he and his ministers realised just how dangerous an Anglo-French alliance really might be and were panicked into action. It seems that in July there was a similar realisation that Henry's support would have to be earned, not merely assumed. It was an important, if belated, decision by the emperor because, having got himself into the game at last, his preponderant power did indeed turn it in his favour – but that was not until some two years later when the international situation faced by Henry and Wolsey had changed radically.

Immediately after the Field, Francis moved south to Abbeville, hunting in the forest of Crécy and elsewhere as he travelled. On or about 1 July, he and Queen Claude were again conveyed upon the river Somme from Abbeville back to Picquigny, a mercy to the heavily pregnant queen no doubt, and from there they came to Amiens. There the king ordered new fortifications at the northern approaches to the city.[13] Sir Richard Wingfield, the English ambassador still, travelled with the court and Amiens's municipal records reveal that a number of other English gentlemen and their wives either accompanied the king or travelled into Picardy soon after him, at his invitation. One Didier de la Varenne and eight colleagues were paid 8 *livres*, 16 *sous tournois* between them for escorting 'plusieurs seigneurs et dames d'Engleterre' from Abbeville to Amiens. One Jean Charpentier and companions were paid 8 *livres* for fish presented to the English in accordance with the king's command that they be received and feasted well.[14] From Amiens, Francis made his way to Chantilly and on to the royal château of Saint-Germain-en-Laye, arriving by 10 July. There, a month later, the long-suffering Queen Claude was delivered of her fifth child, Madeleine.[15]

Francis was also aware of Wolsey's talk at the Field of a tripartite peace. He played up to the English cardinal fully, even offering to return to the border of his kingdom and seek no place of honour for himself in conference with the other two kings if only Wolsey could bring about such a concord between them. He gave this dramatic undertaking confident that it would never be required of him. As a mutually agreed expression of trust between the two kings, Anne de Montmorency accompanied Henry to Calais to witness all that went on there and then travelled with him back to England. By 19 July, with Montmorency's return to France, Francis knew for certain that the imperial overtures for an immediate alliance had failed and he expressed his gratitude to Henry through Wingfield.[16]

The optimistic spirit in the French court at this time was encapsulated in a book written by the king's former tutor, François Demoulins's, which dates from November 1520. This is the third volume of his *Commentaires de la guerre gallique*, now in the Musée Condé at Chantilly.[17] In this work, the events at Guînes and Ardres frame and contextualise what is, in effect, a praise of Francis I's imperial status. Like the first two volumes of this work which were completed in 1519, the third begins with a fictitious meeting between Francis and Julius Caesar which supposedly took place on Saturday 27 February 1520. It opens with Francis at the royal château at Cognac which is also referred to as 'la maison de Daedalus'. The name of the house symbolises the inventiveness necessary for Francis to play Daedalus to Charles V's Minos.[18] Outside is the park and forest of Craige, near Angoulême. The two towns represent Francis's kingdom and dynasty. In the story, a storm blows up, which is almost certainly an allegory of conflict with Charles V. The king is sure that 'whether the wind comes from Germany or Spain', the two centres of Habsburg power, the forest (of France) is strong enough to withstand it.[19] The king's companions, Bonnivet and Montmorency, urge him to stay close to the château for fear that he will be harmed.

> Nevertheless, because of the magnanimity he possessed and his determination not to be afraid, he went out and entered the forest all alone leaving at the gate the two named gentlemen.[20]

In the forest, Caesar greets Francis as a son. He tells Francis that soon he will go to his town of Ardres near Calais where he will meet a king who will make him joyous and good cheer; you will make him more honour than your power requires of you, but your humility and gracious eloquence will constrain him to love you and this will reduce the arrogance of the islanders. You also will be contented by him at this meeting, for he is a gracious prince.[21]

At the end of the conversation the king 'returns to Angoulême and shortly afterwards sets out on the road to Ardres'. Demoulins's says that he cannot convey the splendour of the Field and refers his readers to Guillaume Budé's greater powers of description – perhaps a reference to the *Campi* [see Bibliography]? He must, however, note three things. The first is the 'virtuous bravery and firm constancy of our wise and loving Caesar'. The second is 'the devotion and clear temperance of our precious and pacific union', which would appear to be the treaty of London alliance, and the third is the means by which this agreement was secured, namely the 'wise knowledge and divine way of achieving of Our Lady Concord'. The phrases 'union precieuse' and 'Madame Concorde' appear frequently in Demoulins's writing as allegorical figures of his patrons, the king's sister and his mother respectively. Louise is particularly flattered for her prudence and dedication to peace. A clear connection is being made here between Francis's apparent status as Caesar's son (and therefore the real 'Holy Roman Emperor') and the recent political events. Caesar has advised Francis how, by gracious and magnanimous treatment of his potential enemy, he will bring the king of England into his allegiance.[22]

This is, of course, a retrospective and highly politicised reading of Francis's behaviour at the Field, and rather ignores the irony of the stormy winds knocking down the French tents there. The emphasis on the king's personal bravery in leaving safety to encounter his destiny is perhaps intended to recall Francis's unannounced visit to Henry at Guînes. Demoulins's poem is evidence that in the months afterwards, the Field of Cloth of Gold was presented by scholars in the king's circle as the event at which Francis had personally and effectively co-opted the English into a celebration of his own power. In this view, by his conduct and magnanimity, Francis had compelled the support of Henry in the achievement of his own ambitions.

Soon after his return to the French capital with the court, Wingfield was succeeded as resident ambassador by his fellow Knight of the Body in the Privy Chamber, Sir Richard Jerningham. This change reflected the wish to emphasise the steadily growing importance of the Chamber representatives and, through them, the more personal links between the two sovereigns so recently strengthened at the Field. Jerningham's instructions incorporated a full report of what had gone on at Calais, confirming that Henry had not agreed to any kind of offensive alliance against Francis. The report was intended to reassure Francis while alerting him once more to the value of Henry's alliance. The implied narrative was direct and simple. Henry had kept faith with Francis as he had promised; let Francis now keep faith with him and do nothing to upset the equilibrium so favourable to Henry.[23]

Upsetting the equilibrium was, however, exactly what Francis I felt bound to do as the implications of Charles V's election as Holy Roman Emperor and of the Universal Peace became clearer. Francis's problem with Charles was less the fear that he would invade France itself than that his encircling power would threaten Francis's hold on the duchy of Milan and prevent him pursuing his claim to the kingdom of Naples as successor to Charles VIII and Louis XII. By 1520, the treaty of Noyon, agreed in 1516 to resolve their many competing claims, was a dead letter. Francis fretted under the knowledge that the longer he waited to return to Italy, the more time he gave Charles V to consolidate his financial and military power there. Francis expected the English king to support his claim to Naples as a 'good brother and friend', but preventing Francis doing anything more in Italy had been one of the driving forces in the Universal Peace and the Field of Cloth of Gold for Wolsey and Henry. In the winter of 1520 the king of France evidently decided that even if he could not himself move immediately against Italy, he must at least prevent Charles from doing do. Not the least of his considerations in taking what proved to be a disastrous decision was the fact that at Aachen, on 23 October 1520, Charles was crowned as the elected ruler

of the German lands and acclaimed as 'King of the Romans'. This was
the first of a two-part formalisation of his full imperial status. The final
stage would be, theoretically, to receive the imperial crown itself and
title of 'Holy Roman Emperor' from the pope – in Rome.[24]

In early February 1521 Robert II de La Marck, duc de Bouillon and
seigneur de Sedan, a disaffected vassal of the emperor, arrived at the
French court. Shortly afterwards and with covert support from Francis,
La Marck attacked imperial territory in Luxembourg. At about the
same time, Henri d'Albret and André de Foix, seigneur de Lesparre,
attacked Navarre in support of Henri's claim to that kingdom. As the
French knew he would, the emperor counter-attacked. They hoped to
present this as unprovoked aggression against Francis and to call for
assistance under the terms of the Universal Peace. By the end of May,
Charles V's commander, Henri de Nassau, had thrown La Marck out of
Luxembourg, overrun the lordship of Sedan and threatened France
itself. Meanwhile Lesparre overreached himself. After initially taking
Navarre, he attacked Castile only to be forced into a rapid withdrawal,
leaving Navarre in Castilian hands. To cap this disastrous sequence of
events, Pope Leo X, who had been allied to the French king since 1515,
now publicly repudiated him. Worse still for Francis, he formally invited
Charles to enter Italy to receive the imperial crown.[25]

Wolsey's initial response in March to the outbreak of war and
requests for assistance from both sides was that Henry's power was best
served by arbitrating the dispute, as required by the Universal Peace,
rather than entering into it himself. As he told the king:

> In thys controversy betwext thes two princes yt shalbe a me[rvelous
> great prayse] and honor to your grace so by your hye wisdo[m] and
> authority to passe betwen and stey them bothe, that ye be nat by ther
> [contention and variance brought] onto the wer.[26]

Wolsey arranged for a conference between the parties chaired by himself
to meet at Calais. He arrived there on 2 August 1521 armed with ample
powers from Henry, the pope, the emperor and the king of France to

arbitrate and, if possible, make the Universal Peace a reality. Wolsey apparently worked hard to this end and his personal international standing was, if anything, even higher than it had been at the Field during the previous summer. Yet, as Peter Gwyn has demonstrated, for all Wolsey's 'shuttle diplomacy' between the parties, conducted with that mix of pomposity, earnestness and charm that was his trademark, he could not resolve their differences. He and Henry realised soon enough that nothing could be done to maintain a peace advantageous to Christendom and so to England. Whatever their hopes in March, by August 1521 they knew that Henry must be drawn into the conflict. At all costs, he must do so on his own terms and be kept on the winning side.[27]

Shortly after his arrival, therefore, Wolsey began covert talks with the imperial representatives to conclude an anti-French alliance. An agreement was reached quite quickly. It provided that the emperor would marry Princess Mary, she receiving a substantially higher settlement than the French had offered. Charles would provide an 'indemnity' to cover Henry's loss of the French pension. Henry would not even have to declare war on Francis until March 1523, almost two years later, unless the present war had not ended by November. Henry would, however, immediately assist Charles to return to Spain whither he was desperate to go to reassert his authority after the revolt of the *comuneros* in 1520.[28] The treaty gave all the advantages to Henry. The contracted delay would allow England to play for more time and even, conceivably, turn once more towards France if changed circumstances made it in Henry's interests to do so. More important still, it allowed time for the careful preparation of a really serious double invasion of France such as had not been attempted in the war of 1513. Wolsey could reprise his role as quartermaster-general to the English army and, with his eye for detail, plan so devastating a co-ordinated attack that it must sweep all before it, striking the crown of France into Henry's hands.

The consequence of Francis's ill-calculated moves against the emperor, therefore, was that Charles obtained in the summer of 1521 all that he had sought without success only one year earlier. By the end of the year Charles's armies had deprived Francis of the city of Tournai, so recently repurchased from Henry, and the entire duchy of Milan.[29] These were bitter blows and Francis partly blamed the two men by whom he now felt deeply betrayed, Wolsey and Henry. He was right so to do, for almost the last thing Wolsey did before he left Calais at the end of November was to agree to an amplified alliance with Charles in which Pope Leo was now also included.

Henry VIII, meanwhile, had put pen to paper in defence of that same pope against Luther. His 1521 book *Assertio septem sacramentorum* was greeted warmly by Leo X, who expressed his thanks by bestowing upon Henry the personal title of *Fidei Defensor*. The bull promulgating it was published in Rome in October and in England the following February.[30] By then, Leo was dead but plans were soon in hand for Charles to make his second visit to his uncle's kingdom as he journeyed from the Netherlands to Spain. Travelling with a retinue of 2,000, Charles arrived at Dover on 26 May 1522, and was accompanied by Henry from there to Greenwich. On 6 June Charles made a formal entry into London for Mass at St Paul's Cathedral, and was greeted by the whole civic establishment. En route, king and emperor were presented with pageants that highlighted the commonality of their descent from John of Gaunt, their potential as allies against the enemies of Christendom and Henry's new title of Defender of the Faith. The following week was taken up with hunting, banquets and anti-French pageants. Among the most pointed was one given at a banquet at Windsor in which figures representing Friendship, Prudence and Might together tamed a wild horse, bridled it and made it obey their commands – an obvious allusion, Hall assures us, to the king of France. On 15 June the two allies publicly committed themselves to a joint invasion of France. They aimed, they said, to subdue the disturber of Christian peace as the necessary precondition for an expedition against the Turks. The king then escorted his guest, hunting all the way, from Windsor via Winchester to Southampton, where Charles embarked for Santander on 6 July.[31]

At Lyon, on 29 May 1522, Clarenceux King of Arms had declared war on Francis I. Henry VIII defied Francis on the grounds that he had broken the treaties of London and of Ardres, principally by his covert and overt attacks on the emperor in Luxembourg and on Navarre and by stopping the annual payments due to Henry. The war that followed lasted for three years. English armies under the duke of Suffolk invaded France in 1522 and 1523 but the projected descent on Paris by an Anglo-Imperial army never materialised due to confused aims and logistics.[32] Francis once more crossed the Alps in the autumn of 1524, determined to take back Milan. Instead, his army was crushed at the Battle of Pavia on 24 February 1525, the emperor's twenty-fifth birthday. The defeat saw the greatest slaughter of the French nobility since Agincourt. Francis himself was unhorsed in a failed cavalry charge and surrendered to the imperial commander on the battlefield. He was eventually taken to Spain as Charles V's prisoner.[33]

The French defeat delighted Henry, who eagerly pressed Charles for the 'Great Enterprise' of another joint, full-scale, invasion of France which now lay virtually defenceless before them. Charles, however, was no longer interested in such a plan. He knew his decisive victory at Pavia to be God-given and that with it came a divinely ordained opportunity to settle the neuralgic Habsburg–Valois disputes. Urged on by his Chancellor, Charles determined not to divide France with Henry, but to unite Christendom through his own magnanimity to its defeated king. Restored to an admittedly smaller kingdom, shorn of those lands to which the emperor laid claim, a chastened and grateful Francis would, Charles imagined, join with him and his brother England against the Ottomans. Together, under Charles's leadership, the three great Renaissance princes would force their common enemy back beyond Hungary and the Balkans, liberate the Holy Land, and Charles would become – in fact as well as name – truly the Holy Roman Emperor.

This was a vision of a very different sort of 'universal peace' from that Wolsey had tried to make. It may have been compelling for Charles and his advisors but was deeply troubling to the rest of Europe. In the aftermath of Pavia, Charles now looked far too powerful for comfort. As Francis soon realised, this suddenly made him the rallying-point for all those whose interests were threatened by the emperor's preponderant power, including the king of England. Henry was absolutely furious at a second betrayal by an unreliable Habsburg ally. While he stormed and stamped, Wolsey, who had accepted far more quickly than his master that the bid for glory in war in 1522–5 had failed, knew that Henry's best interests now lay in recovering the role of arbiter and at minimal cost. After all, Henry had acted strictly according to the rules of the 1518 Universal Peace. He had, in the end, gone to war against a pronounced aggressor, who had been defeated in battle and taught a lesson. Motivated by no personal ambition, Wolsey could claim, Henry now sought the best for all in another international peace under his aegis.

The reality was rather more prosaic. Finding himself isolated again, Henry did as he had done in 1514 and made a complete about-turn, agreeing to peace with France under the treaty of The More signed on 30 August 1525.[34] As under the treaties of London of 1514 and 1518, the king of France had to pay for peace. Henry demanded two million gold *écus* in annual instalments of 100,000 *écus*, partly funded through a share of the profitable French salt trade.[35] An Anglo-French truce was proclaimed at Lyon on 25 September. Francis finally gained his freedom by the treaty of Madrid, agreed with Charles in January 1526. Among other things, it required him to restore the duchy of Burgundy to Charles, to give up all his Italian and Flemish claims and to marry Charles's sister, Eleanor of Portugal. His two eldest sons were also to be held as hostages in Spain for their father's fulfilment of the treaty. It was a heavy price to pay for his freedom – too heavy, in fact. No sooner had Francis returned to France in March 1526 than he repudiated the treaty of Madrid. Despite the risk to the young hostages, Francis rejected the agreement as one signed under duress and sought allies against Charles. Wolsey, who had encouraged Francis to do exactly this, hurriedly swung Henry behind him. He helped to build a new anti-Habsburg alliance between France, the papacy, Venice, Milan and Florence in the League of Cognac agreed in May 1526. Henry did not join the League himself but became its 'protector'.

Wolsey encouraged French overtures for a fuller alliance based on the marriage of Francis, or more likely one of his sons, to Princess Mary. Before he would discuss any marriage, however, he demanded that the French confirm, once and for all, Henry's huge pension agreed under the treaty of The More. This, in effect, meant buying out Henry's ancestral claim to the French throne. Only by offering a permanent or 'eternal' peace, as it would soon be called, could Henry demand such a high price. Hence Wolsey's insistence to the astonished ambassadors that the marriage negotiations which they had come to complete must await a totally renegotiated peace agreement and his extraordinary statement that neither the 1518 treaty of London nor the treaty of The More was ever intended to be anything other than a short- to medium-term expedient![36] The king of France had once more to acknowledge the English king's rights in France and the value of his alliance.

The treaty that ensued created no mechanism for a 'universal peace' such as the agreement of 1518. Neither did the pope play any role, notional or otherwise, in it. Had Wolsey tired of elaborate peace plans? Subsequent evidence suggests not. However, this time he seems to have looked to build solid foundations for the agreement rather than elaborately carved rhetorical keystones. Although Wolsey employed the language of 1518 in the spring of 1527, he was not making a second attempt to impose peace on Europe. In April, the treaty of Westminster was agreed between Henry and Francis. Henry would lend Francis assistance in having his two sons, still prisoners in Spain, released by the emperor. The key to the settlement was that Henry's French pension was increased and the two kings forswore war between them permanently. Mary's marriage would be to Francis's second son, Henri, duc d'Orléans. Henceforward, each habitually referred to the other as not only his 'good friend and brother' but his 'perpetual ally'.

As in 1518, large embassies were exchanged to ratify the Eternal Peace. Henry built a temporary banqueting house and a disguising theatre at Greenwich as showcases for the technical and artistic talent marshalled at his court. The pageants presented to the French during the several banquets at Greenwich in May 1527 combined some rhetorical elements reminiscent of those employed in 1518 and 1520. They were intended as reminders to them of Henry's recent magnanimity towards Francis and warnings to honour him in keeping the peace.

All were carefully contrived to show Francis as the supplicant for the 1527 peace, Henry as its bestower and Wolsey as its mediator. Princess Mary took part in one of the pageants, which featured a 'riche mounte', an allusion to the Tudor dynasty familiar at the English court since 1513. The absence from the mountain on this occasion of any symbolic plants, other than those of England, contrasted with the profusion of dynastic emblems displayed on the one that had appeared in 1518, underscoring the limited nature of the new agreement.[37] As celebrations for the renewed alliance got under way at Westminster, news reached England of the Sack of Rome by rebellious imperial troops and Clement VII's escape, first to the Castel Sant'Angelo on the Tiber, and then to the hilltop retreat of Orvieto.

At the end of May 1527, Arthur Plantagenet Viscount Lisle, Thomas Boleyn (now Viscount Rochford), Anthony Browne and John Clerk were commissioned to go to France at the head of a large English delegation and there to receive Francis I's ratification of the April treaty. The king of France received them in the Salle de Saint-Louis in the Louvre on 8 June. At Mass the next day, Francis swore to uphold the treaty. Brilliantly illuminated, the documents of his ratification of the treaty of Eternal Peace depicted, among other things, the two royal coats of arms, heraldic flowers and Francis's salamander emblems. The document of Francis's final ratification of the treaty incorporated a new three-quarter-length portrait of him based on one done by Jean Clouet on the king's return from Spain in 1526.[38] The following Thursday the ambassadors were entertained at a banquet before which Francis met them and spoke 'very gentylly and discusyd with us of huntyng and buldyng and of dyver odyr thinges'. The pageant of the 'Ruin of Rome' was presented on this occasion. It was not described in Lord Lisle's account of the embassy, but its subject is easily imagined from its title.[39]

On 11 July 1527 Wolsey crossed the Narrow Sea and once more arrived in France as English plenipotentiary and legate *a latere*. He hoped to turn the Sack of Rome to Henry's advantage by amplifying the treaty of Westminster into a full Anglo-French alliance. He wanted to secure the pope's release from effective captivity by the imperial troops who had ruined the Eternal City. He also wanted the pope's agreement to an international peace and to an annulment for Henry VIII. Francis I personally oversaw plans for Wolsey's reception. At Boulogne, Montreuil-sur-Mer, Abbeville and finally Amiens, Wolsey was presented with a succession of street pageants and orations in which he was praised as *Cardinalis pacificus*, cardinal peacemaker, and saviour of the Church. As he had been seven years earlier, Wolsey was acutely conscious of the responsibility of his vice-regal status. His gentleman usher, George Cavendish, reports that Wolsey told his household officers that when they were in France, he expected them to give him 'all such service and reverence as to his highness's presence is meet and due'. On 4 August, as Wolsey approached Amiens he was informed that Francis was coming to meet him. An old roadside chapel stood close by and there he 'newly apparelled him into more richer apparel'.[40] Still mounted on his mule, Wolsey then greeted the king as an equal, just as he had done at Ardres in 1520. As Cavendish describes the encounter, it was almost as fraught with tension about relative status as that between Henry and Francis had been in 1520. When they came within 200 yards of each other, both men stopped and Wolsey would not move again until Francis had first moved towards him. At Amiens, Wolsey told Henry, he found his lodgings 'richely and pomposely apparelled with the Frenche Kinges oun stuff' of plate and furnishings brought to Amiens from his châteaux at Blois and Amboise.[41] Wolsey received a number of very expensive ecclesiastical gifts from Francis. One account of items made for the legate runs to a total of over 3,220 *livres*.[42] On 18 August, Wolsey and Francis signed and swore to a new Franco-English alliance under the treaty of Amiens. Afterwards, Wolsey went to Compiègne where he negotiated the details of joint Anglo-French action against the emperor with the French council.[43]

It was this connection between peace and profit which Wolsey later emphasised to Henry VIII's council, to the mayor and aldermen of London and to the king's judges when he addressed them in the Star Chamber at Westminster after his return from France. He said that

Henry would, by this peace and alliance, 'have more treasure out of France yerely then all his revenewes and customes amount to' and thereby become the 'richest prince of the world'. It is significant that in his attempt to impress his audience, Wolsey made no mention of international peace as such or of the honour to Henry from managing the affairs of Christendom. Instead, Wolsey told his audience that he had turned a military war into a monetary one and that Henry was its acknowledged victor. The implied promise was that the kind of annoying parliamentary subsidies that had been demanded in 1522 were, perhaps, things of the past.[44]

A second large French embassy to England came in the autumn to receive Henry's ratification of the treaty of Amiens. It was led by Anne de Montmorency, now the *Grand Maître* of France, and was escorted into London on 20 October by Henry Courtenay, now Marquess of Exeter, Viscount Rochford, William Blount, Lord Mountjoy, and Cuthbert Tunstall, Bishop of London. As in 1518, the French were accommodated at the bishop's palace and in surrounding merchants' houses. Henry received the French at Greenwich on 22 October and swore to uphold the new alliance at Mass celebrated by Wolsey on All Saints' Day.[45] At Francis I's insistence, the two kings finally exchanged membership of each other's chivalric orders. On 10 November at Greenwich, Henry was presented with the collar and mantle of the Order of St Michael. After a tournament that afternoon, the French were entertained in the same banqueting and disguising houses built to entertain the April embassy. These had been entirely renovated and the pageants presented after the banquet recalled those which had greeted Wolsey in France. They played up his supposed role in delivering the pope and the two French princes from captivity.[46] However flattering the vision of the omnicompetent churchman was intended to be, Wolsey was actually trying to project an altogether different image of himself to his French guests. A few days before the Greenwich festivities, he had given a banquet at Hampton Court, which, as he explained to his household, was designed to give the French such triumphant cheer as they may not only wonder at it here, but also make a glorious report in their country to the King's honour and of this realm.[47]

Wolsey displayed his own wealth to an unprecedented degree on this occasion. Cavendish assures us that Hampton Court was laden with gold and silver plate, 'very sumptuous and of the newest fashions' and his guests ate as they would have done at a royal banquet.[48]

A final reciprocal embassy to deliver to Francis the insignia and robes of the Order of the Garter was dispatched in November. Once more the king took personal charge of its reception. On 2 November he wrote to Montmorency advising him that from Boulogne to Paris the English ambassadors would be received as befitted the perpetual friendship between himself and Henry. He would personally receive them, 'le plus privement et honorablement qu'il me sera possible'.[49] The king's secretary Robertet also congratulated Montmorency on his mission and assured him that the English would be well received. In January 1528, nearly a decade after he first sought to be so, Francis became the first French king to be admitted formally to the highest rank of English chivalry. In St George's Chapel, Windsor, he was installed by proxy as a knight of the Order of the Garter.[50]

The rhetoric and presentation of the second great Anglo-French rapprochement of Henry's reign was splendidly optimistic, and publicly the English king and his chief minister rejoiced that the alliance in defence of the papacy was proof that Henry was once again at the centre of European affairs and had recovered that pre-eminence and influence which he had enjoyed seven years earlier at the Field of Cloth of Gold. As always, the reality was less marvellous than they pretended. Even as Wolsey arranged this extravagant Franco-English reconciliation, Henry had decided upon a course of action which would hazard the very prominence that Wolsey had laboured so hard to regain. For, in the midst of so much else that year, Henry finally determined to obtain an annulment of his marriage to Katherine, the aunt of Charles V. His repudiation of his wife alienated the most powerful dynasty in Europe and precipitated Henry's break with Rome. His friendship with Charles, tenuous at the best of times, completely collapsed. Whether he liked it or not, Francis was now Henry's only major ally in the face of an emperor who had the pope entirely at his command.[51] Almost a decade after its great inauguration at the Field of Cloth of Gold as the key to the Universal Peace of Christendom, Henry VIII discovered that his alliance with Francis I was more important to his international status as king of England than it had ever been before.

Epilogue: A Renaissance Peace Conference?

A CAPACITY TO make an honourable, 'chivalric' peace was essential in establishing the new concord between Henry VIII and Francis I in 1527 that became the Anglo-French 'Eternal Peace'. For almost twenty years thereafter, virtually an eternity in the turbulent world of sixteenth-century European dynastic politics, the two kings sank their differences. As we have seen, Henry's competitive relationship with Francis, expressed in extravagant claims of friendship and gift exchange, was given structure through the alliances of 1514 and 1518 and expressed most dramatically at the Field of Cloth of Gold. The many displays of friendship which followed in the later 1520s and 1530s such as the sending and receiving of large embassies, entertaining each other's intimate companions, exchanging personal letters and astronomically expensive gifts, continually expressing mutual praise and a desire to meet again, all took their inspiration from the personal meeting in 1520. The Field therefore gave a dynamic impulse to England's engagement with the Continental Renaissance which predated Henry's reign but reached its highest point under him.

With Henry's break from Rome, Francis became his only effective European ally. The two kings met again at Boulogne and Calais over the course of a week in October 1532 in a somewhat scaled down and slightly more middle-aged version of the Field. There was no tournament on that occasion, the feasting and dancing were on a less prodigious scale, but gift-giving and effusive praise and expressions of mutual regard punctuated this meeting quite as much as they had done that of

1520.[1] The French king did make some efforts to endorse Henry's view of his first marriage and to press the papacy for its annulment, but Henry's high hopes of Francis's more active political support in his campaign were disappointed. Nevertheless, isolated as he was, Henry had little choice but to maintain relations with Francis, even if these were often rancorous and always difficult.[2] As the Henrician royal supremacy took hold in the later 1530s, Henry found the several wars fought between Francis and Charles very useful in distracting mainland attention from what he was up to in England. The dissolution of the monasteries in these years gave him windfall profits which were invested in maintaining the navy, building a chain of defensive fortifications along the length of his kingdom's southern coast and constructing the palace of Whitehall. On Henry's death, Whitehall was the largest royal residence in Europe. It became the principal public stage of his personal power and glory, much in the way Fontainebleau was for Francis and, later, Versailles was for Louis XIV.

For his part, Francis never got the military and financial support from Henry against Charles V that the grand settlements of 1527 seemed to promise. Gradually, he all but stopped paying the debts he owed to Henry under the various treaties between them. Yet he could not afford to alienate Henry entirely, lest his 'perpetual ally' once more throw in his lot with Charles. Frustrated by Francis's indifference, Henry finally did exactly that. In 1544 English armies invaded France for the fourth time, allied to the forces of the Habsburg emperor. Henry commanded the siege and conquest of Boulogne in August and September, but at the cost of any co-ordinated strategy with Charles. The emperor was ready to sweep down on Paris through the north-east of France, even as Henry carried on the siege. Running short of money, and with his English ally nowhere to be seen, Charles made peace with Francis, leaving Henry isolated – just as he had done twice before.

Outraged by the loss of Boulogne, Francis launched a retaliatory strike against Portsmouth or Southampton in July 1545. Henry defended the south coast effectively enough, even if he lost his prized warship, the *Mary Rose*, in the process. Exhausted, the two kings made their final peace agreement in 1546. Had they lived, they would almost certainly have been at war again before too long. In the event, both died the following year, within months of each other, Henry in January and Francis in March 1547. Although the rhetoric surrounding their final peace, its exchange of splendid embassies and promises of mutual regard, echoed all that had gone before in spirit, the reality was that there was no longer much real belief in the idea of 'magnificent peace' inaugurated all those years ago at the Field of Cloth of Gold.

The Field has become a byword for extravagant display and ostentatious consumption in early-modern Europe. The numbers of people involved on both sides in all their various capacities were indeed extraordinary, as was the range of human industry required to stage such an event. The difficulty for anyone looking at it from this distance is to identify what its meaning or significance was for its participants. People in any age do not usually invest hugely in an event that means little or nothing to them. In seeking to explain its meaning, historians have striven for analogies and comparisons with later events.

Something of the spirit of the Field was rekindled at the 1532 meeting between Francis and Henry. We have noted Francis's behaviour at his meeting with Charles at Aigues-Mortes in 1538. Little over eighteen months later, during the winter of 1539–40, Francis invited the emperor to pass through France from Spain to the Netherlands. Although confined to a litter at times due to ill health, Francis personally escorted Charles through his kingdom, entertaining him in the châteaux of the Loire Valley, spending Christmas with him at Fontainebleau, and spending the early weeks of 1540 with the emperor in royal residences in and around Paris. Francis's gracious reception of Charles recalled his treatment of Henry in 1520. It was predicated upon the belief that it would help to secure Milan permanently for the French crown; if not for Francis personally, then at least for his youngest son, Charles d'Angoulême. In that respect it somewhat echoes the dynamics of the Field where, for a brief time at least, the prospect of an advantageous peace between two erstwhile foes captured the imagination of their courts and councils. Once more, however, the hopes of peace were finally disappointed.[3]

In 1559, the treaty of Cateau-Cambrésis was signed which was intended to bring to an end more than half a century of Franco-Habsburg warfare. It was, in a sense, another attempt at a 'universal peace' which had eluded the generation of 1520. England, under the young Queen Elizabeth, was comprehended in the peace but was hardly its arbiter this time around. Once again there was a summer tournament, held on 30 June on the rue St-Antoine in Paris, to celebrate the end of war. Tragically, the death of Henri II, following horrific head injuries suffered at the lists, plunged France into civil war. The treaty that the tournament inaugurated once more brought no lasting resolution to endemic conflict in Western Europe.

The sporting emphasis of the Field, in the tournament, archery, wrestling and equestrian display, has prompted comparison with the modern Olympic Games. This is hard to sustain on closer inspection. The Games of the 29th Olympiad, however, do offer an interesting comparison with the Field of Cloth of Gold. The Opening Ceremony of the Beijing Olympics on 8 August 2008 was a truly global event. It was witnessed by 91,000 people in the Bird's Nest stadium and by billions across the globe who saw it live on television and on the internet. The scale of its highly choreographed artistic presentations of Chinese history astonished all who saw it. The ceremony involved thousands of extras, many of them troops of the People's Liberation Army. The entire ceremony elided a nationalistic vision of the significance of Chinese history with its imagined place in the future world and the so-called 'Olympic ideals' of international brotherhood and friendship. Of course every opening ceremony of every modern Olympics has advertised the claims to fame of the host city and nation. Yet that of Beijing 2008 was exceptional, even by Olympic standards.[4] The Beijing rhetoric was earnest, even intense, in its presentation of China's new offer of co-operation on the international stage – on its own terms. As so often in human history, the medium was the message. In having at their disposal the vast numbers of people and the material resources required to host the Games in such an extravagant manner, the Chinese proclaimed their proudest achievements, hid perceived weaknesses, and advertised their future potential in a 'new world order'.

Something very similar was going on in the fields between Guînes and Ardres in the summer of 1520. Vast sums of money were spent hosting a short-lived event which declared to a wide audience beyond those participating in it, the capacity, confidence and competence of the hosts and protagonists. Their potential to be enemies or to be friends and thus leaders of an advantageous peace throughout Christendom was the message of the meeting. Necessarily imprecise though they are, the estimates of costs offered here demonstrate that, for both kings, the Field represented a serious investment. For each king it was an utterly self-conscious display of the material and human resources at his command, designed both to impress and to intimidate his rival into co-operation. The Field was a showcase of the building, sporting and personal prowess, not just of the kings themselves, but of the elite of two nations. It was not, as Russell characterised it, 'in fact merely an excuse for a party on a grand scale'. It is accurately described as extravagant but cannot rightly be dismissed as frivolous.

Like the Bird's Nest stadium in 2008, the temporary palace of 1520 was intended to be a demonstration of the technical expertise and confidence of its builders. Whether it was designed by Wolsey, by Henry, or both of them working together, it was meant to announce the king of England's awareness of classical decorative design and his capacity to innovate. It was a dramatic statement in brick and timber, in canvas and glass, of his potential in all other fields of royal endeavour. Because it was temporary, it could be far more daring and impressive than a more prosaic permanent building might be. The monumental gateway of the palace with its huge scallop-shell pediment flanked by English roses and its roundels of classical figures was a visually impressive statement of Renaissance chic. The acres of glass which lit the building from every side anticipated the style of the 'prodigy houses' of the Elizabethan period. Within its light, airy and perfumed rooms, whose floors were strewn with rushes, hundreds of the French nobility were shown the wealth of the Tudor monarchy in the tapestries and hangings which decorated its walls, in the display of gold and silver plate on buffets and in the abundant food served at the three major banquets and other meals besides.

The French and other observers were very impressed by what they called 'the crystal palace'. Perhaps this suggests another apt analogy for the Field. The Great Exhibition of 1851 was held in the temporary structure called the Crystal Palace designed by Joseph Paxton and erected in Hyde Park. Organised in part by Prince Albert, the Exhibition featured technology from around the world but was primarily intended to display British design and to emphasise Britain's role as an industrial leader. As in 1520, the temporary building was itself regarded as a technological marvel and sufficient proof of superior British design. Critics of the Great Exhibition, including Karl Marx, attacked it as so much posturing and 'trumpery', condemning the waste of resources on such a temporary event – rather as Bishop Fisher did the meeting of 1520.

The subsequent patterns of exchange and influence should alert us to the fact that while the English temporary palace carried the palm in 1520, the same spirit of innovation it embodied also inspired the French encampment. Based on the latest Italian designs essayed in Paris in 1518 and Amboise the following year, the decoration of the temporary banqueting house so impressed the English that they would adapt it for the banqueting houses built to receive the French at Greenwich in 1527. The French king's monumental tent at the Field was also, in its own way, every bit as avant-garde as the English palace. It, too, was designed to impress with its sheer scale and daring as a temporary structure. To contemporary eyes, the soaring vertical planes of canvas, held aloft as high as a ship's mast, covered in deep blue velvet and festooned with thousands of gold *fleurs-de-lis*, were as awe-inspiring as a ship in full sail.

In the veritable sea of rich fabrics upon which it seemed to float, the French king's magnificent pavilion, and those of the great nobles that clustered close to it, did indeed symbolise the power of the French monarchy and nation as if it were a great warship to set mightily against anything that could sail across the Narrow Sea from England. As the Mantuan ambassador observed of the pavilions, 'they were the pride of France; who thus counterbalanced the English pride generated by the house described above'.[5] Unfortunately for the French, the winds that fill sails also brought down their gorgeous tents in the storms of mid-June. Perhaps this was indeed an omen for the storm of war that would sweep over France the following year, but as Bishop Fisher reminds us, the magnificently dressed tents of most of Henry's own entourage were also flattened by the same winds.

The competitive material display between Francis and Henry galvanised by the Field continued throughout the rest of their reigns. During the 1530s, when Henry's finances allowed him to patronise ambitious projects, he was largely isolated in Europe by the break with Rome. Throughout that decade Henry was kept well informed by his ambassadors of Francis's architectural and artistic patronage and a number of artists and artisans who had worked for Francis also worked for Henry. These included Nicolas Bellin of Modena, who had worked at Fontainebleau and came to England in about 1539–40, where he worked on the decoration of Nonsuch Palace. Conscious of the extraordinary portraits Jean and François Clouet produced for Francis and his court, Henry secured one of the greatest European artists ever to serve an English monarch. In Hans Holbein he found an artist of truly international standing whose iconic images of Henry helped to make him the most famous king in English history.

For the French historian Jules Michelet, the Field stood between the two different worlds of the Renaissance and the Reformation. He ascribed subsequent Anglo-French enmity to Francis's unfortunate throwing of Henry in their wrestling bout described by Florange. While that is doubtful, the sense of transition is not. The Field of Cloth of Gold did lie between two worlds. It looked backwards towards an imagined, or at least idealised, world where the values of chivalry could serve Christian unity, and concerted action by princes in the service of a single religious ideal was thought possible and desirable; a world which Leo X, Wolsey and perhaps even the kings themselves were trying to bring about by the Universal Peace. The particular circumstances of having three young, reasonably dynamic and ambitious kings on three of Europe's principal thrones at the same time paradoxically heightened the potential for unity. It made it seem, perhaps, more tangible than it had ever been, and yet also made that unity impossible because of the intense rivalry between them. By the time the kings met in 1520, the possibility of Christendom forged into united action by the will of individual kings, popes and cardinal legates *a latere* was already lost – if indeed it had ever really existed. The authority of the papacy was being scrutinised as never before. Its capacity to command the sort of international consensus required for a universal peace was in decline and had been so long before Martin Luther raised his insistent voice against it.

Nevertheless, the idealism of the Field was as real as any in human experience and deserves to be ranked with other aspirational moments in European, indeed world, history. Writing in the aftermath of the First World War and within two years of the start of the Second, Garrett Mattingly usefully described the 1518 treaty of London as an 'early non-aggression pact'. Grand international peace treaties and attempts to regulate international violence have rarely worked, or rarely for very long. Yet even the total failure of the League of Nations, and the less than complete success of the United Nations since its foundation in 1949, do not prove that attempts at creating organisations or systems for international conflict resolution and peace-keeping were not genuine. Similarly, that the Field did not bring in its wake a universal peace of Christendom to match the high-flown rhetoric of the occasion does not prove insincerity on every side, nor that such ambitions were not serious – as has been the traditional reason for describing it as inconsequential.

Henry and Francis were not committed to war with each other in 1520 but neither were they committed to peace with each other purely for its own sake. In 1520 Henry and Wolsey were doing through this event what they had done through Mary Tudor's marriage to Louis XII in 1514 and in the lavish entertainments provided for the French ambassadors who had come to London in 1518 to conclude the treaty of Universal Peace. For Henry, the Field was an offer of peace matched with a warning that if Francis broke the rules of the treaty so favourable to the king of England, he would be attacked. For his part, Francis offered peace and alliance with Henry as the price for his co-operation in allowing the English king any effective role in Europe beyond the boundaries of his island domain. His threat was to leave Henry isolated and marginalised if he broke the agreement between them. In 1520, Francis was also doing again what he had done at the end of 1518. He welcomed Englishmen to France and entertained them as supporters of his own claims to international prominence as the victor of Marignano and natural leader of Christendom. Francis was genuinely hopeful that his offer of friendship would be accepted by Henry on the basis that, at the Field, he also showed him his strength and determination to be the king of France in deed as well as name. He was frustrated by Henry's evident reluctance to commit himself. Hence the dramatic early-morning visit he made to Henry, designed at once to disarm and to persuade, to disconcert and to reassure his rival. Henry's decision to ally with Charles V came a year after this event and only after Francis launched a pre-emptive strike against the emperor in 1521. It was prompted by the realisation that, for all Henry's posturing as international arbiter, he could not finally prevent a Franco-Habsburg war and had better ensure that he was on the winning side.

In focusing attention on the kings in the way it did, the Field achieved its intended purpose for each of them. It is perhaps pointless seeking to find the type of 'outcome' or 'consequence' of the encounter that would satisfy the dictates of conventional 'diplomatic history' and render the meeting 'significant' in those terms. In this it has much in common with other historical 'summit' meetings of the past and those of our own time. With their jousting, dancing and the like at the Field of Cloth of Gold, Henry and Francis can seem very remote from the ways of our own world leaders – and indeed in many ways they are. Yet, despite the manifest changes in the institutions and practices of government and society since the sixteenth century, the fundamentals of communication between contemporary national leaders are perhaps in essence not so different from those of the Field. Nor are the politics of display as remote from us as we might imagine. Some of the most important decisions or shifts in patterns of international relations of the twentieth century were initiated in high-profile 'summit' meetings, of which the Field was a Renaissance forerunner.

The outcomes of the Tehran, Yalta and Potsdam conferences at the end of the Second World War were strongly informed by the

personalities and interactions of Stalin and Churchill, Roosevelt, Truman
and Attlee. With some justification, Richard Nixon described his
personal visit to China in February 1972 and his meeting with Mao
Tse-Tung as 'the week that changed the world'. His visit, prearranged
through a series of secret discussions conducted by Henry Kissinger in
1971, initiated the normalisation of relations between the United States
of America and the People's Republic of China after two decades of
mounting tension. The freeing up of these relations had implications for
the position of the Soviet Union and preceded by only a few years the
dramatic economic reforms initiated by Deng Xiaoping. Their ramifica-
tions are still working themselves out in the early twenty-first century.
In 1986 another summit, between Ronald Reagan and Mikhail
Gorbachev, at Reykjavik in Iceland, also 'changed the world'. Although
the conference itself was described as a failure due to a breakdown in
talks, it nevertheless began a process of arms reduction between the
superpowers and better relations between them – despite Reagan's stri-
dently anti-Soviet rhetoric. It is arguable that the perceived reduction in
the threat posed as a result of the arms agreements played its part in
allowing Gorbachev's reform programmes of *glasnost* and *perestroika* to
take hold, with profound implications for the Soviet Union and the rest
of the world.

As Sir Christopher Meyer, the former British ambassador in
Washington, observed in his memoirs of his time there, the personal
mode of dealing between leaders is still, today,

> the meat and drink of everyday relations between states; and it
> cannot be carried out at several thousand miles' range. It needs
> people on the spot: feet on the ground, faces across a table, a tennis
> court, on a golf course, eyeball to eyeball . . . It is the normal practice
> of great multinational corporations.[6]

One could add, in reference to the sixteenth century, 'on a tournament
field and in a banqueting hall'. In other words, it is now a commonplace
of early-modern cultural history to observe that the size of a king's

retinue, the lavish hospitality he provided for his guests and his personal demeanour with them were all crucial elements in displaying a winning magnificence which expressed his personal power. Nevertheless, in the end, the explanation for the Field of Cloth of Gold need not be any more, or less, complicated than this.

Contrary to the general assumption, the encounter in 1520 was not intended primarily to be a celebration of Anglo-French peace which neither side believed in and which was ruined by irrepressible rivalry. Neither was it merely two weeks of wasted time and money with no purpose other than entertainment for its own sake. Nor yet was it a deliberate deception of the French designed to mask Henry VIII's 'real' intention, already decided upon, of allying with Charles V against Francis I. The meeting is best understood as a 'field' in the sixteenth-century senses of the word: a place, an event and a battle. It was literally and metaphorically a war game which depended on spectacle for success. It was a very conspicuous piece of royal Renaissance 'self-fashioning', of ostentatious material display and political theatre, designed to present the power of monarchy in a dynamic and compelling way. Ultimately, the meaning of the event is declared by its name – the Field of Cloth of Gold.

Appendix A
Bodleian Library MS Ashmole 1116, fos 95–99

[fo. 95r] The appointment for the king and queene at Canterburie and so to Callis and Guynes to the meeting of the french king 1520

[total retinue]

The lord legatt	xii chapplins l gentilmen ccxxxvii servants cl horses	300 men 150 horses
the archbishopp of Canterburie	v chapplins x gentilmen lv servants xxx horses	70 men 30 horses
dukes	eyther of them	
the duke of Buckingham the duke of Suffoulk	v chapplins x gentilmen lv servants xxx horses	140 men 60 men
earles	everie earl	

the earle of Shrewsbury
    Devonshire
    Westmoreland
    Stafford
    Kent
    Northumberland
    Essex
 	
    Wiltshire
    Worcester
    Oxonford
	iii chaplains
	vi gentilmen
	xxxiii servants
	xx horses
	
	xxx men above his number for his office marshall
		450 men
		230 horses

[fo. 95v]

	ether of them	
the marquis of Dorsett	iiii chappelins	112 men

the bishop of Duresme	viii gentilmen	52 horses
lord privie seale	xliiii servants	
	xxvi horses	

Bishopps	everie bishop	

the Bishop of Elie	iiii chapplins	172 men
the Archbishopp of	vi gentilmen	80 horses
Armacan [Armagh]	xxxiii servants	
the Bishopp of [Chi] Chester	xx horses	
the Bishopp of Excester		

Barons	everie Baron	

the earle of Kildare	ii chapplins	462 men
the lord of St Johns	ii gentilmen	252 horses
the lord Roos	xviii servants	
the lord Matravers	xii horses	
the lord Fitzwater		
the lord Burgaveny [Abergavenny]		
the lord Montague		
the lord Hastings		
the lord fferrers		
the lord Barnesse [Berners]	[did not go to the Field]	
the lord Darcy	[did not go to the Field]	
the lord Lawarre		
the lord Brooke		
the lord Lumley		
the lord Herbert		
the lord John Grey		
the lord Richard Grey		
the lord Leonard Grey		
the lord Dawbenye		
the lord Edmond Howard		
the lord Curson		

[fo. 96r]

knyghts of the garter	everie of them	

Sir Edward Pnyngs [Poynings]	ii chapplins	66 men
Sir Henry Marney	ii gentilmen	36 horses
Sir William Sands	xviii servants	
	xii horses	

councellors spirituall	everie of them	

maister secretarie	i chapplin	48 men
the master of the rowles [rolls]	xi servants	32 horses
the deane of the kings chappell	viii horses	
maister aulmonier		

knights bachelors	everie knight	

Sir Nicholas Vaux	i chapplin	996 men
Sir T Boleyne	xi servants	602 horses
Sir J Cutte	viii horses	
Sir Tho Wyndham		
Sir An Windsore		

Sir Mo Brackley [Barcklay]
Sir Tho Nevell
Sir John Husey
Sir John Heron
Sir Richard Weston
Sir J Dancy
Sir Henry Guildford
Sir W Kingston
Sir N Waddam
Sir E Chamberlein
Sir W Aparre [Parr]
Sir E Nevell
Sir Pierce Egecomb
Sir W Morgan
Sir Thomas Cornuall
Sir J Hungerford
Sir E Wadeham

[fo. 96v]

Sir William Ascu
Sir X [Christopher] Willoughbie
Sir W Hansard
Sir Tho West
Sir E Hungerford
Sir Henry Long
Sir J Heydon
Sir Robert Brandon
Sir A Wingfield
Sir Ro Drury
Sir Ri Wingfeild [*sic* but almost certainly Robert Wingfield]
Sir Jo Peche
Sir Davy Owen
Sir Wistan Browne
Sir Ed Balknappe [Belknap]
Sir W fitzWilliam
Sir W Compton
Sir R. Jerningham
Sir W Essex
Sir A Plantagenet
Sir W Barrington
Sir Ed Guildford
Sir Edm Walsingham
Sir John Talbot yonger
Sir J Ragland
Sir Raue [Ralph] Egerton
Sir An Poyntz
Sir Tho Newport
Sir W Hussey
Sir T burg yonger
Sir R Constable
Sir ffynche
Sir J Senior
Sir T Audeley
Sir W Paston

Sir Ri Wentworth
Sir Ar Hopton
Sir Ph Tilney
Sir John Veer
Sir J Marny
Sir Ri Sacheverell

[fo. 97r]

Sir Richard Carew
Sir John Gainsford
Sir John Neville
Sir John Gyfford
Sir Thomas Lucie
Sir Edward Grey
Sir William Smythe
Sir Rowland Vielle
Sir Edward Bouleyn
Sir John Rainsford
Sir Gi Stranways
Sir William Skevington
Sir E Braye
Sir G Harvy
Sir Gi Chappel [Capel]
Sir E ffererrs
Sir Gilbert Talbott
Sir John Burdett
Sir William Perpoint
Sir Griffthe Doone

Esquires	everie esquire	
Thomas More	i chapplin	168 men
Thomas They	xi servants	120 horses
William Gascoigne	viii horses	
John Mordant		
Edward Pomery		
Henry Owen		
Godfrey ffoulgeham		
Thomas Cheney		
William Courtney		
William Coffyn		
John Cheny		
Richard Cornvaile		
Nicholas Carew		
ffrauncis Brian		

[fo. 97v]

knights
Sir Henry Wyot [Wyatt]   vi men
over and above his   vi horses
number for the
business of his office

knights scurers [scourers]   these iii shall have a
Sir Griffithe Rice   c men and a

Sir William Bulmer	c horses to be
Sir Richard Tempest	light horseman for scurers

Ambassadors		
The Emperours	xx men	
ambassadors	xviii horses	
the ambassadors	xviii men	
of Venise	xvi horses	
Chapplins	everie chapplin	
the deane of Sarum	vi servants	60 men
	iiii horses	30 horses

the archdeacon of Richemont
doctor Taylor
doctor Knight
doctor ffelle

maister Stokeslye
maister Higons
Doctor Rauson
doctor Powell
doctor Cromer

Secretaries	
John Meawtis french secretarie	v men
	vi horses
Brian Tuke [Master] of	iii servants
the Posts	iiii posts
	viii horses
	either of them
two clarks of the signet	iii servants
two clarks of the privie seal	iiii horses

[fo. 98r]

sergeants of arms xii	everie of them
	i servant
	ii horses
kings of arms	everie of them
Gartier [Garter]	iii servants
Clarencieux	iii horses
Norrey	
heraults of arms	everie of them
Windsore	i servant
Richmont	ii horses
Yorck	
Lancaster	
Carley [Carlisle]	
Montorgeul	
Somersett	
pursuyvants	everie of them
Rougecrosse	i horse
Blewmantell	
Porterculis	

Rougedragon
Calleys [Calais]
Risebanck
Guisnes
Hames

minstrells
trumpetts   [Lambeth MS gives a total of 30]

the garde

cc yeman of the gard whereof c had horses

the kings chamber
lxx personns   cl servants
                                             c horses

the king's household   ccxvi servants
                                             lxx horses

the kings stable or armory
ccv persons which shall have ccxi horses of the
kings and their owne

[fo. 98v]

For the Queene
The Earle of Derbie   vi chapplins
                                             xxxiii servants
                                             xx horses

Bishopps   everie bishop

The Bishopp of Rochester   iiii chapplins
The Bishopp of Herford   vi gentilmen
The Bishopp of Landast [Llandaff]   xxxiii servants
                                             xx horses

Barons   everie baron

The Lord Montioye   ii chapplins
The Lord Willowghbie   ii gentilmen
The Lord Cobham   xxviii servants
The Lord Morley   xii horses

Knights   everie knight

Sir Ro Pointz	Sir Edw Darell	i chapplin
Sir Tho Tirrell	Sir Tho ffetiplace	xi servants
Sir John Lysle	Sir Georg ffoster	viii horses
Sir Adrien fforestcue [sic]	Sir Wat Stoner	
Sir Edw Griville	Sir Georg Selenger	
Sir John Hampden	Sir John Kukeham	
Sir Mar Constable	Sir Myles Busy	
Sir Ra[lph] Verney yonger	Sir Henrie Willowghbie	
Sir Paris	Sir William Reed	
Sir Ra Chamberlein	Sir Robert Johns	
Sir Ra Clere	Sir John Shelton	
Sir John Heningham	Sir Ph Calthropp	
Sir Roger Wentworth	Sir William Walgrave	
Sir John Villeirs	Sir Tho Lynde	

Sir John Ashton   Sir Nat Browne
Sir Henry Sacheverell   Sir John Mordant

Chapplins   everie chapplin
Chapplins six   iii servants
                                     ii horses

[fo. 99r]
Duches

The Duchess of Buckingham   iiii gentlewomen
                                     vi menservants
                                     xii horses

Countesses   everie countesse

The countess of Stafford   iii gentilwomen
        Westmoreland   iiii menservants
        Shrewsbury   viii horses
        Devonshire
        Darbie

The countess dowaiger   iii gentilwomen
    of Oxonford   xvi menservants
                                     xx horses

Baronesses   everie baronesse

The ladie fitzwalter   ii weomen
        Boleyn   iii menservants
        Willowbie   vi horses
        Burgavenny
        Cobham
        Elizabeth Grey
        Ann Grey
        Scrope
        Morley
        Hastings
        Montagew
        Dawbney
        Montioye
        Grey, lord John's wife
        Broke
        Guildford the elder

Knights wyffes   everie knights wyfe
The Ladie Vaux   i weomen
        ffetiplace   ii men servants
        Parre wydew   iiii horses
        Rice   and they that have
        Darell   no husbands to
                                     have
        Giulford the yonger [sic]   i woemen
        Selenger   viii men servants
        Parre wyffe   viii horses
        Compton
        ffinche
        Hopton

Tilney
Wingfeild Sir Richard's wife
Owen
    Bulleyn, Sir Edw wyfe
    Wingfeild, Sir Anthonie's wyfe
    Cleare
    Neville Sir Johns wyfe

[fo. 99v]

Gentilweomen		everie gentil-weomen to have
Mistress	Carew	i weomen
	Cheyney	ii men servants
	Courtney	iii horses
	Norrys	
	ffitzwaren	
	Wotton	
	Browne	
	ffynche	
	Cornwales	
	Coke	
	Parris	
	Victoria	
	Appliard	
	Cary Lord fftzwaters daughter	
	Coffyn	
	Parker	
	Jerningham widowe	
	Bruce	
	Danet	
	Points, Sir Anthonie's daughter	
	Catherine Mountoria	
	Laurence	
	Anne Wentworth	
	Brigett Longan	

Chamberers	everie chamberer
Mistress Kempe	i man servant
Margett	ii horses
Margery	

The Garde
L [50] yeomen of the gard   L [50] horses

The queens chamber
L [50] personns   xx servants
                             xxx horses

The queens stable
Lx [60] personnes which shall have Lxx [70] horses of the queenes and their owne

Appendix B
BNF, Manuscrit Français 21,449, fos 49r–60r[1]

[fo. 49r]

Chapelle

François de Moulins, grand aumônier	1200lt
Guillaume Paruy, éveque de Troyes, confesseur	800lt
Symphorien Buliod, éveque de Glandeves	600lt
Ithier Bouverot	400lt

[fo. 49v]

Ouduart Hennequin, archdiacre de Puysais	240lt
Robert de Cocquebourne	400lt
Louis de Rochebeaucourt	240lt
Antoine Taucourt, *dit* Villernoul	240lt
Guillaume Cretin	240lt
Tousaints Fere, père de St Radegeonde, sous doyen de Poitiers	120lt
Jerome Arzegus, éveque de Nice	120lt
Jean de la Motte, pronotaire	120lt
Jean de Bidault, pronotaire	120lt
Jacques Terrail, frère de Bayard	120lt
Jean Baptiste Bonjehan, éveque de Vence	240lt
Loys Robertet	120lt
Jean de La Romagiere, pronotaire	120lt
François de Dinteville, éveque d'Auxerre	no wage recorded
Giles de Pontbriant, doyen de Clery	no wage recorded
Denis Briçonnet, éveque de Saint-Malo	no wage recorded
Pierre de Martigny, éveque de Castres	no wage recorded
Martin Baucher, abbé de St-Jean-de-Chartres	no wage recorded

[fo. 50r]

Maîtres d'Hôtel

Mellin de Saint-Gelais, chlr St-Severin	800lt
François de Pontbriant, chlr, sr de La Villate	600lt
Jean de Bremonds, chlr, sr de Balensac	800lt
Robert de la Marthonnie, chlr, sr de Bonnes	800lt

Jacques du Fou	600lt
Jean de Picart, chlr, sr de Radeval, *dit* bailly d'Estelan	600lt
M. Philippe de la Platierre, chlr, sr de Bordes	800lt
Gaucher de Dinteville, sr de Polissy, bailly de Troyes	600lt
René de Clermont, chlr	600lt
Jacques de Conigan, sr de Chevreux, mort en Juin	300lt
Michel de Luppe, chlr, sr d'Yenville, en sa place 1er Juillet	300lt
Bertrand le Voyer, chlr, sr de la Court, capitaine de Brest	600lt
Estienne des Ruaux, chlr	600lt
Loys de Barres, *dit* le Barrois, chlr	
Jean François de Cardonne	800lt
Palemon de Casenove	600lt

[fo. 51r]

Jean de Rostaing	400lt
Jean de Tournon, le jeune	400lt
Marron Dosserans	240lt
Antoine de Lamet, chlr, sr du Plessis	600lt

Pannetiers

René de Cossé, chlr, sr de Brissac, premier	800lt
Antoine de Guy, sr de Breuil	400lt
Charles Alleman, sr de Laval	400lt
Georges de Villebrenier	400lt
Pierre Le Roy, sr de Chavigny	400lt
Michel Galliard, sr de Longjumeau	400lt
Charles Dache, chlr, sr de Cerquigny	400lt
François, comte de La Rochefoucalt	400lt
Antoine de Rochechouart, chlr, sr de St-Amand	400lt
André de Crussol, sénéschal de Beaucaire	400lt
Jean de Pujol, dit de Saint-Chamans, sénéschal des Lanes	400lt
Odet Daydie, fils aine de Capitaine Odet	400lt
François de Teligny, chlr, sénéschal de Rouergue	400lt
Pierre de Rostain	400lt
Jean Poussart, sr de Fors	400lt
François, sr de Bourdeilles	400lt
François de Peruse, sr d'Escars	400lt
Guillaume du Plessis, sr de Savonnieres	400lt
Christophe de Chaunoy, mort le 9 Octobre	320lt

Eschansons

Adrien de Hangest, chlr, Ier	600lt

[fo. 51v]

Jacques de Giverlay	400lt
Marin de Montchenu	400lt
Antoine de La Rochefoucault	400lt
Antoine de Clermont, Tallart	400lt
Claude d'Annebault, sr de Saint-Pierre	400lt
Antoine de Saint-Gelais, sr de Mamont	400lt
Giles le Roy, sr du Chillou	400lt

Jean, sire de Rembures	400lt
Jean de Saint-Aulaire	400lt
Hector de Bourbon, de Lauedan	400lt
Galiot de La Tour	400lt
Jean de Sains, sr de Marigny	400lt
Gabriel de La Guiche	400lt
François de La Rochebeaucourt	400lt
Charles de Vendôme, sr de Graville	400lt

Varlets Tranchans

François de Silly, chlr, bailly de Caen, Ier	600lt
Guyot de Refuge	400lt
Antoine de Ancienville, sr de Villers	400lt
Guyon de Clermont de Lodeve	400lt
Michel d'Aubeterre, sr de Saint-Martin	400lt
Jacques Blondel, sr de Turbinghen, bailly d'Etaples	400lt
François de Vavasseur, sr d'Esquilly	400lt
Jean de Santerre, sr de Fontenilles	400lt
Jean de Rochefort, bailly de Dijon	400lt
Raoulin de Marteau, sr de Vilette	400lt
François du Puydufou, chlr	400lt
Jean d'Acigny	400lt
Antoine de Tournon, l'aine	400lt
René de Montjean	400lt

[fo. 52r]

Escuyers d'Escurie

Regnaud de Refuge, chlr, sr de Villaine	600lt
Jean de Jussac, *dit* le Marafin	400lt
Dordert de la Roque	400lt
Guy de Maugeron, *dit* le legat	400lt
Charles de Refuge, *dit* Boucal	400lt
Pierre Françisque de Nosset, d'Alexandrie	400lt
Pierre de Tardes, seneschal de Leon *dit* le Basque	400lt
Antoine de Lafayette	400lt
Ayme d'Aurillac, *dit* Pauquedenare, sr de Ravel	400lt
Pierre d'Arthie [Ouarty]	400lt
Charles de Saint-Severin	400lt
Belin de Cremone	400lt
Jean de Montepezat, *dit* Carbon	400lt
Claude d'Urfé	400lt
Le marquis de Seue	400lt
Jean Albert, *dit* Merveilles	400lt

Enfans d'honneur

Jean de Grammont, fils de M. de Grammont	240lt
François d'Estançon	240lt
Jacques Stuard, comte de Mourray	240lt
Antoine de Clermont, Tallart	240lt

Jean Ferme, de Trivulce comte de Melfe, neveu du sr Jean Jacques   240lt
Joachim de Chabannes, Curton   240lt
Robert de Montal fils Maury de Montral   240lt

[fo. 52v]

François de Breil   240lt
Antoine de Bohier, sr de la Chesnaye   240lt
Antoine de Hallwin, Piennes   240lt
Philbert Ferrier, fils de Mons de Condé   240lt
François de Salezart, sr de Saint-Just   240lt
Loys de Rochechouart-Mortemart   240lt
Loys de la Fayette   240lt
René de Bar, fils du sire de Baugy   240lt
Loys de Bruges, fils du sr de La Gruthuse   240lt
Henry de Lenoncourt, bailly de Vitry   240lt
Loys de Ridoux   240lt
Jacques de La Haye, Hoto   240lt
François de Chastel   240lt
Loys du Bellay, fils du sr de La Forest   240lt
Jean, sire de Thaix, fils de feu M. de Taire   240lt
Charles de Vivonne, La Chasteigneraye   240lt
Jean de Levis, fils du sénéschal de Carcasonne   240lt
Giles du Chastellier   240lt

Gentilshommes de la Chambre

M. Anne de Montmorency, chlr, sr de La Rochepot   600lt
Pierre de Pontbriant, chlr, sr de Montreal   400lt
M. Philippe de Chabot, chlr, sr de Brion   400lt
M. François de Saint-Marsault, chlr   400lt
M. Jacques de Genouillac, dit Galiot, sénéschal d'Armagnac,   400lt
    maître et capitaine general de l'artillerie

[fo. 53r]

M. Charles du Solier, chlr, sr de Morette   400lt
M. Antoine de Raffin, dit Potjon, chlr, sr de Pecalvary,   400lt
    sénéschal d'Agenois
Bernadin de Clermont, sr de Taillart   400lt
M. Michel de Poysieu, *dit* Capdorat, chlr, sr de Saint-Meme   400lt
M. François de Crussol, chlr, sr de Beaudine   400lt
Bernard de Villeneufe, capitaine de Beaucaire   400lt
M. Jean de Levis, sr de Châteaumorant   400lt
M. Jean Loue   400lt
M. Regnaud de Loue, chlr, sr de Berry   400lt
M. Loys de Vendôme, visdame de Chartres   400lt
M. René d'Anjou, chlr, sr de Mézières   400lt
M. Adrien de Tiercelin, chlr, sr de Brosse   400lt
M. Loys de Raguier, chlr, sr de La Motte   400lt
M. Claude de Gouffier, fils du sr de Boisy   400lt
Jean de La Barre, bailly de Rouen   400lt
Antoine de Lettes, *dit* des Prez, sr de Montepezat   400lt
François de Montmorency, sr de Thoré   400lt
Charles de Mouy, sr de Mailleraye   400lt
Claude de Savoy, comte de Villars   400lt

Varlets de Chambre

Guillaume de Moyne	240lt
Jean Baucheron	120lt
Robert Gousselin	240lt
Loys Le Mercier	240lt
Adrian du Ferte	240lt

[fo. 53v]

Loys Senot	240lt
Jean Verdot, *dit* Montmorillon	240lt
André Leroy	240lt
M. Seraphin du Tillet	240lt
Guillaume Feau	180lt
Philibert de Babou, sr de La Bourdesiere	240lt
Hillaire Berroneau	400lt
François Planchette	240lt
Antoine de Longeuval	240lt
Antoine Canart	180lt
Oudin de Mondoucet	240lt
Jean de La Chesnaye, sr de Bouly	240lt
François d'Allegre, sr de Presy	240lt
Laurans Meigret	180lt
Jacques de Saint-Pol, sr de Reveux	240lt
Gilbert Tariel	180lt

Varlets de Chambre Extraordinaire

Pierre Salla	120lt
Arnaton D'Artie, arbalestrier	240lt
Guillaume des Marquets, *dit* le ceinturer	180lt
Mathurin Viart	240lt
Lambert Meigret, *dit* le Tresorier	120lt
Antoine le Riche, *dit* le Chantre	180lt
Henry Richard, *dit* le Maire de Cognac	180lt
François d'Olivier dast	240lt
Jean Paulle	240lt
Philippe Marie, viscontin	240lt

[fo. 54r]

Maître de la Garderobe

M. Jean de La Barre, chlr, bailly de Rouen	400lt

Varlets de Garderobe

Claude de Briues	180lt
Jean Mauhilaire, *dit* Pasdeye	180lt
Barthelemy Guet, *dit* Guyot, peintre	200lt
Felix Martel	120lt
Jacques des Poussins, *dit* flamenc	120lt
Charles Popillart, portmanteau	240lt
Jacques Maudyon, *dit* de Rancoigne, portmanteau	180lt

Charles de la Primaudaye	180lt
Jean Valette	180lt
Jean Marot	240lt
Loys de Brabant	180lt
Jean d'Escobleau, sr de Sourdis	180lt
Loys Perinet	120lt

Varlets de Garderobe Extraordinaire

Jean Perreal, *dit* Paris peintre	240lt
Jean Bourdichon, peintre	240lt
Nicolas Belin de Modena, peintre	120lt
Janet Clouet, peintre	180lt
Thierry Remond, tailleur	180lt
Pierre Durand	120lt

[fo. 54v]

Jacques Jourdin, *dit* Trepillon, chaussetier	120lt
Jean Robichet, *dit* d'Auvergne, pelletier	120lt
Hubert Spalter, jouer de luths	120lt
Jacques Berthet, qui fait les fusees	120lt
François de Bugats, jouer de luth	240lt
Hughes Menessier	120lt
Antoine Gillier	180lt

Secretaires de la Chambre

Nicolas de Neufville, chlr, sr de Villeroy et Audiencer de France	400lt
François de Robertet	400lt
Antoine Bohier	400lt
Jean Robertet	400lt
Guillaume Budé	400lt

[fo. 60r]

Tapissiers

Richard le Cordier, *dit* Gousselin	150lt
Briçet Dupré	240lt
Pierre du Gart	180lt
Michel Dumain	150lt
Gabriel de Hierbannes	150lt
Jacques Valart	120lt

... etc. to end of roll, fo. 61v. Made at Saint-Germain-en-Laye,
8 September 1520, countersigned Neufville.

Note on Names, Currencies, Coins and Measures

Names

With the exception of Francis I, all French names are given in their accepted French forms.

Money of Account

At the time of the Field of Cloth of Gold, the English money of account was the pound sterling divided into 20 shillings, each shilling worth 12 pence. The French money of account was the *livre tournois* divided into 20 *sous*, each *sou* worth 12 *deniers*.

One *livre tournois* was valued at about *two* English shillings so there were 10 *livres* to one pound sterling

Coins

The main French gold coin was the *écu d'or au soleil*, worth about 40 *sous tournois* in 1520.

The main silver coin was the *teston* which featured an image of the king's head in profile (hence its name) worth about 10 *sous tournois* in 1520. Other smaller coins, of mixed silver and copper, included the *douzain* (12 *deniers tournois*) and the *double* (2 *deniers tournois*).

The main English gold coin was the crown, worth 4 shillings.

Comparative Values of English Coins in 1525[1]

English Crown	4s.
Venetian Ducat	4s. 6d
Ecus d'or au soleil	4s. 4d
Gold Carolus	6s. 10d
Florin	3s. 3d

Measurements of Cloth

English linear measurements for cloth were the foot, the yard (3 feet or 0.9m) and the slightly longer ell (45 inches or 1.1m).

French linear measurement for cloth was the *aune* (3.96 feet or 1.188m).

Measurements of Drink

Quart = 2 pints
Potell = 4 pints
Gallon = 8 pints

One tun contained 252 'wine gallons' or 210 imperial gallons (955 litres). There were two butts, each of 105 imperial gallons (477.50 litres) to the tun. There were four hogsheads, each of 52½ gallons (238 litres) to the tun.

Abbreviations

AMA	Archives Municipales d'Amiens
AN	Archives Nationales de France, Paris
Anselme	*Histoire généalogique et chronologique de la maison royale de France, des pairs, grands officiers de la Couronne, de la Maison du Roy et des anciens barons du royaume*, by Père Anselme de Sainte-Marie, continued by H. Du Fourny (9 vols: Paris, 1726–33)
APDC	Archives Départementales de Pas-de-Calais
Archaeologia	'Two papers relating to the interview between Henry the Eighth of England and Francis the First of France', ed. John Caley, *Archaeologia* 21 (1827): 176–91
Barrillon	*Journal de Jean Barrillon, secrétaire du chancelier Duprat 1515–21*, ed. P. de Vaissière (2 vols: Paris, 1897–9)
BL	British Library, London
BNF	Bibliothèque Nationale de France, Paris
Bodl.	Bodleian Library, Oxford
CAF	*Catalogue des actes de François Ier* (Académie des Sciences Morales et Politiques, ed. P. Marichal et al.), 10 vols (Paris, 1887–1908)
Campi	*Campi convivii / atque ludorum agonisticorum ordo / modus / atque descriptio* (without place or date;

	[Paris, Jean de Gourmont, 1520]. Copy consulted BL C. 33 e. 27
Chronicle of Calais	The Chronicle of Calais, in the reigns of Henry VII and Henry VIII, to the year 1540, ed. John Gough Nichols (London, 1846)
Colvin	The History of the King's Works, ed. H. M. Colvin (6 vols: London, 1933–82)
CSP Sp.	Calendar of State Papers, Spanish, ed. P. de Gayangos, G. Mattingly, M.A.S. Hume and R. Tyler (15 vols in 20: London, 1862–1954)
CSP Ven.	Calendar of State Papers and Manuscripts Relating to English Affairs, Existing in the Archives and Collections of Venice etc., ed., R. Brown, C. Bentinck and H. Brown (9 vols: London, 1864–98)
DBF	Dictionnaire de biographie française
Description	La Description et ordre du camp et festins et ioustes des trescrestiens et trepuissans roys de France & Dangleterre. Lan Mil. ccccc. et vingt, Au moys de Juing (without place or date; [1520]). Copy consulted BL G.1209
Du Bellay	Mémoires de Martin et Guillaume Du Bellay, ed. V.L. Bourrilly and F. Vindry, 4 vols (Paris, 1908–18), I
Dubois	Francisci Francorum Regis et Henrici Anglorum Colloquium by Jacobus Sylvius (Jacques Dubois) (Paris, Josse Badius, 1521), ed. and tran. Stephen Bamforth and Jean Dupèbe, Renaissance Studies V (1–2) (March–June 1991)
EHR	The English Historical Review
Florange	Mémoires du Maréchal de Florange dit le jeune adventureux, ed. R. Goubaux and P.A. Lemoisne (2 vols: Paris, 1913–24) I
Hall	The Union of the Two Noble and Illustre Famelies of York and Lancastre (1809 edn)

HJ	*The Historical Journal*
JBP	*Journal d'un bourgeois de Paris sous le règne de François Ier 1515–1536*, ed. Louis Lalanne, Paris, 1854
L'Ordonnance	*L'Ordonnance et ordre du tournoy / ioustes / & combat / a pied / & a cheval. Le tresdesire & plusque triumphant rencontre / entrevue / assemblee / & visitation / des treshaultz / tresexcellens princes / les Roys de France / & de Angleterre* ... (Paris, Jean Lescaille (for Pierre Vidoue), without date [1520]). Copy consulted BL C. 33. d. 22 (1)
LP	*Letters and Papers, Foreign and Domestic of the Reign of Henry VIII, 1509–1547*, ed. J.S. Brewer, J. Gairdner and R.H. Brodie (21 vols and addenda: London, 1862–1932)
Montfaucon	*Les monuments de la monarchie française* selected by Bernard de Montfaucon (5 vols: Paris, 1729–33)
ODNB	*Oxford Dictionary of National Biography*
ODRF	*Ordonnances des rois de France: Règne de François Ier*, Académie des Sciences Morales et Politiques, 9 vols, ongoing (1902–).
Rawdon Brown	*Four Years at the court of Henry VIII. Selection of despatches written by the Venetian ambassador Sebastian Giustinian ... 1515 to 1519*, trans. L. Rawdon Brown (2 vols: London, 1854)
Rutland Papers	*Original Documents illustrative of the Courts and Times of Henry VII and Henry VIII from the private archives of the Duke of Rutland, selected by W. Jerdan*, Camden Society (London, 1842)
Rymer	*Foedera, Litterae, Conventiones* ... ed. T. Rymer (20 vols: London, 1727–35)
SCJ	*Sixteenth Century Journal*
SR	*Statutes of the Realm*, ed. A. Luders et al. (11 vols: London, 1810–28)

STC	*A short-title catalogue of books printed in England, Scotland and Ireland, and of English books printed abroad 1475-1640. Second edition, revised and enlarged, begun by W.A. Jackson and F.S. Ferguson, completed by K.F. Pantzer. London: Vol. I (A–H). 1986. Pp. 620. Vol. II (I–Z). 1976. Pp. 504. Vol. III (Indexes, addenda, corrigenda). 1991*
St. P.	*State Papers Published under the Authority of his Majesty's Commission, King Henry VIII* (11 vols: London, 1830–52)
TNA	The National Archives, Kew
TRHS	*Transactions of the Royal Historical Society*

Notes

Introduction: Why the Field of Cloth of Gold?

1. Sophie-Anne Leterrier, 'The Field of Cloth of Gold in Popular Imagination and Historical Imagery during the Nineteenth Century', in Charles Giry-Deloison (ed.), *1520 Le Camp du Drap d'Or* (Paris, 2012), pp. 65–85.
2. Joycelyne G. Russell, *The Field of Cloth of Gold: Men and Manners in 1520* (London, 1969); Geoffrey R. Elton, *Reform and Reformation, England 1509–1558* (London, 1977), pp. 84–5; Sydney Anglo, *Spectacle, Pageantry and Early Tudor Policy* (Oxford, 1969; 1995).
3. A note on these sources and their importance for this study may be found at the start of the Bibliography.
4. M. Keen, *Chivalry* (New Haven, CT, and London, 1984).
5. Garrett Mattingly, 'An Early Non-Aggression Pact', *Journal of Modern History*, 10(1) (1938): 1–30.
6. *Matthew Paris's English History from the year 1235 to 1273*, tr. J. A. Gileso (3 vols: London, 1854), III, pp. 105–11, at p. 110.
7. Ibid.
8. Nigel Saul, *Richard II* (New Haven, CT, and London, 1997), pp. 229–34 and 253–4.
9. Ruth Karras, *From Boys to Men: Formations of Masculinity in Late Medieval Europe* (Philadelphia, 2003), pp. 20–66.
10. Charles was regent for his mother, Juanna, in Castile. He was elected the 'King of the Romans' or 'German-Roman king' by the Electors of the Empire in June 1519. Technically, he only assumed the title of Holy Roman Emperor at his coronation by Pope Clement VII at Bologna in 1530. He was, however, generally known as 'the emperor' long before this date.
11. Kristen Neuschel, *Word of Honor: Interpreting Noble Culture in Sixteenth-Century France* (Ithaca, NY, and London, 1989); see also Roy Strong, *Art and Power: Renaissance Festivals 1450–1650* (London, 1984).
12. BNF, MS fr. 5500, fo. 226 [*CAF* VII, 25519], powers given to Châtillon, undated; BL, Cotton MS Caligula D VII, fos 180–81 [*LP* III i, 677], Francis I to Wolsey, Châteauneuf, 13 March 1520. Châtillon's eldest son, Gaspard II, seigneur de Coligny, became the Admiral of France and a prominent Protestant leader. A bungled assassination attempt upon him in August 1572 was a critical factor in provoking the St Bartholomew's Day massacre.
13. Ibid., *ODNB sub* 'Charles Somerset'.
14. *Archaeologia* 21: 176–7; *Chronicle of Calais*, p. 18.
15. Walter C. Richardson, *Tudor Chamber Administration* (Baton Rouge, LA, 1952), pp. 195–215. Belknap had first served Henry VII from 1499 as an esquire of the body. He was knighted after the fall of Tournai and he died in 1521: *ODNB sub* 'Rastell John'.

16. *ODNB*, 'Vaux of Harrowden'. He was made Baron Vaux of Harrowden by April 1523 but died scarcely a month later.
17. *LP* I i, 1176, retinues for war in 1512; TNA, SP1/22, fo. 254 [*LP* III ii, 1437], Pace to Wolsey, 24 July 1521; Maurice Howard and Edward Wilson, *The Vyne: A Tudor House Revealed* (London, 2003), pp. 40–8. Sandys had been a Knight of the Body to Henry VII and fought at Blackheath in 1497. In January 1510 he was made Constable of Southampton Castle and in November the same year, Sheriff of Hampshire. He was 'treasurer of war' in 1512–14. He died in 1540.

1 European War and 'Universal Peace'

1. Rawdon Brown, I, p. 79.
2. Richard Hoyle, 'War and Public Finance', in Dairmaid MacCulloch (ed.), *The Reign of Henry VIII: Politics, Policy and Piety* (Basingstoke, 1995), pp. 75–99, at p. 77.
3. Rymer XII, 493; John M. Currin, '"To Traffic with War"? Henry VII and the French Campaign of 1492', in David Grummitt (ed.), *The English Experience in France c.1450–1558: War, Diplomacy and Cultural Exchange* (Aldershot, 2002), pp. 106–31 on the background to this treaty.
4. André-Joseph Ghislane Le Glay, *Négociations diplomatiques entre la France et l'Autriche* (2 vols: Paris, 1845), I, p. 294; *CSP Ven.* II, 52; Rymer, XIII, 271. On Henry's reluctance to remain at peace with France as reported by the Spanish ambassador Luiz Caroz, see *LP* I i, 476.
5. David Carlson, 'Royal Tutors in the Reign of Henry VII', *SCJ*, 22 (2) (1991): 253–79; David Starkey, *Henry: Virtuous Prince* (London, 2008), pp. 67–73, 118–35, 172–83. On a suggested role in Henry's education of Margaret Beaufort, see John J. Scarisbrick, *Henry VIII* (London, 1968), p. 6.
6. *CSP Ven.* II, 1287, Giustinian's report on England to the Venetian Senate, October 1519.
7. BL, Additional MS 6113, fo. 79b [*LP* I i, 670, 674], reports of the baptism of Prince Henry and the presentation of gifts from Louis XII of France as the child's godfather; [*The*] *Great Tournament Roll of Westminster*, ed. Sydney Anglo (2 vols: Oxford, 1968).
8. Charles G. Cruickshank, *Army Royal, Henry VIII's Invasion of France 1513* (Oxford, 1969); see also G. Phillips, 'The Army of Henry VIII: A Reassessment', *Journal of the Society for Army Historical Research*, 75 (1997): 8–22.
9. Scarisbrick, pp. 50–6.
10. Ibid.
11. Charles Giry-Deloison, 'France and England at Peace, 1475–1513', in Glenn Richardson (ed.), *The Contending Kingdoms, France and England, 1420–1700* (Aldershot, 2008), pp. 43–60 for the background to the 1514 treaty of London.
12. Charles Giry-Deloison, '"Une haquenée ... pour le porter bientost et plus doucement en enfer ou en paradis": The French and Mary Tudor's marriage to Louis XII in 1514', in Grummitt, *The English Experience in France*, pp. 132–59.
13. *CSP Ven.* I, 510, 511.
14. AN, KK 240, fos 1–104, 'Compte septième de Pierre de La Place écuyer et argentier de Mons de Valois, comte d'Angloulême'.
15. Frederick J. Baumgartner, *Louis XII* (Basingstoke, 1996), p. 238.
16. Dorothy M. Mayer, *The Great Regent, Louise of Savoy* (London, 1966), pp. 24–8, 35–7.
17. Baldassare Castiglione, *The Book of the Courtier*, tr. George Bull (Harmondsworth, 1967), p. 88.
18. BL, Cotton MS Caligula B II, fo. 36 [*LP* I ii, 3342], Norfolk to Wolsey, Montreuil, 7 October 1514.
19. Hall, p. 610.
20. Theodore Godefroy, *Le Cérémonial françois* (2 vols: Paris, 1649), I, pp. 245–75 for details of the king's coronation and entry to Paris.

21. Anne-Marie Lecoq, *François Ier imaginaire: Symbolique et politique à l'aube de la Renaissance française* (Paris, 1987), pp. 67–100, esp. pp. 35–45 for the origins of the salamander myth and its use as an Angoulême family emblem.
22. Glenn Richardson, 'Anglo-French Political and Cultural Relations during the Reign of Henry VIII', University of London PhD dissertation (1996), pp. 62–5.
23. Baumgartner, pp. 200ff. Louis had made good the Orléans family's claim to Milan. In 1499 he had captured the duchy and city of Milan from Ludovico Sforza and then ruled it for a dozen years until forced to relinquish it in 1512.
24. Rawdon Brown, I, pp. 76, 79–81; see also 84–7.
25. Philippe Contamine, 'Les Industries de guerre dans la France de la Renaissance: L'exemple de l'artillerie', *Revue Historique*, 271 (1984): 249–80; David Potter, *Renaissance France at War: Armies, Culture and Society c.1480–1560* (Woodbridge, VA, 2008), pp. 152–7.
26. Robert J. Knecht, *Renaissance Warrior: The Reign of Francis I* (Cambridge, 1994), pp. 62–87.
27. *LP* II ii, 2965, 2968, 3437; Scarisbrick, pp. 57–69.
28. *LP* II ii, 3812/3, letters between Wolsey and the Bishop of Worcester in Rome, November 1517.
29. BNF, MS fr. 2964, fo. 6, Francis I to Pope Leo X, Paris, 2 February [1518].
30. BL, Cotton MS Caligula D VII, fo. 2 [*LP* II ii, 4046] (the ambassadors were Jean Gobelin, the Bishop of Paris's secretary, and Nicholas de Neufville, seigneur de Villeroy); TNA, E36/216, fo., 9v (Gobelin received a reward of £10); SP1/16 fo. 283, Memorandum of fees and rewards to messengers for these negotiations.
31. Rawdon Brown, II, p. 177.
32. BL, Cotton MS Caligula D VII, fos 9–17 [*LP* II ii, 4303, 4293, 4304]; *CAF* I, 864, 868, Villeroy's commission for the alliance, Angers, 3 July 1518.
33. Knecht, *Renaissance Warrior*, pp. 170ff.
34. On the origins of the Universal Peace, see Introduction.
35. Knecht, *Renaissance Warrior*, p. 165.
36. BL, Cotton MS Caligula D VII, fos 2, 8 [*LP* II ii, 4064, 4166]; MS Caligula E I, fo. 124ff. [*LP* II ii, 4254–5].
37. TNA, SP1/17, fos 61–2 [*LP* II ii, 4432], Sandys to Wolsey, Calais, 14 September 1518; BNF, MS fr. 5761, fo. 10r. On Bonnivet see P. Carogue, 'Artus (1474–1519) et Guillaume (1482–1525) Gouffier à l'émergence de nouvelles modalités de gouvernement', in Cedric Michon (ed), *Les Conseillers de François Ier* (Rennes, 2011), pp. 229–53.
38. Hall, p. 594, but cf. Rawdon Brown, II, pp. 218, 233. Hall says the ambassadors entered London on 27 September but the Venetian ambassador gives the date of 23 September, as does Niccolo Sagudino in a letter to Alvise Foscari. Given that Bonnivet's letter from Sandwich was dated 18 September, this seems the more likely date.
39. Hall, p. 594; TNA, SP1/17, fos 150–5 [*LP* II ii, 4549], payments of £130 2s.10d paid by Henry's treasurer for entertaining the ambassadors 'in the 10th year of the reign of King Henry the VIII'. The Keeper of Taylors' Hall received 4s. 4d for 'making clean divers houses there afore the coming of the ambassadors and after their departing'.
40. BNF, MS fr. 5761, fo. 11, Francis I to his ambassadors in England, Morlaix, 24 September 1518.
41. Rawdon Brown, II, p. 233. Sagudino gives the date as 26 September; Hall, p. 594, has 'on the last day of Septe[m]ber'.
42. Hall, p. 595; TNA, E36/216, fo. 21v: Richard Gibson was paid £230 4s. 4d for costumes and scenery for this pageant and for those used in the 'mummery' presented at Westminster at the banquet Wolsey gave there on 3 October.
43. Richard Pace, *Oratio Ricardii Pacei in pace nuperrime composita* (London, 1518), tr. D.A. Russell, in Joycelyne G. Russell, *Peacemaking in the Renaissance* (London, 1986), pp. 234–41 (*STC* 19081A).
44. Anonymous, *Oration Nuptiale de Messire Richard Pace*, printed by Jean Gourmont (Paris, 1519).

45. Russell, *Peacemaking in the Renaissance*, pp. 234–41.

46. Pace, fo. A ii v [Russell, *Peacemaking*, p. 235].

47. Ibid., fo. A vi r [Russell, *Peacemaking*, p. 238]. Pace also refers to Henry's tactical planning and the impregnability of his camp, both less than subtle allusions to the sieges of Tournai and Thérouanne and to the Battle of the Spurs.

48. Ibid., fos A iv r – Bl r [Russell, *Peacemaking*, pp. 236–9].

49. Ibid., fo. B ii v [Russell, *Peacemaking*, p. 240].

50. Ibid., fo. B iii r [Russell, *Peacemaking*, p. 241].

51. *ODNB sub* 'Pace, Richard'; Jervis Wegg, *Richard Pace, A Tudor Diplomatist* (London, 1932), pp. 77–90 and p. 138. Pace was deputising for the Dean of St Paul's, John Colet, whose strong empathy with Erasmus suggests he would have preached a more pacific sermon.

52. *LP* II ii, 4559, 4580; *JBP*, p. 71 notes that those who had gone to England 'had been very well received by the king of England'. On Worcester, see Introduction.

53. BL, Cotton MS Caligula D VII, fos 43–46 [*LP* II ii, 4638]; BNF, MS fr. 2943, fo. 13, Francis I ordered the ambassadors to be delayed at Boulogne and Amiens; Barillon, II, p. 112.

54. Bernardino Rincio, *Oraison en La Louenge du marriage de Monsieur le Dauphin de Gaulles* (Paris, 1519).

55. Bernardo Dovizi (1470–1520) was made Cardinal Bibbiena by Leo X. Painted by Raphael, as cardinal, he took the name of his native Tuscan town.

56. *Le Livre et forest de messire Bernardin Rince Millanoys: Docteur en medecine contenant et explicant briefuement lappareil, les leux et le festin de la Bastille*, printed in Paris in 1519 by Jean Gourmont. Several copies of the French translation of the Latin original survive. See BL, *Printed Books Catalogue* 811.d.31.9 (i). Hereafter cited as Rincio. The text is in all important respects identical to one published as A. Bonnardot (ed.), *Les Rues et églises de Paris vers 1500, une fête à la Bastille en 1518* (Paris, 1876), pp. 57–78. The British Library copy has a different decorative woodcut 'P' on folio A ii from the one in Bonnardot and its final page has a woodcut of a king.

57. Rincio, *Oraison*, fo. C iv.

58. Rincio, fo. A iv r, 'grand félicité pour les présent et temps advenir'.

59. Ibid., fo. B iii v.

60. *LP* III i, 94; Anselme, VI, p. 74: La Bastie had first travelled to England with the Admiral Bonnivet's embassy in 1518.

61. G. Richardson, '"Most highly to be regarded": The Privy Chamber of Henry VIII and Anglo-French Relations, 1515–1520', *The Court Historian* 4 (2) (1999): 119–40, for more detail on the disputes about hostages and the transfer of Tournai.

62. BL, Cotton MS Caligula D VII, fos 91–6 [*LP* III i, 701], Thomas Boleyn to Henry VIII, Paris, 9 February 1519.

63. Ibid., fos 96–8, 99–100, 101–3 [*LP* III i, 100, 118, 121, 122], Thomas Boleyn's letters to Wolsey and Henry VIII, dated 28 February, 11 and 14 March. Among other things, Francis promised to make Wolsey pope if he was elected.

64. *CSP Ven.* II, 1287, Giustinian's final report on his mission to England; *St. P.* I, p. 8, was Richard Pace's letter to Wolsey, dated Penshurst, 11 August, reporting Henry's reaction in front of the hostages, with whom he was playing tennis, when he received the news that Charles had been elected.

65. BL, Cotton MS Caligula D VII, fos 111–12, 125–6 [*LP* III i, 170, 289], Thomas Boleyn to Wolsey, dated 9 April and 7 June; TNA, E36/216, fo. 40: £100 'unto the French queen's midwife and to the nursery there'.

66. *LP* III i, 212, Boleyn to Henry VIII, Paris, 14 March 1519.

67. *LP* III i, 416, Boleyn to Wolsey, Melun, 14 August 1519; 514, Boleyn to Wolsey, Blois, 16 November 1519.

68. BL, Cotton MS Caligula D VII, fo. 170 [*LP* III i, 549], Thomas Boleyn to Wolsey, Blois, 11 December 1519.

69. Ibid., fo. 182 [*LP* III i, 665], Wingfield to Henry VIII, Cognac, undated but about 8 March 1520.
70. *ODNB sub* 'Wingfield, Sir Richard'.
71. Ibid.
72. TNA, SP1/19, fo. 121 [*LP* III i, 543], Francis I to Wolsey, credence for Marigny, Blois, 10 December 1519; BNF, MS fr. 21,449, fo. 38r. Marigny is listed as an 'eschanson' in the household.
73. BL, Cotton MS Caligula D VII, fo. 169, a list made at Blois on 10 December 1519 [*LP* III i, 547]; Richardson, 'Anglo-French Relations', pp. 113–15, for the names and backgrounds of these hostages.
74. *ODRF*, I, pp. 409–30, for the treaty of Noyon, August 1516. Its principal provisions were the payment of an annual tribute to Francis for the kingdom of Naples, which implicitly recognised him as its suzerain, and compensation to Catherine d'Albret, the widow of King Jean of Navarre, for the loss of part of the kingdom on the Spanish side of the Pyrenees, annexed by Ferdinand of Aragon in 1512. Charles was also to marry Francis's daughter, Louise.
75. *LP* III, 551, Charles V to the Bishop of Elna, 12 December 1519; *CSP Sp.* II, 274 [*LP* III i, 740–41], treaty documents dated London, 11 April 1520; *CSP sp.* II, 279, Juan Manuel, imperial ambassador in Rome to Charles V, 12 May 1520; Karl Brandi, *The Emperor Charles V* (London, 1965), pp. 116–19.
76. BL, Cotton MS Caligula D VII, fos 196–202 [*LP* III i, 722–7], Wingfield to Wolsey; Francis and Bonnivet to Wolsey, Blois, 7 April 1520. On Robertet see Bernard Chevalier, 'Florimond Robertet (v.1465–1527)', in Michon, *Les Conseillers de François Ier*, pp. 99–116.
77. *LP* III i, 728, De la Sauch to Chièvres, London, 7 April 1520; *CSP Sp.* II, 274 [*LP* III i, 740–1].

2 Two Stars in One Firmament

1. *Archaeologia*, p. 176.
2. *CAF* I, 1140; on the artillery and its organisation under de Genouillac, see Potter, *Renaissance France at War*, pp. 152–7; R.J. Knecht, 'Jacques de Genouillac dit Galiot (v.1465–1546)', in Michon, *Les Conseillers de François Ier*, pp. 155–70.
3. BNF, MS fr. 10,383, Account of Guillaume de Saigne.
4. *DBF, sub* 'Charles de Bourbon'; see also David Potter, *War and Government in the French Provinces: Picardy 1470–1560* (Cambridge, 1993), pp. 67–73, and Philippe Hamon, 'Charles de Bourbon, connétable de France (1490–1527)', in Michon, *Les Conseillers de François Ier*, pp. 95–7.
5. BNF, MS fr. 10,383, fo. 29v. The armour consisted of 'halcetz' and 'ecrivisses' (different kinds of iron body armour to protect the chest and midriff). In 1521 the English would object strongly to Ardres's further refortification by the French.
6. *LP* III i, 642, Francis I to La Bastie, Cognac, 27 February 1520; 869 in *Description*.
7. BNF, MS fr. 5761, fo. 18; MS 2934, fos 11, 13, 15, 74, 77, for examples of these letters.
8. *LP* III ii, 3229, letter of the Council at Calais reporting that 'Ponderemy and Fayete are at variance. The French king favours the latter against Ponderemy, Dourrier and other gentlemen of Picardy'. On the redating of this letter to 1517 and the rest of La Fayette's brief career at Boulogne see David Potter, *Un homme de guerre au temps de la Renaissance: La vie et les letters d'Oudart du Biez, Maréchal de France, Gouverneur de Boulogne et de Picardie (vers 1475–1553)* (Arras, 2001), pp. 18–21.
9. Hall, pp. 543, 551–2.
10. *CAF* V, 17217, Humieres's appointment dated 10 January 1520; Potter, *War and Government*, pp. 117–22, 137.
11. BNF, MS fr. 10,383, fo. 29r. See Potter, *Renaissance France at War*, for weights and calibres of these types of cannon.

12. BNF, MS fr. 10,383, fos 23v and 29r, payments to officers and the secretary of the artillery for journeys made to take inventories.

13. *Chronicle of Calais*, p. 83. On the identities of the three commissioners, see Introduction.

14. *LP* III i, 825, English Commissioners to Wolsey, Guînes, 21 May 1520.

15. Bernard Chevalier, *Tours: Ville royale, 1356–1520* (Tours, 1975), pp. 16–17, 72–6, 201–9. On relations between the monarchy and towns more generally see his *Les Bonnes Villes de France du XIVe au XVIe siècle* (Paris, 1982).

16. *Gallia Christiana in provincias ecclesiasticas distributa: qua series et historia archiepiscoporum, episcoporum, et abbatum franciae vicinarumque ditionum / opera & studio Domni Dionysii Sammarthani* (16 vols: Paris, from the Libraria S. Congregationis de Propaganda Fide, 1870–[1874]), 14, p. 132. Brillac died in August 1520 and was succeeded by Martin de Beaune: *CAF* V, 17,334.

17. BNF, MS fr. 10,383, fo. 10r. A majority of items on the accounts are specified to have been delivered to Dupré, suggesting that he took overall responsibility for the work; BNF, MS fr. 21,449, fos 60r and 114–15. Dupré was the highest-paid 'tapissier du roi' in 1520, receiving 240 *livres tournois* in annual household wages. He remained in the household until his death on 24 May 1524.

18. Natalie Zemon Davis, 'Women in the Crafts in Sixteenth-Century Lyon', *Feminist Studies*, 8 (1) (1982): 46–80; Susan Broomhall, 'Identity and Life Narratives of the Poor in Later Sixteenth-Century Tours', *Renaissance Quarterly*, 57 (2004): 439–65.

19. BNF, MS fr. 10,3838, fos 39r–132r. Some of the women at Boulogne received only 3 *sous* per day.

20. BNF, MS fr. 10,383, fos 10r–14r, 17v–19v; Russell, *Field*, p. 25, for the overall estimate of the amount of canvas used.

20. BNF, MS fr. 10,3838, fos 39r–132r.

21. *CAF* VI, 19080 dated 15 March 1526, V, 15127 dated 14 June 1546.

22. BNF, MS fr. 10,383, fos 182–5.

23. S. Schneelbalg-Perelman, 'Richesses du garde-meuble parisien de François Ier: Inventaires inédits de 1542 et 1551', *Gazette de Beaux-Arts*, 6th ser., vol. 78 (1971): 253–304.

24. BNF, MS fr. 10,383, fo. 14v.

25. Ibid., fo. 39ff.

26. Arlette Jouanna, *La France du xvie siècle 1483–1598* (Paris, 1996), pp. 8–11.

27. BNF, MS fr. 10,383, fos 31r–v.

28. H.A. Dillon, 'Calais and the Pale', *Archaeologia*, 53 (1893): 289–388, at p. 332.

29. *Chronicle of Calais*, p. 85, Sir Nicholas Vaux to Wolsey, Guînes, 18 May 1520.

30. *LP* III i, 825, English commissioners to Wolsey, 21 May 1520.

31. Florange, I, p. 263: 'et fit faire le roy de France à Ghines trois maisons, l'ugne dedans la ville d'Ardre qui fut toutte bastiez de neufz, qui estoit asses belle pour ugne maison de ville, et y avoir assés grant logis, et en ce dict lieu fut festoyé le roy d'Angleterre'.

32. Hall, p. 607; Dubois, p. 77.

33. Pierre Lesueur, *Dominique de Cortone dit Boccador* (Paris, 1928), pp. 62–3.

34. Dubois, pp. 77 and 160–5; *CSP Ven.* III, 69, at p. 54.

35. Hall, p. 615.

36. *Mémoires ou Journal de Louise de Savoye, Duchesse a'Angoulesme, d'Anjou et de Valois, Collection Universelles des Mémoires Particuliers Relatifs à l'Histoire de France*, vol. XVI (Paris, 1786), p. 428.

37. APDC 3P 038/27, 1832 Ardres, *cadastre section C 1re feuille*. Despite the many references in contemporary sources to the construction of a royal *hôtel* in the town, Ardres's municipal authorities maintain that no building was ever made for Francis I and that he relied only on the pavilion in the fields below the town. This, despite the fact that the tents blew down within days of being erected and were unusable for most of the fortnight of the Field. No archaeological investigation has ever been done to search for a possible location of a residence built for the 1520 meeting.

38. Hall, p. 607.
39. Florange, I, p. 263; Hall, p. 607; Dubois, p. 79.
40. Lesueur, p. 25.
41. Anne-Marie Lecoq, 'Une fête italienne à la Bastille en 1518', in *Il se rendit en Italie: Etudes offertes à André Chastel*, ed. Giuliano Briganti (Rome, 1987), pp. 149–68. Florange, I, p. 263, states bluntly of the banqueting house: 'Touttes fois elle ne servit de riens.'
42. Simon Thurley, 'The Banqueting and Disguising Houses of 1527', in D.R. Starkey (ed.), *Henry VIII: A European Court in England* (London, 1991), pp. 64–9.
43. *CSP Ven.* II, 94; Hall, pp. 607 and 615; Montfaucon, IV, p. 164: 'fut la planter & dresser son camp, tentes & pavillons pres d'une petite riviere dehors ladite ville'.
44. APDC 3P 038/27, 1832, Ardres, *cadastre section C 1re feuille*.
45. See pp. 66–9.
46. BNF, MS fr. 10,383, fo. 26r.
47. Ibid., fos 26r and 20r.
48. Ibid., fos 186r–87v; 191v–192r; see also Philippe Hamon, 'Semblançay homme de finances et de Conseil (v.1455–1527)' in Michon, *Les Conseillers de François Ier*, pp. 117–30.
49. BNF, MS fr. 10,383, fo. 20r; Bourdichon was paid a total of 1,066 *livres* 6 *sous* and 8 *deniers* for his work: fo. 195r.
50. *CSP Ven.* III, 94; *LP* III I, 750, 890; *Chronicle of Calais*, pp. 82–5.
51. *Chronicle of Calais*, p. 19, spelling modernised. On Worcester, see Introduction.
52. Dillon, 'Calais and the Pale', 289–388; J. Munby, 'The Field of Cloth of Gold: Guînes and the Calais Pale Revisited', edited text of a lecture delivered to the Royal Archaeological Institute, 8 December 2010. I am grateful to Dr Munby for allowing me to use this text and for discussions with him on the location of the temporary palace at Guînes.
53. BL, Cotton MS Caligula D VII, fo. 186 [*LP* III i, 678], Wingfield to Wolsey, Angoulême, 13 March 1520.
54. S. Thurley, 'The Domestic Building Works of Cardinal Wolsey', in S.J. Gunn and P. Lindley (eds), *Cardinal Wolsey, Church State and Art* (Cambridge, 1991), pp. 76–102, at pp. 94–6.
55. *LP* III i, 700, 825, commissioners to Wolsey, Guînes, 21 May 1520, in which they refer to the plans being discussed by Henry and Wolsey.
56. *Chronicle of Calais*, pp. 79–82, Belknap and Vaux to Wolsey, Guînes, 26 March 1520; also p. 18; TNA, E36/216, fos 86r, 87v.
57. Du Bellay, vol. 1, p. 101, states that Henry had a building made 'qu'il avoit faict charpenter en Angleterre et amener par mer toute faicte'; *Chronicle of Calais*, p. 18.
58. *Chronicle of Calais*, p. 18, my italics.
59. Starkey, 'Ightham Mote', pp. 153–63; *The National Trust Guide to Ightham Mote, Kent* (1998).
60. L.F. Salzman, *Building in England down to 1540* (Oxford, 1952; reprinted 1992), pp. 350–1, 195–209.
61. *Chronicle of Calais*, pp. 82–3, Vaux to Wolsey, Guînes, 10 April 1520.
62. Ibid., pp. 84–5, Vaux to Wolsey, Guînes, 18 May 1520.
63. Ibid.; *LP* III i, 825, Commissioners to Wolsey, Guînes, 21 May 1520. On confusion in previous accounts due to mistaking Vaux's word 'rofes' for 'roses' see Russell, *Field*, p. 34.
64. Colvin, IV, pp. 286–88; I am grateful to Dr Alasdair Hawkyard for his advice on this point.
65. TNA, E 101/203/21, 'Expenses of making furniture against the king's voyage, for his Banquet Chambers at Guysnes', dated April–May; 11–12 Henry VIII [i.e. 1520] for the account of Thomas Busch 'groom porter of the king's house'; fo. 4 for total of the account.

66. TNA, SP1/20, fos 79r–80v [*LP*, III i, 826], Fowler's account of advances made.
67. Bernard W. Alford and Theodore C. Barker, *A History of the Carpenters' Company* (London, 1968), pp. 43–4.
68. *Chronicle of Calais*, p. 81; TNA, E36/216, fo. 89v; on William Vertue see *ODNB sub* 'Vertue, Robert' where he is discussed in the context of his brother's career.
69. *SR*, Stat. 11 Hen VII c.22.
70. Julian C.K. Cornwall, *Wealth and Society in Early Sixteenth-Century England* (London, 1988), pp. 7–29.
71. Ibid., pp. 79–82; more generally on patterns of labour in medieval towns see Gervase Rosser, 'Crafts, Guilds and the Negotiation of Work in the Medieval Town', *Past & Present*, 154 (1997): 3–31.
72. Salzman, pp. 74–81; Christopher Dyer, *Standards of Living in the Later Middle Ages: Social Change in England c.1200–1520* (Cambridge, 1988), pp. 219–33.
73. Dyer, p. 205; E.H. Phelps Brown and S.V. Hopkins, 'Seven Centuries of the Prices of Consumables, Compared with Builders' Wage-Rates', *Economica*, New Series 23 (92) (November 1956): 296–314; and by the same authors, 'Wage-Rates and Prices: Evidence for Population Pressure in the Sixteenth Century', *Economica*, New Series 24 (94) (November 1957): 289–306.
74. Sydney Anglo, 'The Hampton Court Painting of the Field of Cloth of Gold Considered as an Historical Document', *Antiquaries Journal*, 46 (1966): 285–307.
75. Hall, p. 605; *OED sub* 'entrayled' and 'albin' (the latter was an opaque white mineral, a variety of apophyllite).
76. Hall, p. 605.
77. D.W. Crossley, 'The Performance of the Glass Industry in Sixteenth-Century England', *Economic History Review*, New Series, 25 (3) (August 1972): 421–33; see also Charles Ashdown, *The History of the Worshipful Company of Glaziers of the City of London* (London, 1918), pp. 20–2.
78. Florange, p. 265; Du Bellay, p. 101.
79. *CSP Ven.* II, 94; Thurley, 'The Domestic Building Works of Cardinal Wolsey', p. 95: Thurley's conjectural plan shows the layout of rooms contrary to Soardino's description but cf. his *The Royal Palaces of Tudor England: Architecture and Court Life 1460–1547* (New Haven, CT, and London, 1993), p. 46 where another conjectural plan does conform to the Mantuan ambassador's report.
80. Hall, p. 606; *Chronicle of Calais*, p. 80.
81. *CSP Ven.* II, 50 at p. 23.
82. Hall, p. 605; Dubois, pp. 70–1.
83. Hall, pp. 606–7.
84. TNA, E36/216, fo. 90r; A.W. Reed, *Early Tudor Drama: The Medwall, the Rastells, Heywood, and the More Circle* (London, 1926), pp. 7–18 (Armstrong was also a prolific writer of reformist religious tracts, known to Cromwell; he died in 1536); *ODNB sub* 'Rastell'; S.T. Bindoff, 'Clement Armstrong and his Treatises of the Commonweal', *Economic History Review*, 14 (1) (1944): 64–73.
85. *ODNB sub* 'Barclay, Alexander'; Barclay was also regarded as something of an expert on the French language. In 1521 he produced his *Introductory to Write and to Pronounce French*, later used (although not uncritically) by John Palsgrave in preparing his more famous 1530 work, *L'esclaircissement de la langue francoyse*.
86. *Chronicle of Calais*, p. 83, Vaux to Wolsey, Guînes, 10 April 1520; Russell, *Field*, p. 34.
87. The suggestion has been made by Dr Kent Rawlinson, Curator of Historic Buildings at Hampton Court Palace. I am grateful to Dr Rawlinson for sharing his research on this point.
88. Dubois, pp. 70–1.
89. Hall, pp. 605–6; *Chronicle of Calais*, pp. 82–5, Vaux to Wolsey, Guînes, 10 April and 18 May 1520; Thurley, *Royal Palaces*, pp. 93–8.
90. TNA, E36/216, fos 84v, 90v.

91. Thomas P. Campbell, *Henry VIII and the Art of Majesty: Tapestries at the Tudor Court* (New Haven, CT, and London, 2007), pp. 143–55, at p. 146.
92. *CSP Ven.* III, 20.
93. Campbell, pp. 149–55.
94. *CSP Ven.* III, 69, 88.
95. Anglo, 'Hampton Court Painting', p. 290, and further explanation in footnote 6 citing *CSP Ven.* III, 94, Soardino to the Marquess of Mantua, 26 June 1520: 'In the middle of the long entrance hall a small building was added, containing two oratories for the King and Queen, looking down on the very large church below where High Mass was occasionally celebrated.'
96. TNA, SP1/19, fo. 267, list of members of the chapel present at the Field of Cloth of Gold; Fiona Kisby, '"When the King Goeth a Procession": Chapel Ceremonies and Services, the Ritual Year, and Religious Reforms at the Early Tudor Court, 1485–1547', *Journal of British Studies*, 40 (2001): 44–75, at pp. 47–8 and pp. 55–61.
97. Colvin, IV, pp. 53–8; Thurley, *Royal Palaces*, pp. 40–4.
98. BL, Cotton MS Augustus III, fos 11, 18, 19.
99. BL, Cotton MS Augustus I, ii, fo. 76.
100. TNA, E36/216, fos 87v, 90v, 93v.
101. BL, Cotton MS Augustus III, fo.18; Susan Doran (ed.), *Henry VIII: Man and Monarch* (London, 2009), p. 96 (foldout) for a superb reproduction of folio 18.
102. *LP* III i, 738, commission to deal with French commissioners dated Greenwich, 10 April 1520.
103. TNA, SP1/20, fos 1–2 [*LP* III i, 746], Worcester to Wolsey, Calais, 18 April; BN, MS fr. 5761, fos 37–8, Francis I to Châtillon, Chambord, 20 April 1520; *LP* III i, 765, Worcester to Wolsey, Calais, 26 April 1520.
104. TNA, SP1/20, fos 42–3 [*LP* III i, 806], Wingfield to Henry VIII, Crèvecoeur, 13 May 1520.
105. *Chronicle of Calais*, pp. 86–8, Worcester to Henry VIII, Calais, 19 May 1520.
106. Hall, p.611; *CSP Ven.* III, 50; Anglo, 'Hampton Court Painting', pp. 300–3.
107. *Chronicle of Calais*, pp. 88–9, Châtillon to Worcester, Ardres, 23 and 24 May 1520.
108. TNA, SP1/20, fos 44–7 [*LP* III i, 807], Wingfield to Henry VIII, undated memorandum; from context, probably May 1520.
109. *Diarii*, vol. 19, p. 235 [*CSP Ven.* III, 50].

3 Equal in Honour

1. Hall, p. 600.
2. BNF, MS fr. 5761, 39r–42r, 'Articles pour l'entrevue du roy et du roy d'angleterre faicte à ardre'; for the formal treaty agreeing to these articles see Rymer, VI, 180–1; *ODRF*, II, pp. 565–75, Francis I's confirmation of the treaty, dated Châtellerault, 26 March 1520 [*LP* III i, 702].
3. *Archaeologia*, pp. 184–91 at p. 190.
4. Hall, pp. 601–2 [*LP* III i, 673], proclamation dated 12 March 1520; BNF, MS fr. 5761, fo., 32v Bonnivet to Wolsey, Cognac, 23 February 1520.
5. Ibid., p. 602. King John the Good of France had been brought to England as Edward III's prisoner in 1356 and died in captivity.
6. BL, Cotton MS Caligula D VII, fos 180–1 [*LP* III i, 677], Francis I to Wolsey, Châteauneuf, 13 March 1520; see also *LP* III i, 643 [Bonnivet?] to [Wolsey], Cognac, 10 March? 1520. Wolsey's proclamation referred to Francis incorrectly as the 'most Christened king' rather than 'the most Christian king'; BNF MS fr. 5761, fo., 34r Bonnivet to Wolsey, Cognac, 18 March 1520.
7. Charles de La Roncière, *Histoire de la marine française*, 2nd edn (6 vols: Paris, 1909–32), III, pp. 164–8.
8. *St P.* VI, pp. 57–60, Wingfield to Henry VIII, Blois, 18 April 1520.

9. Ibid., pp. 57–8.
10. Ibid., p. 60.
11. Ibid., p. 59; Jean-Pierre Babelon, *Châteaux de France au siècle de la Renaissance* (Paris, 1989), pp. 110–15. This terrace was probably the one shown in Du Cerceau's drawing of the château, running along the front of buildings which then stood on the court at right angles to the François Ier wing (then still under construction) and opposite the Louis XII wing. This range and its terrace were demolished between 1635 and 1638 when Gaston d'Orléans built the neoclassical wing now found there.
12. *St. P.* VI, pp. 61–2, Wingfield to Henry VIII, Beaugency, 20 April 1520. Charles V was appointed to the Order of the Garter in 1508 as archduke of Burgundy.
13. *LP* III i, 786; Anselme, VI, p. 174. La Bastie's biographical details are scarce. He is recorded only in reference to his wife, Marguerite Dubois, *dame* de Barlin. He had first travelled to England with the Admiral Bonnivet in September 1518.
14. TNA, SP1/20, fos 42–3 [*LP* III i, 806], Wingfield to Henry VIII, Crèvecoeur, 13 May 1520; BL, Cotton MS Caligula D VII, fo. 222 [*LP* III i, 808], Wingfield to Henry VIII, Crèvecoeur, 14 May 1520.
15. See Chapter 6; BNF MS fr. 5761, fos 37–8 Francis I to Châtillon, Chambord.
16. *LP* Appendix, 2, Thomas Boleyn to Wolsey, 19 March 1519; *CSP Ven.* II, 1182, Antonio Giustinian to the Venetian Signory, 24 March 1519; see also *LP* III i, 718 and 131, French note of arrangements, undated, calendared in 1520 but refers to meeting planned for 1519. It may be the 'paper in French' that Boleyn reported sending to Wolsey on 21 March 1519.
17. *Archaeologia*, p. 184.
18. Rymer, XIII, 713 [*LP* III i, 702 (no.4)].
19. James Sharpe, 'Economy and Society', in Patrick Collinson (ed.), *The Sixteenth Century* (Oxford, 2002), pp. 17–44.
20. David Potter, *A History of France, 1460–1560* (Basingstoke, 1995), pp. 170–1; see also Robert J. Knecht, 'The French and English Nobilities in the Sixteenth Century: A Comparison', in Richardson, *Contending Kingdoms*, pp. 61–78, for a concise review of the structure of the two nobilities.
21. *Archaeologia*, p. 180.
22. Bodl. MS Ashmole 1116, fos 95r–99v (also published by Russell, *Field of Cloth of Gold*). The other two lists are in Lambeth Palace Library, MS 285, and in the *Rutland Papers*, pp. 28–38. A review of numbers from these sources confirms the figures published by Russell, *Field of Cloth of Gold*, in 1969. As Russell observes, p. 49 note 1, the Bodleian and Rutland lists are almost identical. The Lambeth list is the only one that includes musicians and trumpets. It omits some of the knights attendant on the queen and gives a higher figure by 1,100 of the total number of horses.
23. Bodl. MS Ashmole 1116, fo. 95r/v. Thomas Ruthall, Bishop of Durham, was allowed more as Lord Privy Seal.
24. BL, MS Caligula D VII, fos 238–40 [*LP* III i, 895, 896], letters from the Council in England to Wolsey and Henry VIII, 2 July 1520; *ODNB sub* 'Bourchier, John'. In November 1520 Henry appointed Berners Deputy of Calais and he remained in that post until 1526.
25. *Chronicle of Calais*, pp. 90–4, letters from the Council in England to the king and Wolsey, 28 June and 2 July respectively.
26. Montfaucon, IV, p. 186, for the names of Edmund Howard's team at the tournament.
27. Robert J. Knecht, *The French Renaissance Court* (New Haven, CT, and London, 2008), pp. 33–40.
28. BNF, MS fr. 21,449, fo. 49r; Russell, *Field*, pp. 207–8; Pierre Benoist, 'Le Clergé de cour et la décision dans la première moitié du xvié siècle', in *La Prise de décision en France (1525–1559)*, ed. Roseline Claerr and Olivier Poncet (Paris, 2008), pp. 53–68.
29. Cédric Michon, 'René, Grand Bâtard de Savoie (v.1473–1525)', in his *Les Conseillers de François Ier*, pp. 255–63. René was half-brother to Louise de Savoie.

30. Anselme, I, p. 217, VIII, p. 453, for Claude d'Orléans who was killed, aged seventeen, in November 1524 during the siege of Pavia; William Weary, 'La Maison de la Trémoille pendant la Renaissance: une seigneurie aggrandie', in *La France de la fin du xvème siècle: Renouveau et apogée*, ed. Bernard Chevalier and Philippe Contamine (Paris, 1985), pp. 197–214. He was married to the very much younger Louise, Duchess of Valentinois, the daughter of Cesare Borgia.

31. Olivier de la Marche, 'L'Etat de la maison de duc Charles de Bourgogne', in *Collection complète des mémoires relatifs à l'histoire de France*, ed., Petitot (Paris, 1820), X, pp. 479–556, esp. p. 492. 'Bouche' of court was the right to have meals there.

32. BNF, MS fr. 21,449, fo. 53r for all names; BL, Cotton MS Caligula D VII, fo. 235 [*LP* III i, 894], Wingfield to Wolsey, 7 July 1520; TNA, E36/216, fos 95–7 [*LP* III i, pp. 1541–2].

33. Anselme, I, pp. 313, 316–17. Charles III de Bourbon-Montpensier acquired his title by marriage to Suzanne de Beaujeau, daughter of Pierre, duc de Bourbon. The couple had three children, all of whom died in childhood.

34. Potter, *A History of France*, p. 351, cf. Russell, *Field*, p. 72, who says that there were only three marshals in 1520 and that Odet de Foix, seigneur de Lautrec, had by then been replaced as marshal by his brother Thomas de Foix, seigneur de Lescun. Potter notes that this did not happen until 1521. See also Cédric Michon, 'Odet de Foix, vicomte de Lautrec (v. 1483–1528)', in his *Les Conseillers de François Ier*, pp. 265–72. On Palisse, see in the same volume Robert J. Knecht, 'Jacques II de Chabannes, seigneur de La Palisse ou La Palice (v.1470–1525)', pp. 163–70.

35. Montfaucon, IV, p. 191; Norman MacDougall, *An Antidote to the English: The Auld Alliance, 1295–1560* (East Linton, 2001), pp. 96, 118–26. Robert married his cousin Anne, the daughter of Bérault Stuart d'Aubigny. He was made a marshal in 1514.

36. *LP* III i, 704 (4); Knecht, *Renaissance Court*, p. 38; Potter, *Renaissance France at War*, p. 68; *JBP*, pp. 157–60. Saint-Vallier was implicated in Bourbon's rebellion in 1523. Found guilty of treason and sentenced to death, he was reprieved on the scaffold, probably due to his son-in-law's intervention. His daughter Diane, the future mistress of Henri II, had married Louis de Brézé in March 1515.

37. Christine Cazaux, *La Musique à la cour de François Ier* (Paris, 2002), pp. 127–37; BNF, MS fr. 21,449, fos 53v, 54v.

38. Monique Chatenet, *La Cour de France au xvi* siècle: Vie sociale et architecture* (Paris, 2002), p. 27.

39. BL, Cotton MS Caligula D VII, fo. 222 [*LP* III ii, 808], Wingfield to Henry VIII, Crèvecoeur, 14 May 1520]; *DBF sub* 'Claude de France'. The queen's first child, Louise, had died in September 1517, aged two. As might be expected, there is no record that any of her three infant children, Charlotte (aged three), François the dauphin (aged two, whom Wingfield had met) or Henri (aged 16 months), were at Ardres.

40. Pierre Jourda, *Marguerite d'Angoulême duchesse d'Alençon et reine de Navarre* (2 vols: Paris, 1930).

41. *CSP Ven.* III, 94, Soardino to the Marquess of Mantua.

42. Anselme, III, p. 379; Knecht, *Renaissance Warrior*, pp. 116–17; Malcolm Walsby, *The Counts of Laval: Culture, Patronage and Religion in Fifteenth- and Sixteenth-Century France* (Aldershot, 2007), p. 87; Raffaele Tamalio (ed.), *Federico Gonzaga alla corte di Francesco I di Francia nel carteggio privato con Mantova (1515–1517)* (Paris, 1994), pp. 256–7, Federico Gonzaga to Francesco Gonzaga, Chambéry, 17 June 1516; pp. 277–8, Stazio Gadio to Isabella d'Este, L'Arbresle, 11 July 1516.

43. Anselme, III, pp. 315–16: he was married to Renée de Bourbon-Montpensier, the younger sister of the Constable; Stuart Carroll, *Martyrs and Murderers. The Guise Family and the Making of Europe* (Oxford, 2009), pp. 22–4.

44. Anselme, III, p. 327; Carroll, pp. 24–46, on the life and career of Claude de Lorraine. He was married to Antoinette de Bourbon-Vendôme, the sister of Charles de Vendôme. In 1527 Claude became the first duc de Guise and a peer of France.

45. Anselme, III, pp. 275 and 328.
46. Robert Harding, *Anatomy of a Power Elite: The Provincial Governors of Early Modern France* (New Haven, CT, and London, 1978), pp. 21–31; Potter, *Renaissance France at War*, pp. 67–85.
47. Hall, p. 602; see also *Archaeologia*, p. 184.
48. *Chronicle of Calais*, pp. 78–9; *LP* III i, 705, undated draft warrant in similar terms.
49. *LP* I i, 1176 [2] for Fortescue's inclusion in Sandys's retinue in 1512; *Chronicle of Calais*, pp. 205–6. In April 1527, Henry asked Fortescue to contribute ten men to the garrison at Guînes, the castle of which was then commanded by Sandys.
50. H. Suggett, 'The Use of French in England in the Later Middle Ages', *TRHS*, 4th series, 28 (1946): 61–84.
51. TNA, E36/219, fo. 89v; Maria Hayward, *Dress at the Court of King Henry VIII* (Leeds, 2007), pp. 226–7; Henry did give Henry Bouchier, Earl of Essex, £333 6s. 8d towards the costs of going to Calais with him.
52. *Henry VIII* Act 1 sc. 1; Du Bellay, I, pp. 101–2.
53. *ODNB sub* 'Fortescue, Sir Adrian'. He was executed in July 1539 after being implicated, somewhat obscurely, in the 'Courtenay conspiracy'.
54. *LP* III i, 841 proclamation by Francis I, dated Montreuil, 26 May 1520; on La Chastre, see Anselme, VII, p. 367.
55. Christophe Vellet, 'Entre légistes et ministres: Antoine Duprat (1463–1535), conseiller technicien de François Ier', in Michon, *Les Conseillers de François Ier*, pp. 211–27.
56. *A collection of ordinances and regulations for the government of the royal household made in diverse reigns* (London, 1790).
57. Archives Municipales d'Amiens CC 97, fos 174 for the wages of Lannoy as captain of the town and 194v for the expense of accommodating Longueval in the town: 60 *sous*, 3 *deniers*.
58. BL, Cotton MS Caligula D VII, fo. 229 [*LP* III i, 851]. Margaret Baynham owned a large rentable property in the vicinity of the main market square.
59. Hall, pp. 615–16.
60. *CAF* V, 17,249, mandate to Sebastian de Mareau to pay 2,471 *livres tournois* to the *fournisseurs* of the household for provisions for the banquet; see also 17,246.
61. Barillon, II, pp. 165–6; *LP* III i, 752, 797; TNA, SP1/20, fos 42–3, 222 [*LP* III i, 806, 808].
62. Archives Municipales d'Amiens, CC 97, fos 196v–197r.
63. *Inventaire sommaire des municipales antérieures à 1790* by A. Ledieu (Abbeville, 1902), p. 152; *CAF* IV, 17,260; IX, p. 431. cf. Russell, *Field*, p. 66, who, following Barillon's editors, says he arrived at Montreuil on 24 May. The king had already been to Abbeville once since his accession, in 1517, and so did not make a formal entry to the town.
64. BNF, MS fr. 5761, fo. 42, Francis I to La Bastie, undated but from context 25 May 1520, corroborated by Wingfield's letter of the same date; BL, Cotton MS Caligula D VII, fos 230–1 [*LP* III i, 835, 841], Wingfield to Wolsey, Montreuil, 25 May 1520.
65. Hall, pp. 603–5; *CSP Ven.* III, 50; *Chronicle of Calais*, p. 28.
66. Pascale Bréemersch and Jean-Yves Léopold, *Armorial du Pas-de-Calais: Communes des arrondissements de Béthune, Boulogne-sur-Mer, Calais, Lens, Montreuil, Saint-Omer* (Arras, 1996), p. 186.
67. Barrillon, II, p. 167; BNF MS fr. 21,449, fo. 52v. Saint-Marsault was killed at Pavia. He was later succeeded as *sénéchal* of Périgord by Antoine des Près, seigneur de Montepezat.
68. *LP* III, 828, John Hereford, Customer of Plymouth, to Henry VIII, Plymouth, 23 May 1520; *Archaeologia*, p. 180. Hall, p. 604.
69. *Archaeologia*, p. 180. Apart from the *Mary Rose* it is not certain, however, that he used these particular vessels as the two 'Barks' are also included on a list of expenses submitted in October 1520 for six ships prepared 'for carrying the King and Queen to Calais and back'. Perhaps having been used as part of a pre-emptive defensive sweep, the ships were then used for transport, or perhaps Fitzwilliam used other vessels altogether. He oversaw these preparations with John Hopton, Clerk Controller of the King's Ships since 1512.

70. TNA, 36/216, fos 91r and 94r. Sir Henry Guilford, as Constable of the Castle, received £66 13s. 4d towards repairs for Henry's stay and a further £200 afterwards.

71. *CSP Ven.* III, 50, at pp. 14–20; *LP* III i, 836, La Bastie to Francis I, Canterbury, 25 May 1520.

72. TNA, E36/216, fo. 89v: the organisers were paid £700 between them in May and June for hiring hoys; fos 84, 90 and 93v show that in May John Hopton was also paid £200 for wages for the crew of the *Sweepstake* and for rigging the king's ships and £40 for 'cutting the docks' to bring them out.

73. TNA, E36/11, fos 101–15 [*LP* III i, 1009], list of expenses for ships used on the crossing, dated 2 October 1520; Arthur Nelson, *The Tudor Navy: The Ships, Men and Organisation 1485–1603* (London, 2001), pp. 46–7.

74. Ibid., fos 71–88 [*LP* III i, 558], expenses for building the *Katherine Plesaunce*, 20 December 1519.

75. Ibid., fos 101–15 [*LP* III i, 1009], list of expenses for preparing six ships, dated 2 October 1520, which includes items for furnishing the *Katherine Plesaunce;* David Loades, *The Tudor Navy, an Administrative, Political and Military History* (Aldershot, 1992), p. 71.

76. *Archaeologia*, p. 180.

77. TNA, E36/09, fo. 8v [*LP* III ii, 1115].

78. *LP* III i, 919 at p. 334, costs of carriage of the king and queen's wardrobes of robes and beds between Calais and Guînes and back; Maria Hayward, 'The Packing and Transportation of the Possessions of Henry VIII, with Particular Reference to the 1547 Inventory', *Costume*, 31 (1997): 8–15.

79. TNA, E36/216, fo. 93v for payment to 'Trewlove' of the *Christopher; The Anthony Roll of Henry VIII's Navy*, Occasional Publications of the Navy Records Society vol. 2, ed. C.S. Knighton and D. M. Loades (Aldershot, 2000), Appendix II for details of some of these vessels.

80. TNA, E36/217, fo. 170 [*LP* III ii, p. 1556], revels miscellaneous accounts 1519–20.

81. Montfaucon, IV, pp. 165–7 [*LP* III i, 869]; Dubois, pp. 57–61; *CSP Ven.* III, 58, 59.

82. Hall, p. 607. The book to which Hall refers is probably *L'Ordonnance et ordre du tournoy*, summarised in *LP* III i, 870. The description of the cardinal's procession to which Hall refers is on pp. B iii verso to C i recto.

83. Hall, pp. 607–8.

84. Rymer, XIII, 719–20 [*LP* III i, 861].

85. Barillon, II, pp. 167–8.

4 Right Chivalrous in Arms

1. Hall, p. 602.

2. *CSP Ven.* III, 67, anonymous letter to the Signory; 68, letter to Pietro Montemerlo, 7 June 1520.

3. Hall, p. 608; *CSP Ven.* III, 67, 68, 69.

4. Oliver Millar, *The Tudor, Stuart and Early Georgian Pictures in the Collection of Her Majesty the Queen* (London, 1963), pp. 55–6; Anglo, 'Hampton Court Painting'. I am grateful to Dr Jennifer Scott, Curator of Paintings at the Royal Collection, for her advice on these points.

5. Montfaucon, IV, pp. 201–6, describes the bas-reliefs which are illustrated by line drawings. They were once thought to represent the assembling of the Council of Trent or the reception of Charles V in France in 1539. Montfaucon states that they were first identified as scenes from the Field of Cloth of Gold by one Abbé Noël in 1726.

6. Adrien was the brother of Artus de Gouffier, seigneur de Boisy, Francis's former governor, and of Guillaume de Gouffier, seigneur de Bonnivet, the Admiral of France.

7. *CSP Ven.* III, 68, 70, Giovanni Badoer and Antonio Giustinian to the Venetian Signory, Ardres, 8 June 1520; Montfaucon, IV, pp. 169–70; *L'Ordonnance*, pp. C ii v–C iii r [*LP* III i, 870].

8. Hall, p. 609.

9. *CSP Ven.* III, 73.

10. Bodl. Ashmole MS 1116, fo. 100v.

11. This area is identified as the site of the Field on the 1: 250 000 scale map of the area produced by the Institut Géographique National, *Carte de randonnée* 2103 ET IGN. 1: 25 000; 1cm = 250m.

12. Hayward, *Dress at the Court of King Henry VIII*, p. 106. Henry had a number of chammers made for him. The garment was in vogue only during the 1520s.

13. Hall, p. 610; *CSP Ven.* III, 60.

14. The most famous portrait of the king, painted in 1526 by Jean Clouet, shows him dressed in a very similar combination of white, silver, cream, black and gold. He wears a black velvet bonnet with a jewelled brim and a white ostrich plume. That the king chose to have himself portrayed in clothing of this colour combination suggests it was one he favoured.

15. Hall, p. 610, my italics.

16. Du Bellay, I, p. 99.

17. *CSP Ven.* III, 60.

18. Hall, p. 610; *CSP Ven.* III, 60, 67, 68, 69.

19. BNF, MS fr. 32,753, *Armorial d'Urfé*. A tournament of three rounds had been staged successively at sites near Saint-Omer (then in French-held Artois) some 14 kilometres from Calais, near Ardres (then in English hands) and near Calais itself. Knights of England, Hainault and France met in a local competition known only from the surviving list of participants.

20. Steven Muhlberger, *Deeds of Arms: Formal Combats in the Late Fourteenth Century* (Highland Village, TX, 2005), pp. 187ff.

21. Jean Froissart, *Chronicles*, tr. Geoffrey Brereton (London, 1968), pp. 373–81; Muhlberger, pp. 215–22.

22. *Great Tournament Roll of Westminster*, ed. Sydney Anglo (2 vols: Oxford, 1968), pp. 27–8.

23. BNF, MS fr. 2692; Sydney Anglo, *The Martial Arts of Renaissance Europe* (New Haven, CT, and London, 2000), pp. 208–9; Richard Barber and Juliet Barker, *Tournaments: Jousts, Chivalry and Pageants in the Middle Ages* (Woodbridge, VA, 1989), pp. 107–37.

24. *Great Tournament Roll*, pp. 27–8.

25. *L'Ordonnance*, fo. Ai r [Russell's translation, p. 109].

26. Ibid., fos Aiiv–Aiii v [*LP* III i, 870]; Bodl. Ashmole MS 1116, fo. 108ff.

27. TNA, SP1/20, fos 44–7 [*LP* III i, 807], 'Memorial' of regulations for 1520 tournament.

28. Catalogue number II 6, Royal Armouries, Tower of London; Claude Blair, *European Armour circa 1066 to circa 1700* (London, 1958), p. 164.

29. BL, Cotton MS Caligula D VII, fo. 187 [*LP* III i, 685], Wingfield to Henry VIII, place unclear, 16 March 1520.

30. Catalogue number II 7, Royal Armouries, Tower of London; Thom Richardson, *The Armour and Arms of Henry VIII* (Leeds, 2002), pp. 18–22; Claude Blair, 'King Henry VIII's Tonlet Armour', *The Burlington House Fair Catalogue* (London, 1983), pp. 16–20; for good photographs of both 1520 armours see *Dressed to Kill*, souvenir magazine of the exhibition of the same name at the Tower of London (London, 2009), pp. 9–19; on the subsequent history of the king's armour see Christopher Highley, 'The Remains of Henry VIII', in Mark Rankin, Christopher Highley and John King (eds), *Henry VIII and his Afterlives* (Cambridge, 2009), pp. 160–89.

31. TNA, E36/09, fos 12v–14r [*LP* III i, 1115].

32. Anglo, *Martial Arts*, p. 211.

33. TNA, E39/09, fos 16v–17v [*LP* III i, 1115].

34. TNA, E36/215, fo. 174v.

35. BL, Cotton MS Caligula D VI, fos 170r and 182 [*LP* III i, 82, 191], Suffolk to Henry VIII, Paris, 21 and 26 February 1515; TNA, E36/215, fo. 174v for the king's payments for the armour. Extraordinarily, the armourer's name is lost at the margin of the page in both of Suffolk's letters.

36. TNA, E39/09, fos 1r–11r [*LP* III i, 1115].

37. BL, Cotton MS Caligula D VII, fo. 221 [*LP* III i, 797], Wingfield to Henry VIII, Paris, 7 May 1520; TNA, E36/216, fo. 95r. 'Parker', later described as 'a gentleman of the French king', was wounded in some way at the Field and given £20 by Henry as compensation.

38. Peter Edwards, *Horse and Man in Early Modern England* (London, 2007), p. 11.

39. Archives Départementales du Nord, Lille, Series B Lettres Missives, fo. 33782ff., instructions from Marguerite de Savoie to the Bishop of Elna and Guillaume de Barres, Ghent, undated, but from context, April 1520; *LP* III i, 802, Marguerite de Savoie to Henry VIII, Ghent, 12 May 1520.

40. Hall, p. 620; *CSP Ven.* III, 60; Florange, I, p. 271.

41. Hall, p. 611; Montfaucon, IV, p. 182. Anthony Knyvet (*c.* 1485–1549) was the younger brother of Sir Thomas Knyvet, the first Master of the Horse to Henry VIII. He was killed in action aboard the *Regent* in a naval battle in 1512.

42. Montfaucon, IV, p. 185, where he is mistakenly called 'duc' de Salusses, and p. 188. He jousted with his younger brother Francesco. Potter, *Renaissance France at War*, p. 147. Saluzzo remained allied to Francis I until his death in 1528. He was succeeded by his brother Gian Ludovico who was himself deposed as marquess by their younger brother Francesco. The last became lieutenant-general for the king in Piedmont in 1536 but defected to Charles V in the prelude to the emperor's invasion of Provence that year and was killed at Carmagnola in 1537.

43. Hall, pp. 571–2; on the 1514 Paris tournament see BN, Additional MS 30,543, fos 73–114, Mountjoy King of Arms' record of the event; fo. 114 for Montmorency's score (6 broken lances, 3 attaints) on that occasion; on the 1517 tournament, see Hall, pp. 591–2, and Rawdon Brown, II, pp. 97, 101–2.

44. Anglo, *Martial Arts*, pp. 133, 173, 201, 214, 237, 271; San Severino was killed at Pavia.

45. BNF, MS fr. 21,449, fo. 52r/v for Piennes; *The Memoirs of Philip de Comines, Lord of Argenton*, ed. A. Scoble (2 vols: London, 1856), II, p. 76; Potter, *War and Government*, pp. 50, 312. He was the scion of a Flemish house in the service of France. His grandfather, Louis, had been governor of Picardy under Louis XII.

46. Montfaucon, IV, p. 186; Anselme, VII, pp. 188–9, for Antoine de Lettes; see also Potter, *A History of France*, p. 81. In 1540 he was made governor of the Languedoc in succession to Montmorency and then became a marshal of France in 1544. For Charles de Mouy see BNF, MS fr. 21,449, fo. 53r *et seq.*; *CAF* III, 8604, 10001; V, 17458; VI, 21064. He eventually became a vice-admiral of France, the governor of Le Havre and the king's lieutenant-general in Normandy.

47. Montfaucon, IV, p. 186; *ODNB sub* 'Thomas Grey'. He was the third of seven sons and ultimately the successor to his father Thomas Grey, the first marquess, who died in 1501. His older brothers died young and Richard, John and Leonard Grey listed for the tournament were his brothers, not sons, as they are called in the *Rutland Papers*. The second marquess himself had four sons, the eldest of whom, Henry (later duke of Suffolk and the father of Lady Jane Grey), was born in 1517. He was therefore only three years old in 1520 and could not have jousted at the Field.

48. Hall, p. 612; Bodl. Ashmole MS 1116, fo. 101v.

49. Dubois, p. 87.

50. Hall, p. 613.

51. Ibid., p. 614.

52. Anglo, *Martial Arts,* pp. 253–68.

53. TNA, E36/217, fo. 161.

54. See p. 124.
55. Anglo, *Martial Arts*, pp. 168–71.
56. Hall, p. 618.
57. Florange, I, p. 272; Anglo, *Martial Arts*, pp. 172–86, esp. p.175.
58. The same was true for female princes. Mary Tudor's beauty as a token of her virtue was praised in an oration made to her by the University of Paris after she became Queen of France in November 1514.
59. Dubois, p. 66. The necklace of shells is an allusion to the collar of the Order of St Michael.
60. Phyllis Mack, 'Political Rhetoric and Poetic Meaning in Renaissance Culture: Clément Marot and the Field of Cloth of Gold', in P. Mack and M.C. Jacob (eds), *Politics and Culture in Early Modern Europe: Essays in Honour of H. G. Koenigsberger* (Cambridge, 1987), pp. 59–83.

5 Generous to a Fault

1. TNA, SP1/20, fos 250–2 [*Rutland Papers*, pp. 41–2], An Estymacion for the Kinges diets and the Quenes' etc.
2. Archives Municipales de Saint-Omer, Correspondance des Magistrats Saint-Omer, Liasse 3, fo. 1148. [The letter is not in *LP*.]
3. *LP* III i, 746, Worcester to Wolsey, Calais, 18 April 1520.
4. AMA, AA 12, fo.138 for the proclamation dated 10 May 1520; BB, fo. 35, Charles de Louvencourt and Pierrie Letonnelier were reimbursed; CC fo. 186r, Roland Nyessart was paid 36 *sous* for several journeys to and from Ardres taking sheep to the king's camp there.
5. TNA, SP1/20, fos 213–26 [*LP* III i, 919], expenses of the household at Guînes.
6. Ibid., fos 236–8.
7. *A Relation or rather a True Account of the island of England*, tr. C.A. Sneyd, Camden Society, 37 (London, 1847), p. 21.
8. BL, Cotton MS Augustus I ii 71; *Chronicle of Calais*, p. xxix; Dillon, 'Calais', p. 312. William Donkerman, described as 'chief brewer', plied his trade at 10d a day. Three men were also paid for use of cellars to store beer and ale either in Middle Way or elsewhere: the accounts are not specific. Alison Sim, *Food and Feast in Tudor England* (Stroud, 1997), pp. 45–57.
9. Felicity Heal, *Hospitality in Early Modern England* (Oxford, 1990), pp. 1–22.
10. Jenny Benham, *Peacemaking in the Middle Ages: Principles and Practice* (Manchester and New York, 2011), pp. 71–89.
11. David Carpenter, 'The Meetings of Kings Henry III and Louis IX', in *Thirteenth Century Studies X: Proceedings of the Durham Conference 2003*, ed. M. Prestwich, R. Britnell and R. Frame (Woodbridge, VA, 2005), pp. 1–30.
12. F.J. Furnivall (ed.), *Early English Meals and Manners: John Russell's 'Boke of nurture'*, Early English Text Society (London, 1868), pp. 48–50.
13. TNA, SP1/20, fo. 142v.
14. *'Boke of nurture'*, pp. 28, 49.
15. TNA, SP1/20, fos 219–26 [*LP* III i, 919].
16. J.M. Fletcher and C.A. Upton, 'Feasting in an Early Tudor College: The Example of Merton College, Oxford', in D. Williams (ed.), *Early Tudor England: Proceedings of the 1987 Harlaxton Symposium* (Woodbridge, VA, 1989), pp. 37–59 at pp. 50–1.
17. Tamalio, pp. 124, 128.
18. Hall, p. 526; Anglo, *Spectacle*, p. 117.
19. Sydney Anglo, 'The Evolution of the Early Tudor Disguising, Pageant and Mask', *Renaissance Drama*, New Series I (1968): 3–44, esp. pp. 4–8.
20. Anglo, *Spectacle*, p. 117.
21. *CSP Ven.* II, 50, pp. 22–3.

22. *L'Ordonnance*, fo. D I r; *CSP Ven.* II, 84, anonymous letter from the French court to Pietro Montemerlo.

23. This impromptu action will be examined in more depth shortly in the context of gift-giving.

24. *CSP Ven.* II, 90, Soardino to the marquess of Mantua, Ardres, 19 June 1520; 91, Giovanni Badoer and Antonio Giustinian to the Venetian Signory, Ardres, 21 June 1520.

25. TNA, SP1/20, fos 188–97 [*LP* III i, 919].

26. Margaret McGowan, *Dance in the Renaissance: European Fashion, French Obsession* (London and New Haven, CT, 2008), pp. 94–8.

27. Ibid., and p. 90.

28. Ibid., pp. 132–43.

29. Hall, p. 615.

30. Sydney Anglo, 'The Barriers: From Combat to Dance (Almost)', *Dance Research*, 25 (2) (Winter 2007): 91–106.

31. Hall, p. 518.

32. *CSP Ven*, 90, 19 June 1520, Hall, p. 619.

33. *Calendar of State Papers and Manuscripts in the Archives and Collections of Milan 1385–1618*, ed. Allen B. Hinds (London, 1912), p. 654, Paulo da Laude, Milanese ambassador to the Emperor Maximilian I to Massimiliano Sforza, Duke of Milan, Lille, 13 September 1513.

34. Ibid., p. 669, Paulo da Laude to Massimiliano Sforza, Tournai, 11 October 1513.

35. Hall, pp. 614–15; *CSP Ven.* II, 90, Soardino to the marquess of Mantua, Ardres, 19 June 1520.

36. AN KK 94, fos 122r–55r, 'Compte Particulier de Maistre Sebastien de Mareau, conseiller du roy notre Seigneur et Maistre de sa chambre aux deniers'.

37. *CAF* V, 17, 304, mandate for payment, 30,434 *livres* 10 *sous*, 5 *deniers tournois*, Saint-Germain-en-Laye, 8 September 1520.

38. AN KK 94, fos 130r/v and 148v.

39. Ibid., fos 129v–130r and 148v.

40. Ibid., fos 128r–129v, 130v–131r, 132r/v.

41. Ibid., fos 143v and 146r–147r.

42. Ibid., fo. 142r, 'à Convault, pour souchees et ramees qu'il a fourny à la maison de la ville aud ardre ou ont mangé les gentilshommes de la chambre du roy d'angleterre'.

43. Ibid., fo. 143r.

44. John L. Nevinson, 'A Show of the Nine Worthies', *Shakespeare Quarterly*, 14 (2) (1963): 103–7. In 1608 the London scrivener Thomas Trevelyon included illustrations of the Nine Worthies in his commonplace book.

45. Hall, pp. 618–20.

46. Ibid.; *CSP Ven.* II, 91, 93, 95.

47. *A collection of ordinances*, p. 150.

48. Hall, p. 620.

49. Ibid., p. 605; *CSP Ven.* II, 83. A replica fountain was made and installed in the Base Court at the Palace in 2010.

50. *CSP Ven.* III, 81, letter of Soardino to the marquess of Mantua.

51. Natalie Zemon Davis, *The Gift in Sixteenth-Century France* (Oxford, 2000), pp. 17–35; M. Mauss, *Essai sur le don* (Paris, 1925).

52. Sharon Kettering, 'Patronage in Early Modern France', *French Historical Studies*, 17 (1992): 839–62; Mark Greengrass, 'Noble Affinities in Early Modern France: The Case of Henri I de Montmorency, Constable of France', *European History Quarterly*, 16 (1986): 275–311; Thierry Rentet, 'Network Mapping: Ties of Fidelity and Dependency among the Major Domestic Officers of Anne de Montmorency', *French History*, 17 (2003): 109–26.

53. *CSP Ven.* III, 50 (p. 27).

54. *CSP Ven.* II, 1088.

55. TNA, E36/216, fo. 19v, £800 'to the gentlemen of the French king amongst them in reward'; fo. 21v, William Holland, John Twisleton and Robert Amadas received between them £1,829 14s. for 'divers parcels of plate' purchased from them as rewards for the ambassadors.

56. BNF, MS fr. 5761, fo. 17: Francis acknowledged receipt of the ambassadors' letter of 11 October 'que avez prenez conge de parte ce jour meme'; Rawdon Brown, II, p. 232; Hall, p. 596; JBP, p. 72.

57. Rawdon Brown, II, pp. 231–2; Hall, p. 596.

58. BL, Cotton MS Caligula D VII, fo. 125 [LP III i, 289], Sir Thomas Boleyn to Wolsey, Paris, 7 June 1519.

59. Kristen B. Neuschel, Word of Honor: Interpreting Noble Culture in Sixteenth Century France (Ithaca, NY, 1989), pp. 85–92, for a discussion of this phenomenon.

60. William Sessions, Henry Howard, Earl of Surrey (Boston, 1986). In the months that followed the 1532 visit, the Dauphin François, Henri duc d'Orléans, and Charles duc d'Angoulême together hosted a prolonged stay in France by Henry's natural son, Henry Fitzroy, Duke of Richmond, and his friend Henry Howard, Earl of Surrey.

61. TNA, SP1/19, fos 5–6, Richard Gibson's account for the New Hall masque; Hall, p. 599.

62. BL, Cotton MS Caligula D VII, fo. 187 [LP III i, 685], Wingfield to Henry VIII, 16 March 1520; BNF, MS fr. 5761, fo. 30. In a letter to Suffolk of 5 December 1519, Bonnivet recalled how he had been with the king at Greenwich when he was shown several arm guards and gauntlets for use with the heavy sword; St. P. VI, p. 54 [LP III i, 698], Wingfield to Henry VIII, Châtellerault, 26 March 1520.

63. St. P. VI, p. 54; BL, Cotton MS Caligula D VII, fo. 216 [LP III i, 749], Wingfield's request addressed to Wolsey on 18 April. Francis looked 'dayle to receive fro hym as well hys measure for the makynge of the curasse as also to receve the vauntbrasse and gauntlet'. On the gauntlets see Henry A. Dillon, 'Arms and Armour at Westminster, the Tower and Greenwich 1547', Archaeologia, 51 (1888): 219–80, esp. p. 260.

64. BL, Additional MS 12,192, fo. 53; Cotton MS Caligula D VII, fo. 187 [LP III i, 685].

65. Richardson, Armour and Arms, pp. 23–4; but see also S.V. Ganscay, 'The Armour of Galiot de Genouilhac', Metropolitan Museum Papers, 4 (1937): 1–38. Genouilhac was thought to be the first owner of the armour but after the identification of a similar suit of Greenwich armour made for Henry VIII in 1540, Turenne was identified as the original recipient. See H. Nickel, '"a harness all gilte"', Metropolitan Museum Journal, 5 (1972): 75–124.

66. Ganscay, pp. 13–14 and Plates X and XI. Ganscay's attribution of the 1527 armour to Louis de Lacque, 'dit Merveilles', the Milanese-born master armourer to Charles VIII, Louis XII and Francis I, is no longer accepted. However, Ganscay was probably right to identify Merveille as the producer, or even the designer, of the ventral supporting plate on the cuirass given to Henry by Francis in 1520.

67. Inventaire sommaire des Archives Départementales du Nord, ed. J. Finot (Lille, 1895), p. 178.

68. CSP Ven. III, 90–4, Giovanni Badoer and Antonio Giustinian, Venetian ambassadors in France, to the Venetian Signory, 21 June 1520; Soardino, the Mantuan ambassador to the marquess of Mantua, 26 June 1520.

69. BL, Harley MS 599, fos 1–116 [LP IV iii, 6184], inventory of Wolsey's Household Stuff; LP VI, 338, 'Plate to be broken by the king's command', 13 April 1533.

70. AN, J 947, fo. 2, 'Inventaire fait à Compiègne après le decese de Louise de Savoie, mère de Francois Ier des meubles de sa chambre, garderobbe, chappelle et offices', dated 3 November 1531.

71. Philippa Glanville, Silver in Tudor and Early Stuart England (London, 1990), pp. 344–5 for the Howard Grace Cup.

72. Timothy Schroder, '"Rich, fierce and greedy for glory": Court Goldsmiths' Work in the Early Years of Henry VIII', Silver Society Journal (Autumn 1996): 435–44.

73. Philippa Glanville, 'Cardinal Wolsey and the Goldsmiths', in Gunn and Lindley, pp. 131–48. Amadas became Master of the King's Jewels from 1526, an office he held until his death in early 1532.

74. I. Toesca, 'Silver in the Time of François Ier: A New Identification', *Apollo*, 90 (1969): 292–7.

75. Michel Bimbenet-Privat, *Les Orfèvres parisiens de la Renaissance (1506–1620)* (Paris, 1992), pp. 508–9 and pp. 544–5.

76. *LP* III, p. 1541, king's payments for June 1520.

77. *LP* III, p. 1556, revels accounts for 1520.

78. Hall, p. 620.

79. *LP* I i, 941; Joan Thirsk, *Horses in Early Modern England: For Service, for Pleasure, for Power. The Stenton Lecture 1977* (Reading,1978), p. 26. I am grateful to Peter Edwards for his advice communicated privately about the various types of horses owned by the two kings. On the derivation of 'hackney' see Giry-Deloison, '"Une haquenée ..."' pp. 132–59.

80. *LP* III ii, p. 1554, Revels accounts for June 1520 lists the saddle and harness presented to Louise.

81. On the bonnets see *LP* III i, 852, account of material supplied to Katherine in April and May 1520 including '2 doz. silk points for the French henchmen 12*d.*, ribbon and aglets for their bonnets, 16d'.

82. Florange, II, pp. 268–70; *CSP Ven.* III, 50, 90, Soardino to the marquess of Mantua; 91, Giovanni Badoer and Antonio Giustinian to the Venetian Signory; Hall, pp. 614–15.

83. Hall, p. 597.

84. Knecht, *Renaissance Warrior*, pp. 386–97, for the wider context of the 1538 *entente* agreed between Francis and the emperor.

85. Xavier Le Person, 'A moment of "resverie": Charles V and Francis I's Encounter at Aigues-Mortes (July 1538)', *French History*, 19(1) (2005): 1–27, at p.13.

86. Ibid., p. 25.

87. *CSP Ven.* II, 90, Soardino to the marquess of Mantua, 'Lisien' [Licques], 19 June 1520, my italics.

88. *Chronicle of Calais*, p. 90.

89. Bodl. Ashmole MS 1116, fo. 102v.

90. Ibid.; Roger Bowers, 'The Cultivation and Promotion of Music in the Household and Orbit of Thomas Wolsey', in Gunn and Lindley, pp. 178–218 at pp. 189–96 on the competence of Wolsey's singers and the close relationship between the music establishments of cardinal and king.

91. BNF, MS fr. 21,449, fo. 53v (see Appendix B); Cazaux, pp. 71–3. Longueval was appointed to the post of 'premier chappellain et maistre de la Chapelle' in the autumn of 1515 in succession to Hilaire de Bernonneau and was still exercising that function as late as 1522. He was most likely succeeded by Claudin de Sermisy in or about 1525, the presumed year of his death.

92. *CSP Ven.* III, 50; Theodore Dumitrescu, *The Early Tudor Court and International Musical Relations* (Aldershot, 2008), p. 45 note 66, and on Opiciis's origins and career pp. 87–95. Why his formal role should have precluded him from performing on such an important occasion for Henry is not obvious.

93. Montfaucon, IV, p. 179; *CSP Ven.* III, 93: *Journal Louise de Savoie*, p. 429. The 'Pax' was an object in wood or metal (often a depiction of the crucifixion) by which, according to the Sarum rite, the peace of God was physically communicated from the celebrant to the congregation with the words 'Pax Domini sit semper vobiscum'. The peace was 'received' by kissing the Pax or by a clerical embrace.

94. Dubois, pp. 95–7; *CSP Ven.* III, 50 (p. 29).

95. Dubois, pp. 95–7 and pp. 28–32 of the Introduction; Anglo, *Spectacle*, p. 157.

96. TNA, E30/1111, Francis I's ratification of the treaty of Westminster.

97. TNA, SP1/20, fo. 80 [*LP* III i, 826].

98. Dubois, p. 96.
99. Philippe Hamon, *L'Argent du roi: Les finances sous François Ier* (Paris, 1994), p. 50.
100. Potter, *A History of France*, pp. 72–4.
101. BNF, MS fr. 4523, fo. 50r; Potter, *Renaissance France at War*, pp. 223–4 and 361.
102. Knecht, *Renaissance Warrior*, p. 186; Hamon, *L'Argent du roi*, p. 558, estimates that Francis had, or at least needed, on average between 6 and 7 million livres per annum across the whole length of his reign. This estimate, however, reflects the fact that costs rose significantly during the 1540s.
103. TNA, E36/216, totals from fos 84r–98r; Frederick Dietz, *English Government Finance 1485–1558* (Urbana, IL, 1921), p. 90.
104. Dietz, pp. 88–93; Loades, *Tudor Court*, pp. 73–83.
105. Dietz S. Jack, 'Henry VIII's Attitude towards Royal Finance: Penny Wise and Pound Foolish?', in Giry-Deloison (ed.), *François Ier et Henri VIII*, pp. 145–63; Hoyle, p. 77.

6 The Cold Light of Day

1. *Here after ensueth two fruytfull sermons, made [and] compyled by the right reverende father in God John Fyssher, Doctour of dyvynyte and Bysshop of Rochester (1532)*, reprinted in *Early History of Religion: Early English Books Online* (Milton Keynes, 2013) fo. Bi v.
2. Ibid., fo. Aiii v.
3. Ibid., fo. Biii v; M. Dowling, *Fisher of Men: A Life of John Fisher, 1469–1535* (London, 1999), pp. 157–8.
4. *CSP Ven.* III, 97, Surian to the Venetian Signory, Calais, 28 June 1520; 'Remembraunce devised for thentervieu bitwixte the most noble Princes the King our souerain lord and the electe Kyng of the Romaynes', *Rutland Papers*, pp. 50–7 [*LP* III i, 804].
5. *LP* III i, 883, Spinelly to Wolsey, Brussels, 27 June 1520.
6. Ibid., 885, Spinelly to Wolsey, Brussels, 28 June 1520.
7. Ibid., 888, Charles V to Wolsey, Brussels, 30 June 1520.
8. *CSP Sp.* II, 281, Juan Manuel imperial ambassador in Rome to the emperor, 13 June 1520.
9. Ibid. and 288, Juan Manuel to the emperor, Rome, 22 July 1520, reporting news heard in earlier in the month.
10. *LP* III i, 866, Spinelly to Wolsey, Ghent, 8 June 1520; *CSP Sp.* II, 283, 286, Juan Manuel to Guillaume de Croy, seigneur de Chièvres, Rome, 5 July, and the same to the emperor, 13 July 1520.
11. *Rutland Papers*, pp. 57–9; Anglo, *Spectacle*, pp. 158–69; C. Giry-Deloison, 'Le Premier Ouvrage imprimé à Arras? Jean (de) Buyens et l'entrevue de Charles Quint et d'Henri VIII à Calais en juillet 1520', in Jean-Pierre Poussou, Roger Baury and Marie Catherine Vignal-Souleyrou (eds), *Monarchies, noblesses, et diplomaties européennes* (Paris, 2005), pp. 167–202.
12. *CSP Sp.* II, 287, treaty between Charles V and Henry VIII dated 14 July 1520. See also *LP* III i, 908, 914.
13. AMA BB 22, fo. 128. Francis ordered the construction of 'ung boulvert de la Porte de Montrescu'. Cf. CC 97, fos 71–103, which notes that construction began in 1520 on the boulvert [a defensive outwork] 'à la porte de Montrescu du costé d'Artois en ensuivant le bon voulliour du Roy'. See also Baron A. De Calonne, *Histoire de la ville d'Amiens* (3 vols: Brussels, 1899, reprinted 1976), pp. 487–9.
14. AMA CC 97, fos 199 r/v.
15. Madeleine of France was born on 10 August. She married James V of Scotland in 1537 but died at Holyrood Palace in July the same year, aged seventeen. On the circumstances of the marriage see MacDougall, pp. 129–31.

16. BL, Cotton MS Caligula D VII, fos 242–3 [*LP* III i, 923], Wingfield to Henry VIII, Poissy, 19 July 1520.

17. Musée Condé MS 1139, *Troisieme Livre de la Guerre gallique*. Demoulins was a long-serving client of Louise de Savoie.

18. Ibid., fo. iv; M.C. Howatson (ed.), *Oxford Companion to Classical Literature* (Oxford, 1989), *sub* 'daedalus' and 'labyrinth'. The 'house of Daedalus' evokes the legendary Athenian who designed the labyrinth made for King Minos of Crete. Minos subsequently refused to free Daedalus. He escaped to Sicily, where another of his inventions killed Minos when the latter pursued him there. The word labyrinth comes from *labrys* which Plutarch says was the Lydian word for the royal symbol of the double-headed axe frequently found in the ruins of Minoan Crete. The Habsburgs' double-headed eagle symbol was known universally in the sixteenth century.

19. 'que le vent de source d'almaigne ou d'espaigne'.

20. Musée Condé MS 1139, fo. i v, 'Neantmoins ainsy que magnanimitie le conduit et le garde d'estre timide, il s'avanca et entre dedands tout seul, lesant a la porte les deux gentilshommes dessus nomez'.

21. Ibid., fo. ii v, 'Joyeuse et bonne chere, vous luy ferez plus d'honneur que votre puissance ne requiret/mais votre humilite et gracieuse faconde de le contraindra de vous aymer et mitiquera l'arrogance des insulaires/ Vous aussi ferez contant de luy en ceste ensemble car Il est gracieux prince'.

22. The word *faconde* used in the reference both to Francis and to Louise means 'gracious or persuasive eloquence': see *[A] Dictionarie of the French and English Tongues* (London, 1611; reprinted University of North Carolina Press, Columbia, 1950), *sub* 'faconde'.

23. TNA, SP1/21, fos 20–7 *[LP* III i, 936], undated draft of instructions.

24. In fact, Charles V was not crowned Holy Roman Emperor in Rome, but in Bologna in 1530 by Pope Clement VII.

25. Knecht, *Renaissance Warrior*, pp. 175–7.

26. BL, Cotton MS Vitellius B XX, fo. 239 [*LP* III i, 1213], Wolsey to Henry VIII.

27. Peter Gwyn, 'Wolsey's Foreign Policy: The Conferences at Calais and Bruges Reconsidered', *HJ* 23 (4) (1980): 755–72.

28. BL, Cotton MS Galba B VII, fos 109–18 [*LP* III i, 1508], Treaty of Bruges, dated 28 August 1521; see also *LP* III i, 1493, undated letter from Wolsey to Henry VIII detailing negotiations with imperial envoys.

29. BL, Cotton MS Caligula D VIII, fos 80–1 *[LP* III ii, 1697], Fitzwilliam to Henry VIII, 21 October.

30. Hall, p. 629.

31. *Rutland Papers*, pp. 50–100; Hall, pp. 637–40; Anglo, *Spectacle*, pp. 184–202.

32. BL, Cotton MS Caligula D VIII, fos 223–4 [*LP* III ii, 2292], Clarenceux's declaration of war against Francis I; S.J. Gunn, 'The Duke of Suffolk's March on Paris in 1523', *EHR* 101 (400) (1986): 596–634.

33. Knecht, *Renaissance Warrior*, pp. 216–48.

34. The treaty was named after the manor house of The More where it was agreed. The More, near Rickmansworth, Hertfordshire, was owned by Wolsey as abbot of St Albans from 1521.

35. TNA, PRO 31/8/137, fos 193–6, 197, 198, 199–200, 201–4 [*LP* II i, 1525, 1531, 1537, 1573, 1578], French ambassadors in England to Louise de Savoie; Rymer, XIV, pp. 48–74 [*LP* IV i, 1600–6]; *ODRF*, IV, 394–5, 398–400.

36. TNA, PRO 31/8/137, fos 296–8, [*LP* IV ii, 2794], the French ambassadors in England to Francis I, 21 March 1527; see also BL, Cotton MS Caligula D X, fos 34–5 [*LP* IV ii, 2980], Clerk to Wolsey, Paris, 24 March 1527.

37. Simon Thurley, 'The Banqueting and Disguising Houses of 1527', in Starkey, *European Court*, pp. 64–9; Hall, p. 724.

38. TNA, E30/1109 [*LP* IV ii, 3356/6a].

39. TNA, SP1/42, fos 70–4 [*LP* IV ii, 3171], Lord Lisle's narrative of the embassy to Paris.
40. *Life and Death of Cardinal Wolsey*, by George Cavendish in *Two Early Tudor Lives* ed. R. Sylvester and D. Harding, p. 50; hereafter cited as Cavendish.
41. Ibid., pp. 55–6; *St. P.* I, p. 239, Wolsey to Henry VIII, Amiens, 11 August 1527.
42. BN, MS fr. 10,390, fos 45–51; cf. *CAF* VI, 19,390.
43. TNA, E30/1112/3/4, treaty for the marriage of Princess Mary and the duc d'Orléans; Mercantile Treaty, treaty to withhold consent to a General Council of the Church while the Pope remains a prisoner, all signed at Amiens, 18 August 1527. On the documents themselves, see M. Orth, 'A French Illuminated Treaty of 1527', *Burlington Magazine*, 122 (1980): 125–6.
44. Hall, p. 732.
45. Ibid.; Cavendish, p. 69.
46. Hall, p. 735. For wardrobe and revels accounts for the event see TNA, E36/227, fos 48–61; TNA, SP1/45, fos 20–41 [*LP* IV ii, 3563, 3564]; Anglo, *Spectacle*, pp. 232–4.
47. Cavendish, p.71.
48. Ibid., pp. 71–3.
49. BNF, MS Clairambault 326, fo. 43; MS fr. 2997, fo. 36 [*LP* IV ii, 3567], Francis I to his ambassadors in England; incorrectly dated in *LP* as 11 November.
50. *The Register of the Most Noble Order of the Garter*, ed. John Anstis (2 vols: London, 1724), I, p. 383.
51. Glenn Richardson, 'The French Connection: Francis I and England's Break with Rome, in Richardson (ed.), *Contending Kingdoms*, pp. 95–115.

Epilogue

1. Père Alfred Hamy, *Entrevue de François Ier avec Henri VIII à Boulogne-sur-Mer en 1532* (Paris, 1898).
2. Glenn Richardson, 'Eternal Peace, Occasional War: Anglo-French Relations under Henry VIII', in S. Doran and G. Richardson (eds), *Tudor England and its Neighbours* (Basingstoke, 2005), pp. 44–73.
3. Knecht, *Renaissance Warrior*, pp. 389–92.
4. The organisers of the 2012 London Olympics wisely opted for a more humorous and sardonic representation of aspects of British history and culture that more endeared than intimidated. The stakes seemed to be so much higher for the Chinese in 2008.
5. *CSPV Ven.* III, 94, Soardino to the marquess of Mantua, [Licques], 28 June 1520.
6. Christopher Meyer, *DC Confidential* (London, 2005), p. 63.

Appendices

1. Chevalier is abbreviated as 'chlr'; seigneur as 'sr'; *livre tournois* as It.

Note on Names, Currencies, Coins and Measures

1. *LP*, IV, 1478 [BL, Harleian MS. 442. fo. 51], 6 July 1525.

Bibliography

Note on the Principal Narrative Sources for the Field of Cloth of Gold

There is voluminous diplomatic correspondence about the Field of Cloth of Gold. The Venetian envoys Badoer, Giustinian and Surian, together with the Mantuan, imperial and papal ambassadors, wrote extensive reports of the happenings at Guînes and Ardres summarised in various calendars produced in the late nineteenth and early twentieth centuries. In addition, there are four principal primary sources for our knowledge of the Field.

The first of these descriptions is in Edward Hall's *The Union of the Two Noble and Illustre Famelies of York and Lancastre*, known usually as his *Chronicle*. It was first published in 1542, twenty-two years after the Field. A second edition followed in 1548. Hall's narrative of the Field remains the longest and most detailed prose account in either French or English. The section dealing with it, and the emperor's visits to Dover and Calais, is one of the longest in the book and runs to twenty-two pages in Ellis's 1809 folio edition. Hall confirms that several French descriptions, 'books' as he called them, were being written during the event. He is likely to have used some of them for his own narrative. Judging from the detailed match between them, he also evidently had access to Richard Gibson's Revels accounts, now in the National Archives, for his descriptions of the masking and tournament costumes. Hall may also have seen copies of ambassadorial correspondence and had eyewitness testimony available to him. In common with the whole *Chronicle*, his description of the Field is relentlessly favourable to Henry, disparaging of Wolsey's pomposity and grudgingly complimentary to Francis. Hall's account evokes the sense of rivalry and competition between the two kings and the two entourages better than any other, particularly in the hesitancy on both sides immediately before the meeting of the two kings on 7 June.

The second important contemporary source is a French description of the Field entitled *L'Ordonnance et ordre du tournoy / ioustes / & combat / a pied / & a cheval*, printed by Jean Lescaille under royal privilege to last a year from 31 July 1520. This was itself a translation of an anonymous narrative in Latin, entitled *Campi convivii / atque ludorum agnonisticorum ordo / modus / atque descriptio*, probably written by Guillaume Budé who was at the Field. Budé was France's leading expert in ancient Greek and a prominent political philosopher. He was a frequent correspondent of Erasmus of Rotterdam, Sir Thomas More and other leading English intellectuals and an authority on the status and powers of the French monarchy.

The third account, entitled *La Description et ordre du camp et festins et ioustes* etc., appeared at about the same time. This pamphlet was based so heavily on the Latin *Campi* as to be virtually plagiarised from it. It was reprinted in the eighteenth century by the antiquarian Bernard de Montfaucon as part of his *Les monuments de la monarchie française*, together with two ballads about the Field.

The fourth and last major literary source is *Francisci Francorum Regis et Henrici Anglorum Colloquium*, a self-consciously elegiac Latin description of the event written by Jacques Dubois, a 30-year-old medical humanist on the fringes of the French court who wrote under the Latin name Jacobus Sylvius. Its dedicatory preface is dated 25 July 1520 although it was not actually published until January 1521. Dubois is known to have consulted 'The Journey of Five Days', a Latin narrative of a visit to Ardres and Guînes undertaken between 18 and 22 June 1520 by an unknown monk of the nearby monastery of Saint-Sauve. 'The Journey' shares a number of specific similarities with Dubois's

Colloquium, not least an elegiac description of Henry's temporary palace and a comparison of the 1520 meeting with the one between Richard II and Charles VI at Ardres in 1396.

There were also a number of short descriptions of the Field in diaries and journals published later. These descriptions stress the colour and spectacle of the event, the magnificent appearance of the two kings, especially Francis, the bravery and skill of those who took part in the tournament and the spectacle of the banquets and entertainments. The accounts in these sources tend to be polite about the English and often very complimentary about Henry himself and are essentially descriptive. They include the *Mémoires* of Robert III de La Marck, seigneur de Florange. A childhood friend of Francis I, he was in the king's retinue at the Field and played an important role in its aftermath. Francis's mother, Louise de Savoie, also kept a journal which provides a few minor details about the Field, as does the journal of Jean Barrillon (*c.* 1485–1552). He was secretary to Chancellor Duprat and married to the latter's niece Claudine. He eventually became a royal secretary.

In England, by sharp contrast, virtually nothing survives about the Field of Cloth of Gold that was not official correspondence, royal council papers, orders, accounts, other administrative records or the heralds' score checks for the tournament. The Welsh solider Elis Gruffudd, who was present at the Field in the retinue of Sir Robert Wingfield, did write an account of it in his native language which in all substantial respects accords with other narratives. A narrative of the event in English, possibly written by Suffolk Herald (Christopher Barker), is preserved as Ashmole MS 1116 in the Bodleian Library, Oxford. There were, however, no descriptions, panegyrics or poems commemorating the event or expressing hopes of continuing Anglo-French peace and amity published under the patronage of the Tudor court. Not even Richard Pace's sermon at the High Mass was published, although his address in St Paul's two years earlier had been.

Bishop John Fisher's two sermons reflecting on the events at the Field were published in 1532 by William Rastell as *Here after ensueth two fruytfull sermons, made [and] compyled by the right reverende father in God John Fyssher, Doctour of dyvynyte and Bysshop of Rochester.* Fisher had attended the Field of Cloth of Gold in the retinue of Queen Katherine and his sermons confirm the lavish scale of hospitality, the personal magnificence on display there, the joyful embraces of the kings and their jousting, although he condemned the extravagance as wasteful. William Rastell was the son of John who had worked on the decoration of the temporary palace at Guînes.

In 1520, the poet Clément Marot was in the household of the king's sister Marguerite de Navarre. It is possible that he was at the Field and he composed two poems that comment on it. The first was his Rondeau XXX, *De la veue des Roys de France et d'Angleterre entre Ardres et Guynes* and the second, the Ballade VIII entitled *Du triumphe d'Ardres et Guignes, faict par les roys de France et d'Angleterre. Du triumphe* was first published in 1532 as part of Marot's collection *L'adolesence Clémentine.* Marot was quite proto-evangelical in outlook and his poem perhaps explores how far flattery of princes can be made ironic and so become criticism of them.

Manuscript Sources

France

Paris, Archives Nationales: J 947; KK 94; 240

Archives Départementales

Achives de Pas-de-Calais, Arras: 3P 038/27 1832 Ardres, *cadastre section C 1re feuille*
Archives Départementales du Nord, Lille: Série B Lettres, Missives

Archives Municipales/Communales

Archives Municipales d'Amiens AA 12; BB 22; CC 97
Archives Municipales de Saint-Omer, Correspondance du Magistrat Saint-Omer, Liasse 3.

Paris, Bibliothèque Nationale

Manuscrits français: 2692; 2934; 2943; 2964; 2997; 4523, 5500; 5761; 10,383; 10,390; 21,449; 32,753
Manuscrit Clairambault 326
Manuscrit Nouvelle Acquisition Française 11,679

Chantilly, Musée Condé 1139

Great Britain

London, The National Archives

State Papers, Henry VIII: SP1/16; 17; 19; 20; 21; 22; 42; 45
Exchequer; Treasurer of Receipt, Diplomatic documents: E30/1109; 1111; 1112; 1113; 1114
Exchequer; Treasury of Receipt, Miscellaneous Books: E36/09; 11; 39; 215; 216; 217; 219; 227
Exchequer; King's Remembrancer, various accounts: E 101/203/21; E101/420/11/12
Transcripts made by the Record Commission for Rymer's *Foedera*: PRO31/8/137

London, The British Library

Additional manuscripts: 6113; 12,192; 30,543
Cottonian manuscripts:
   Augustus I ii, III,
   Caligula B II; D VI; D VII; D VIII; D X; E I
   Cleopatra
   Galba B VII
   Nero
   Titus
   Vespasian
   Vitellius B XX
Harleian manuscripts: 442, 599

Lambeth Palace Library: MS 285

Oxford, Bodleian Library: Ashmole MS 1116

College of Arms, London: MS IST M.6

United States of America

Folger Shakespeare Library, Washington: MS V.b.193

Printed Primary Sources

Anonymous, *Oration Nuptiale de Messire Richard Pace*, printed by Jean Gourmont (Paris, 1519).
[*The*] *Anthony Roll of Henry VIII's Navy*, Occasional Publications of the Navy Records Society vol. 2, eds C.S. Knighton and D.M. Loades (Aldershot, 2000).
[Barrillon], *Journal de Jean Barrillon, secrétaire du chancelier Duprat 1515–21*, ed. P. de Vaissière (2 vols: Paris, 1897–99).
Calendar of State Papers and Manuscripts in the Archives and Collections of Milan 1385–1618, ed. Allen B. Hinds (London, 1912).
Calendar of State Papers and Manuscripts Relating to English Affairs, Existing in the Archives and Collections of Venice etc., ed. R. Brown, C. Bentinck and H. Brown (9 vols: London, 1864–98).
Calendar of State Papers, Spanish, ed. G.A. Bergenroth *et al.* (13 vols: London, 1862–1964).
Campi convivii/atque ludorum agonisticorum ordo/modus/atque descriptio (without place or date; [Paris, Jean de Gourmont, 1520].
Castiglione, Baldassare, *The Book of the Courtier*, tr. G. Bull (Harmondsworth, 1967).

Catalogue des actes de François Ier, ed. P. Marichal (10 vols: Paris, 1887–1910).

[The] Chronicle of Calais, in the reigns of Henry VII and Henry VIII, to the year 1540, ed. J.G. Nichols, *Camden Society Old Series* 35 (1846) (New York, 1968).

[The] Chronicles, by Jean Froissart tr. Geoffrey Brereton (London, 1968).

[A] collection of ordinances and regulations for the government of the royal household made in diverse reigns, published by the Society of Antiquaries (London, 1790).

La Description et ordre du camp et festins et ioustes des trescrestiens et trepuissans roys de France & Dangleterre. Lan Mil. cccc. et vingt, Au moys de Juing (without place or date; [1520]).

[I] Diarii di Marin Saundo, ed. F. Stefano *et al.* (50 vols: Venice, 1897).

[A] Dictionarie of the French and English Tongues by R. Cotgrave (London, 1611; Chapel Hill, 1950).

Early English meals and manners; John Russell's Boke of nurture, ed. F.J. Furnivall, Early English Text Society (London, 1868).

[The] English Housewife by Gervase Markham, ed. M.R. Best (Kingston and Montreal, 1986).

'L'Etat de la maison de duc Charles de Bourgogne' by Olivier de la Marche, ed. L. Petitot in *Collection complète des Mémoires relatifs a l'histoire de France* (Paris, 1820), X, pp. 479–556.

Foedera, conventiones, literae et cuiuscunque generic acta publica, ed. T. Rymer (20 vols: London, 1727–35).

Four Years at the court of Henry VIII. Selection of despatches written by the Venetian ambassador Sebastian Giustinian . . . 1515 to 1519, tr. Rawdon Brown (2 vols: London, 1854).

Francisci Francorum Regis et Henrici Anglorum Colloquium by [Jacobus Sylvius] (Jacques Dubois) (Paris, Josse Badius, 1520), ed. S. Bamforth and J. Dupèbe, *Renaissance Studies*, 5 (1–2) (March–June 1991).

[The] Great Tournament Roll of Westminster, ed. S. Anglo (2 vols: Oxford, 1968).

Here after ensueth two fruytfull sermons, made [and] compiled by the right reverende father in God John Fyssher, Doctour of dyvynyte and Bysshop of Rochester (1532), reprinted in *Early History of Religion: Early English Books Online* (Milton Keynes, 2013).

Houston, A., *L'Ecosse Francoise*, treatise printed in Paris, 1608, in *Papers Relative to the Royal Guard of the Scottish Archers in France*, ed. J. Dunlop (Edinburgh, 1835), pp. 46–84.

Inventaire Sommaire des Archives municipales antérieures à 1790 by A. Ledeiue (Abbeville, 1902).

Inventaire Sommaire des Archives Départementales du Nord, ed. J. Finot (Lille, 1895).

Journal d'un bourgeois de Paris sous le règne de François Ier 1515–1536, ed. Louis Lalanne (Paris, 1854).

Letters and Papers, Foreign and Domestic of the Reign of Henry VIII, 1509–1547, ed. J. Brewer, J. Gairdner and R.H. Brodie (21 vols and addenda: London, 1862–1932).

'Lettres échangées entre François Ier et ses ambassadeurs à Londres (août–octobre 1518)', ed. Monique Garand-Zobel, *Bibliothèque de l'Ecole des chartes*, 112 (1) (1954): 104–25.

[The] Life and Death of Cardinal Wolsey, by George Cavendish in *Two Early Tudor Lives*, ed. R. Sylvester and D. Harding (New Haven, CT, and London, 1962).

Matthew Paris's English History from the year 1235 to 1273, tr. J.A. Giles (3 vols: London, 1854).

Mémoires de Martin et Guillaume Du Bellay, ed. V.L. Bourrilly and F. Vindry (4 vols: Paris, 1908–19).

Mémoires du Maréchal de Florange, ed. R. Goubaux and P.-A. Lemoisne (2 vols: Paris, 1913, 1924).

Mémoires ou Journal de Louise de Savoie, Duchesse d'Angoulesme etc ed. L'Abbé Lambert, *Collection Universelle des Memoires Particuliers Relatifs a l'histoire de France*, vol. XVI, (Paris, 1786), pp. 407–34.

Memoirs of Philip de Commines, Lord of Argenton, ed. A. Scoble (2 vols: London, 1856).

Montfaucon, B de, *Les monuments de la monarchie française* (4 vols: Paris, 1732).

L'Ordonnance et ordre du tournoy / ioustes / & combat/ a pied / & a cheval. Le tresdesire & plusque triumphant rencontre / entrevue / assemblee / & visitation / des treshaultz / tresexcellens princes / les Roys de France / & de Angleterre ... (Paris, Jean Lescaille [for Pierre Vidoue], without date [1520]).

Pace, R., *Oratio Ricardii Pacei in pace nuperrime composita* (London, 1518) (*STC* 19081A).
[*The*] *Register of the Most Noble Order of the Garter*, ed. John Anstis (2 vols: London, 1724).
A Relation or rather a True Account of the island of England, tr. C.A. Sneyd, Camden Society, 37 (London, 1847).
Rincio, B., *Oraison en La Louenge du marriage de Monsieur le Dauphin de Gaulles* (Paris, 1519).
—— *Le Livre et forest de messire Bernardin Rince Millanoys: Docteur en medecine contenant et explicant briefuement lappareil, les leux et le festin de la Bastille* (Paris, 1519).
Rutland Papers: Original Papers illustrative of the courts and times of Henry VII and Henry VIII, ed. W. Jerdan, *Camden Society Old Series* 21 (1842) (New York, 1968).
State Papers Published under the Authority of his Majesty's Commission, King Henry VIII (11 vols: London, 1830–52).
Statutes of the Realm, ed. A. Luders *et al.* (11 vols: London, 1810–28).
Tamalio, R. (ed.), *Federico Gonzaga alla corte di Francesco I di Francia nel carteggio privato con Mantova (1515–1517)* (Paris, 1994).
'Two papers relating to the interview between Henry the Eighth of England and Francis the First of France', ed. J. Caley, *Archaeologia*, 21 (London, 1827), pp. 176–91.
[*The*] *Union of the Two Noble and Illustre Famelies of York and Lancastre*, [1542], ed. H. Ellis (London, 1809).
'Un Voyage à Calais, Guines, Ardres et Boulogne en 1520', ed. G. Servois, *Bibliothèque de l'École des chartes*, 18 (1857): 453–8.

Secondary Sources: Books and Articles

Adams, S., 'England and the World under the Tudors 1485–1603', in J. Morrill (ed.), *The Oxford Illustrated History of Tudor and Stuart Britain* (Oxford, 1996), pp. 397–415.
Alford, B.W. and Barker, T.C., *A History of the Carpenters' Company* (London, 1968).
Allmand, C. (ed.), *War, Government and Power in Late Medieval France* (Liverpool, 2000).
Anglo, S., 'Le Camp du drap d'or et les entrevues d'Henri VIII et de Charles Quint', in *Fêtes et cérémonies au temps de Charles Quint*, ed. J. Jacquot (Paris, 1960), pp. 113–34.
—— 'The Hampton Court Painting of the Field of Cloth of Gold Considered as an Historical Document', *Antiquaries Journal*, 46 (1966): 285–307.
—— 'The Evolution of the Early Tudor Disguising, Pageant and Mask', *Renaissance Drama*, New Series I (1968): 3–44, esp. pp. 4–8.
—— *Spectacle, Pageantry and Early Tudor Policy* (Oxford, 1969 and 1995).
—— *The Martial Arts of Renaissance Europe* (New Haven, CT, and London: Yale University Press, 2000).
—— 'The Barriers: From Combat to Dance (Almost)', *Dance Research* 25 (2) (2007): 91–106.
Anselme de Sainte-Marie, Père, *Histoire généalogique et chronologique de la maison royale de France, des pairs, grands officiers de la Couronne, de la Maison du Roy et des anciens barons du royaume*, continued by H. Du Fourny (9 vols: Paris, 1726–33).
Ashdown, C.H., *History of the Worshipful Company of Glaziers of the City of London* (London, 1914).
Ayloffe, J., 'An Historical Description of an Ancient Painting in Windsor Castle', *Archaeologia*, 3 (1786): 185–229.
Babelon, J.-P., *Châteaux de France au siècle de la Renaissance* (Paris, 1989).
Bakos, A.E. (ed.), *Politics, Ideology and the Law in Early Modern Europe: Essays in Honour of J.H.M. Salmon* (Rochester, NY, 1994).
Barber, R., *The Knight and Chivalry* (London, 1970).
Barber, R. and Barker, J., *Tournaments: Jousts, Chivalry and Pageants in the Middle Ages* (Woodbridge, VA, 1989).

Baumgartner, F.J., *Louis XII* (Basingstoke, 1996).

Beaune, C., *Naissance de la nation France. The Birth of an Ideology: Myths and Symbols of Nation in Late-Medieval France*, tr. S. Ross Hutton (Berkeley, 1991).

Begent, P., *Justes Royale: The Tournament in England* (Maidenhead, privately printed, 1984).

Benedict, P., *Cities and Social Change in Early Modern France* (London, 1992).

Benham, J., *Peacemaking in the Middle Ages: Principles and Practice* (Manchester and New York, 2011).

Benoist, P., 'Le Clergé de cour et la décision dans la première moitié du xvie siècle' in *La Prise de décision en France (1525–1559)*, ed. Roseline Claerr and Olivier Poncet (Paris, 2008), pp. 53–68.

Bentley-Cranch, D. and Marshall, R.K., 'Iconography and Literature in the Service of Diplomacy: The Franco-Scottish Alliance, James V and Scotland's Two French Queens, Madeleine of France and Mary of Guise', in J. Williams (ed.), *Stewart Style: Essays on the Court of James V* (East Linton, 1996), pp. 273–89.

Bimbenet-Privat, M., *Les Orfèvres parisiens de la Renaissance (1506–1620)* (Paris, 1992).

Bindoff, S.T., 'Clement Armstrong and his Treatises of the Commonweal', *Economic History Review*, 14 (1) (1944): 64–73.

Blair, C., *European Armour circa 1066 to circa 1700* (London, 1958).

—— 'The Emperor Maximilian's Gift of Armour to King Henry VIII and the Silvered and Engraved Armour in the Tower of London', *Archaeologia*, 99 (1965): 19–39.

—— 'King Henry VIII's Tonlet Armour', *The Burlington House Fair Catalogue* (London, 1983): 16–20.

Bloch, M., *The Royal Touch: Sacred Monarchy and Scrofula in England and France*, tr. J.E. Anderson (London, 1973).

Bonnardot, A. (ed.), *Les Rues et églises de Paris vers 1500, une fête à la Bastille en 1518* (Paris, 1876).

Bowers, R., 'The Cultivation and Promotion of Music in the Household and Orbit of Thomas Wolsey', in Gunn and Lindley, pp. 178–218.

Brandi, K., *The Emperor Charles V* (London, 1965).

Bréemersch, P. and Léopold, J.-Y., *Armorial du Pas-de-Calais: Communes des arrondissements de Béthune, Boulogne-sur-Mer, Calais, Lens, Montreuil, Saint-Omer* (Arras, 1996).

Britnell, J. and Britnell, R., *Vernacular Literature and Current Affairs in the Early Sixteenth Century: France, England and Scotland* (Aldershot, 2000).

Broomhall, A., 'Identity and Life Narratives of the Poor in Later Sixteenth-Century Tours', *Renaissance Quarterly*, 57 (2004): 439–65.

Buy, E., Curveiller, S. and Louf, J., *Guînes des origines à nos jours* (Balinghem, 2008).

Calonne, Baron A. de, *Histoire de la ville d'Amiens* (3 vols: Brussels, 1899; reprinted 1976).

Campbell, T.P., *Henry VIII and the Art of Majesty: Tapestries at the Tudor Court* (New Haven, CT, and London, 2007).

Carlson, D., 'Royal Tutors in the Reign of Henry VII', *SCJ*, 22 (2) (1991): 253–79.

Carogue, P., 'Artus (1474–1519) et Guillaume (1482–1525) Gouffier à l'émergence de nouvelles modalités de gouvernement', in Michon, *Les Conseillers de Francois Ier*, pp. 229–34.

Carpenter, D., 'The Meetings of Kings Henry III and Louis IX', in *Thirteenth Century Studies X: Proceedings of the Durham Conference 2003*, ed. M. Prestwich, R. Britnell and R. Frame (Woodbridge, VA, 2005), pp. 1–30.

Carroll, S., *Martyrs and Murderers: The Guise Family and the Making of Europe* (Oxford, 2009).

Cazaux, C., *La Musique à la cour de François Ier* (Paris, 2002).

Challis, C.E., *The Tudor Coinage* (Manchester, 1978).

Chatenet, M., *La Cour de France au XVIᵉ siècle: Vie sociale et architecture* (Paris, 2002).

Chevalier, B., *Tours: Ville royale, 1356–1520* (Tours, 1975).

—— *Les Bonnes Villes de France du XIVe au XVIe siècle* (Paris, 1982).

—— 'Florimond Robertet (v.1465–1527)', in Michon, *Les Conseillers de François Ier*, pp. 99–116.

Claerr, R. and Poncet, O. (eds), 'La Prise de décision en France (1525–1559)', *Études et rencontres de l'École Des Chartes 27* (Paris, 2008).

Cockayne, G.E., *Complete Peerage*, ed. V. Gibbs (London, 1910–49).

Cole, A. and John, P., *Local Governance in England and France* (London, 2001).

Collins, J.B., 'The Economic Role of Women in Seventeenth-Century France', *French Historical Studies*, 16 (2) (1989): 436–70.

Colvin, H.M. (ed.), *The History of the King's Works* (6 vols: London, 1933–82).

Contamine, P., 'Les Industries de guerre dans la France de la Renaissance: L'exemple de l'artillerie', *Revue Historique*, 271 (1984): 249–80.

Cornwall, J., *Wealth and Society in Early Sixteenth-Century England* (London, 1988).

Cox-Rearick, J., *The Collection of Francis I: Royal Treasures* (Antwerp, 1995).

Crawford, K., *The Sexual Culture of the French Renaissance* (Cambridge, 2010).

Crossley, D.W., 'The Performance of the Glass Industry in Sixteenth-Century England', *Economic History Review*, New Series 25 (3) (August 1972): 421–33.

Crouch, D., *Tournament* (London, 2005).

Cruickshank, C.G., *Army Royal: Henry VIII's Invasion of France 1513* (Oxford, 1969).

Currin, J.M., '"To Traffic with War"? Henry VII and the French Campaign of 1492', in D. Grummitt (ed.), *The English Experience in France*, pp. 106–31.

Davies, M. and Saunders, A., *The History of the Merchant Taylors' Company* (Leeds, 2004).

Davis, N.Z., 'A Trade Union in Sixteenth-Century France', *Economic History Review*, New Series 19 (1) (1969): 48–69.

—— 'Women in the Crafts in Sixteenth-Century Lyon', *Feminist Studies* 8 (1) (1982): 46–80.

—— *The Gift in Sixteenth-Century France* (Oxford, 2000).

Dietz, F., *English Government Finance 1485–1558* (Urbana, IL, 1921).

Dillon, H.A. 'Arms and Armour at Westminster, the Tower and Greenwich 1547', *Archaeologia*, 51 (1888): 219–80.

—— 'Calais and the Pale', *Archaeologia*, 53 (1893): 289–388.

Doran S., *England and Europe 1485–1603* (London, 1996).

—— (ed.), *Henry VIII: Man and Monarch*, British Library exhibition catalogue (London, 2009).

Doran, S. and Richardson, G. (eds), *Tudor England and its Neighbours* (Basingstoke, 2005).

Dowling, M., *Fisher of Men: A Life of John Fisher, 1469–1535* (London, 1999).

Duffy, E., *The Voices of Morebath: Reformation and Rebellion in an English Village* (New Haven, CT, and London, 2001).

Dumitrescu, T., *The Early Tudor Court and International Musical Relations* (Aldershot, 2008).

Dyer, C., *Standards of Living in the Later Middle Ages: Social Change in England c.1200–1520* (Cambridge, 1988).

Edwards, P., *Horse and Man in Early Modern England* (London, 2007).

Elton, G.R., *Reform and Reformation, England 1509–1558* (London, 1977).

Fletcher, J.M. and Upton, C.A., 'Feasting in an Early Tudor College: The Example of Merton College, Oxford', in D. Williams, *Early Tudor England: Proceedings of the 1987 Harlaxton Symposium* (Woodbridge, VA, 1989).

Fletcher, S., *Cardinal Wolsey: A Life in Renaissance Europe* (London, 2009).

Gallia Christiana in provincias ecclesiasticas distributa: qua series et historia archiepiscoporum, episcoporum, et abbatum franciae vicinarumque ditionum / opera & studio Domni Dionysii Sammarthani (16 vols: Paris, 1870–74).

Ganscay, S.V., 'The armour of Galiot de Genouilhac', *Metropolitan Museum Papers*, 4 (1937): 1–38.

Giesey, R.E., *Rulership in France, 15th–17th Centuries* (Aldershot, 2004).

Giry-Deloison, C. 'Henry VII et la Bretagne: Aspects politiques et diplomatiques', in J. Kehervé and T. Daniel (eds), *1491: La Bretagne, terre d'Europe* (Brest, 1992), pp. 223–42.

—— 'Money and Early Tudor Diplomacy: The English Pensioners of the French Kings 1475–1547', *Medieval History*, 3 (1994): 128–46.

—— 'Histoire de la politique étrangère et de la diplomatie anglaises, fin XVᵉ–mi-XVIIᵉ siècle', in F. Lachaud, I. Lescent-Giles and F.-J. Ruggiu (eds), *Histoires d'Outre-Manche: Tendances récentes de l'historiographie britannique* (Paris, 2001), pp. 57–78.

—— '"Une haquenée … pour le porter bientost et plus doucement en enfer ou en paradis": The French and Mary Tudor's Marriage to Louis XII in 1514', in Grummitt, *The English Experience in France*, pp. 132–59.

—— 'Le premier ouvrage imprimé à Arras? Jean (de) Buyens et l'entrevue de Charles Quint et d'Henri VIII à Calais en juillet 1520', in *Monarchies, noblesses et diplomaties européennes. Mélanges en l'honneur de Jean-François Labourdette*, ed. J-P. Poussou, R. Baury and M.-C. Vignal-Souleyrou (Paris, 2005), pp. 167–202.

—— 'France and England at Peace, 1475–1513', in Richardson, *Contending Kingdoms*, pp. 43–60.

—— (ed.), *François Ier et Henri VIII, deux princes de la Renaissance (1515—1547)*, (Lille, 1994).

—— (ed.), *1520 Le Camp du Drap d'Or* (Paris, 2012).

Glanville, P., *Silver in Tudor and Early Stuart England: A Social History and Catalogue of the National Collection 1480–1660* (London, 1990).

—— 'Cardinal Wolsey and the Goldsmiths', in Gunn and Lindley, *Cardinal Wolsey*, pp. 131–48.

Godefroy, T., *Le Cérémonial françois* (2 vols: Paris, 1649).

Greengrass, M., 'Noble Affinities in Early Modern France: The case of Henri I de Montmorency, Constable of France', *European History Quarterly*, 16 (1986): 275–311.

Griffiths, R., 'The Island of England in the Fifteenth Century: Perceptions of the Peoples of the British Isles', *Journal of Medieval History*, 29 (2003): 177–200.

Grummitt, D., 'Henry VII, Chamber Finance and the "New Monarchy": Some New Evidence', *HJ*, 72 (1999): 229–43.

—— 'The Defence of Calais and the Development of Gunpowder Weaponry in England in the Late Fifteenth Century', *War in History*, 7 (3) (2000): 253–72.

—— (ed.), *The English Experience in France c.1450–1558: War, Diplomacy and Cultural Exchange* (Aldershot, 2002).

—— *The Calais Garrison: War and Military Service in England, 1436–1558* (Woodbridge, VA, 2008).

Gunn, S.J., 'The Duke of Suffolk's March on Paris in 1523', *EHR*, 101 (400) (1986): 596–634.

Gunn, S.J. and Janse, A. (eds), *The Court as a Stage: England and the Low Countries in the Later Middle Ages* (Woodbridge, 2006).

Gunn, S.J. and Lindley, P.G. (eds), *Cardinal Wolsey: Church, State and Art* (Cambridge, 1991).

Gwyn, P., 'Wolsey's Foreign Policy: The Conferences at Calais and Bruges Reconsidered', *HJ*, 23 (4) (1980): 755–72.

—— *The King's Cardinal: The Rise and Fall of Thomas Wolsey* (London, 1990).

Hamon, P., *L'Argent du roi: Les finances sous François Ier* (Paris, 1994).

—— 'Charles de Bourbon, connétable de France (1490–1527)', in Michon, *Les Conseillers de François Ier*, pp. 95–7.

—— 'Semblançay homme de finances et de Conseil (v.1455–1527)', in Michon, *Les Conseillers de François Ier*, pp. 117–30.

Hamy, Pere A., *Entrevue de François Iᵉʳ avec Henri VIII à Boulogne–sur–mer en 1532* (Paris, 1898).

Harding, R., *Anatomy of a Power Elite: The Provincial Governors of Early Modern France* (New Haven, CT, and London, 1978).

Hayward, M., 'The Packing and Transportation of the Possessions of Henry VIII, with particular reference to the 1547 Inventory', *Costume*, 31 (1997): 8–15.

—— *The 1542 Inventory of Whitehall: The Palace and its Keeper* (London, 2004).

—— *Dress at the Court of Henry VIII* (Leeds, 2007).

Heal, F., *Hospitality in Early Modern England* (Oxford, 1990).

Highley, C., 'The Remains of Henry VIII', in M. Rankin, C. Highley and J. King (eds), *Henry VIII and his Afterlives* (Cambridge, 2009), pp. 160–89.

Howard, M. and Wilson, E., *The Vyne: A Tudor House Revealed* (London, 2003).

Howard, S., '"Ascending the Riche Mount": Performing Hierarchy and Gender in the Henrician Masque', in P. Herman (ed.), *Rethinking the Henrician Era: Essays on Early Tudor Texts and their Contexts* (Urbana, IL, 1994), pp. 16–39.

Howatson, M.C. (ed.), *Oxford Companion to Classical Literature* (Oxford, 1989).

Hoyle, R., 'War and Public Finance', in D. MacCulloch (ed.), *The Reign of Henry VIII: Politics, Policy and Piety* (Basingstoke, 1995), pp. 75–99.

Huppert, G., *Les Bourgeois Gentilshommes: An Essay on the Definition of Elites in Renaissance France* (Chicago, 1977).

Ives, E., *Anne Boleyn* (Oxford, 2000).

Jack, S., 'Henry VIII's Attitude towards Royal Finance: Penny Wise and Pound Foolish?', in Giry-Deloison (ed.), *François Ier et Henri VIII*, pp. 145–63.

Jackson, W., 'The Tournament and Chivalry in German Tournament Books of the Sixteenth Century and in the Literary Works of Emperor Maximilian I', in *The Ideals and Practice of Medieval Knighthood: Papers from the First and Second Strawberry Hill Conferences*, ed. C. Harper-Bill and R. Harvey (Woodbridge, VA, 1986), pp. 49–73.

James, M., 'English Politics and the Concept of Honour 1485–1642', *Past and Present* Supplement 3 (1978): 1–98.

Jones, T., 'A Welsh Chronicler in Tudor England', *Welsh History Review*, 1 (1960): 1–17.

Jouanna, A., *La France du XVIe siècle 1483–1598* (Paris, 1996).

Jourda, P., *Marguerite d'Angoulême duchesse d'Alençon et reine de Navarre* (2 vols: Paris, 1930).

Karras, R.M., *From Boys to Men: Formations of Masculinity in Late Medieval Europe* (Philadelphia, 2003).

—— *Sexuality in Medieval Europe* (New York, 2005).

Keen, M., *Chivalry* (New Haven, CT, and London, 1984).

—— *English Society in the Later Middle Ages 1348–1500* (Harmondsworth, 1990).

Kettering, S., 'Friendship and Clientage in Early Modern France', *French History*, 6 (2) (1992): 139–58.

'Patronage in Early Modern France', *French Historical Studies*, 17 (1992): 839–62.

Kisby, F., '"When the King Goeth a Procession": Chapel Ceremonies and Services, the Ritual Year, and Religious Reforms at the Early Tudor Court, 1485–1547', *Journal of British Studies*, 40 (2001): 44–75.

Kjaer L. and Watson, A.J., 'Feasts and Gifts: Sharing Food in the Middle Ages', *Journal of Medieval History*, 37 (2011): 1–5.

Knecht, R.J., *Renaissance Warrior and Patron: The Reign of Francis I* (Cambridge, 1994).

—— 'Le Camp du Drap d'Or', in *Arras et la diplomatie européenne XVe–XVIe siècles*, ed. D. Clauzel, C. Giry-Deloison and C. Leduc (Arras, 1999), pp. 219–230.

—— *The Valois: Kings of France 1328–1589* (London and Hambledon, 2004).

—— *The French Renaissance Court* (New Haven, CT, and London, 2008).

Knecht, R.J., 'The French and English Nobilities in the Sixteenth Century: A Comparison', in Richardson, *Contending Kingdoms*, pp. 61–78.

—— 'Jacques de Genouillac dit Galiot (v.1465–1546)', in Michon, *Les Conseillers de François Ier*, pp. 155–61.

—— 'Jacques II de Chabannes, seigneur de La Palisse ou La Palice (v.1470–1525)', in Michon, *Les Conseillers de François Ier*, pp. 163–70.

Labarge, M.-W., *Saint Louis: The Life of Louis IX of France* (London, 1968).

Larmour, R., 'A Merchant Guild of Sixteenth-Century France: The Grocers of Paris', *Economic History Review*, 20 (3) (1967): 467–81.

La Roncière, C. de, *Histoire de la marine française*, 2nd edn (6 vols: Paris, 1909–32).

Lecoq, A.-M., *François Ier imaginaire: Symbolique et politique à l'aube de la Renaissance française* (Paris, 1987).

——, 'Une fête italienne à la Bastille en 1518', in *Il se rendit en Italie: Etudes offertes à André Chastel*, ed. Giuliano Briganti (Rome, 1987), pp. 149–68.

Le Glay, A.J.C., *Négociations diplomatiques entre la France et l'Autriche* (2 vols: Paris, 1845).

Le Person, X., '"A moment of rêverie": Charles V and Francis I's Encounter at Aigues-Mortes (July 1538)', *French History*, 19 (1) (2005): 1–27.

Lesueur, P., *Dominique de Cortone dit Boccador* (Paris, 1928).

Leterrier, S.-A., 'The Field of Cloth of Gold in Popular Imagination and Historical Imagery during the Nineteenth Century', in C. Giry-Deloison (ed.), *1520: Le Camp du Drap d'Or*, (Paris, 2012), pp. 65–85.

Loach, J., 'The Function of Ceremony in the Reign of Henry VIII', *Past & Present*, 142 (1994): 43–68.

Loades, D.M., *The Tudor Navy: An Administrative, Political and Military History* (Aldershot, 1992).

—— *The Tudor Court* (London, 1986).

Loats, C., 'Gender, Guilds and Work Identity: Perspectives from Sixteenth-Century Paris', *French Historical Studies*, 20 (1) (1997): 15–30.

MacCulloch, D. (ed.), *The Reign of Henry VIII: Politics, Policy and Piety* (Basingstoke, 1995).

MacDougall, N., *An Antidote to the English: The Auld Alliance, 1295–1560* (East Linton, 2001).

McGowan, M., *Dance in the Renaissance: European Fashion, French Obsession* (London and New Haven, CT, 2008).

Mack, P., 'Political Rhetoric and Poetic Meaning in Renaissance Culture: Clément Marot and the Field of Cloth of Gold', in P. Mack and M.C. Jacob (eds), *Politics and Culture in Early Modern Europe: Essays in Honour of H.G. Koenigsberger* (Cambridge, 1987), pp. 59–83.

Marks, R., *Stained Glass in England during the Middle Ages* (London, 1993).

Mattingly, G., 'An Early Nonaggression Pact', *Journal of Modern History*, 10 (1) (1938): 1–30.

—— *Renaissance Diplomacy* (New York, 1955).

Mausi, M., *Essai sur le don* (Paris, 1925).

Mayer, D.M., *The Great Regent, Louise of Savoy* (London, 1966).

Mayhew, N., *Coinage in France from the Dark Ages to Napoleon* (London, 1988).

Meyer, C., *DC Confidential* (London, 2005).

Michon, C., *La Crosse et le sceptre: Les prélates d'état sous François Ier et Henri VIII* (Paris, 2008).

—— (ed.), *Les conseillers de François Ier* (Rennes, 2011).

—— 'René, Grand Bâtard de Savoie (v. 1473–1525)', in his *Les Conseillers de François Ier*, pp. 255–63.

—— 'Odet de Foix, vicomte de Lautrec (v. 1483–1528)', in his *Les Conseillers de François Ier*, pp. 265–72.

—— (ed.), *Conseils, conseillers dans l'Europe de la Renaissance v. 1450–1550* (Rennes, 2012).

Millar, O., *The Tudor, Stuart and Early Georgian Pictures in the Collection of Her Majesty the Queen* (London, 1963).

Miller, H., *Henry VIII and the English Nobility* (Oxford, 1986).

Montfaucon, B. de, *Les Monuments de la monarchie française: qui comprennent l'histoire de France, avec les figures de chaque regne que l'injure des temps a epargnées* (Paris, 1732).

Muhlberger, S., *Deeds of Arms: Formal Combats in the Late Fourteenth Century* (Highland Village, TX, 2005).

Mulryne, J.R. and Goldring, E. (eds), *Court Festivals of the European Renaissance: Art, Politics and Performance* (Aldershot, 2002).

Munby, J., 'The Field of Cloth of Gold: Guînes and the Calais Pale Revisited', edited text of a lecture delivered to the Royal Archaeological Institute, 8 December 2010.

Myers, A.R. (ed.), *The Household of Edward IV: The Black Book and the Ordinance of 1478* (Manchester, 1959).

The National Trust Guide to Ightham Mote, Kent (1998).

Nelson, A., *The Tudor Navy: The Ships, Men and Organisation 1485–1603* (London, 2001).

Neuschel, K.B., *Word of Honor: Interpreting Noble Culture in Sixteenth Century France* (Ithaca, NY, 1989).

Nevison, J.L., 'A Show of the Nine Worthies', *Shakespeare Quarterly* 14(2) (1963): 103–7.

Nickel, H., '"a harness all gilte"', *Metropolitan Museum Journal*, 5 (1972): 75–124.

O'Hanlon, R., 'Military Sports and the History of the Martial Body in India', *Journal of Economic and Social History of the Orient*, 50 (4) (2007): 490–523.

Orth, M., 'A French Illuminated Treaty of 1527', *Burlington Magazine*, 122 (1980): 125–6.

Phelps Brown, E.H. and Hopkins, S.V., 'Seven Centuries of the Prices of Consumables, Compared with Builders' Wage-Rates', *Economica*, New Series 23 (92) (November 1956): 296–314.

—— 'Wage-rates and Prices: Evidence for Population Pressure in the Sixteenth Century', *Economica*, New Series, 24 (94) (November 1957): 289–306.

Phillips, G., 'The Army of Henry VIII: A Reassessment', *Journal of the Society for Army Historical Research*, 75 (1997): 8–22.

Potter, D.L., 'The Luxembourg Inheritance: The House of Bourbon and its Lands in Northern France during the Sixteenth Century', *French History*, 6 (1) (1992): 24–62.

—— *War and Government in the French Provinces: Picardy 1470–1560* (Cambridge, 1993).

—— *A History of France 1460–1560: The Emergence of a Nation State* (Basingstoke, 1995).

—— *Un homme de guerre au temps de la Renaissance: La vie et les letters d'Oudart du Biez, Marchéchal de France, Gouverneur de Boulogne et de Picardie (vers 1475–1553)* (Arras, 2001).

—— (ed.), *France in the Later Middle Ages* (Oxford, 2002).

—— *Renaissance France at War: Armies, Culture and Society c. 1480–1560* (Woodbridge, 2008).

—— 'Politics and Faction at the French Court from the late Middle Ages to the Renaissance: The Development of a Political Culture', Paris, Cour de France.fr, 2011 (http://cour-de-france.fr/article1883.html).

Rankin, M., Highley, C. and King, J.N. (eds), *Henry VIII and his Afterlives* (Cambridge, 2009).

Rawcliffe, C., *The Staffords, Earls of Stafford and Dukes of Buckingham 1394–1521* (Cambridge, 1978).

—— 'A Marginal Occupation? The Medieval Laundress and her Work', *Gender and History*, 21 (1) (April 2009): 147–69.

Raymond, J., *Henry VIII's Military Revolution: The Armies of Sixteenth-Century Britain and Europe* (London, 2007).

Reed, A.W., *Early Tudor Drama: The Medwall, the Rastells, Heywood, and the More Circle* (London, 1926).

The Renaissance at Sutton Place: Exhibition Catalogue (London, 1983).

Rentet, T., 'Network Mapping: Ties of Fidelity and Dependency among the Major Domestic Officers of Anne de Montmorency', *French History*, 17 (2003): 109–126.

Richardson, G.J., 'Entertainments for the French Ambassadors at the Court of Henry VIII', *Renaissance Studies*, 9 (4) (1995): 404–15.

—— '"Most highly to be regarded": The Privy Chamber of Henry VIII and Anglo-French Relations 1515–1520', *The Court Historian*, 4(2) (1999): 119–40.

—— *Renaissance Monarchy: The Reigns of Henry VIII, Francis I and Charles V* (London, 2002).

—— 'Eternal Peace, Occasional War: Anglo-French Relations under Henry VIII', in S. Doran and G. Richardson (eds), *Tudor England and its Neighbours* (Basingstoke, 2005), pp. 44–73.

—— (ed.), *The Contending Kingdoms: France and England, 1420–1700* (Aldershot, 2008).

—— 'The French Connection: Francis I and England's Break with Rome', in his *The Contending Kingdoms*, pp. 95–115.

Richardson, T., *The Armour and Arms of Henry VIII* (Leeds, 2002).

Richardson, W.C., *Tudor Chamber Administration* (Baton Rouge, LA, 1952).

Roch, J.-L., 'De la nature du drapier médiéval. L'exemple rouennais', *Revue Historique*, 302 (2000): 3–31.

Rose, S., *Calais: An English Town in France, 1347–1558* (Woodbridge, VA, 2008).

Rosser, G., 'Crafts, Guilds and the Negotiation of Work in the Medieval Town', *Past & Present*, 154 (1997): 3–31.

Russell, J.G., *The Field of Cloth of Gold: Men and Manners in the 1520s* (London, 1969).

—— 'The Search for Universal Peace: The Conferences at Calais and Bruges in 1521', *Bulletin of the Institute of Historical Research*, 44 (110) (1971): 162–93.

—— *Peacemaking in the Renaissance* (London, 1986), pp. 234–41.

Salmon, J.H., *Society in Crisis, France in the Sixteenth Century* (London, 1975).

—— 'A Second Look at the *Noblesse Seconde*: The Key to Noble Clientage and Power in Early Modern France?', *French Historical Studies*, 25 (4) (2002): 575–93.

Saltzman, L.F., *Building in England Down to 1540* (Oxford, 1952; reprinted 1992).

Saul, N., *Richard II* (New Haven, CT, and London, 1997).

Scarisbrick, J. J., *Henry VIII* (London, 1968)

Schalk, E., *From Valor to Pedigree: Ideas of Nobility in France in the Sixteenth and Seventeenth Centuries* (Princeton, NJ, 1986).

S. Schneelbalg-Perelman, 'Richesses du garde-meuble parisien de François Ier: inventaires inédits de 1542 et 1551', *Gazette de Beaux-Arts*, 6th ser.; vol. 78 (1971): 253–304.

Schroder, T., '"Rich, Fierce and Greedy for Glory": Court Goldsmiths' Work in the Early Years of Henry VIII', *Silver Society Journal* (Autumn 1996): 435–44.

Scott, J., *The Royal Portrait: Image and Impact* (London, 2010).

Scouloudi, I. (ed.), *Huguenots in Britain and their French Background 1550–1800: Contributions to the Historical Conference of the Huguenot Society of London, 24–25 September 1985* (Basingstoke, 1987).

Sessions, W., *Henry Howard, Earl of Surrey* (Boston, 1986).

Sharpe, J., 'Economy and Society', in Patrick Collinson (ed.), *The Sixteenth Century* (Oxford, 2002), pp. 17–44.

Sharpe, K., *Selling the Tudor Monarchy: Authority and Image in Sixteenth-Century England* (New Haven, CT, and London, 2009).

Sim, A., *Food and Feast in Tudor England* (Stroud, 1997).

—— *Masters and Servants in Tudor England* (Stroud, 2006).

Small, G., *Late Medieval France* (Basingstoke, 2009).

Smith, M., 'Les Diplomates italiens, observateurs et conseillers artistiques à la cour de François Ier', *Histoire de l'Art*, 35–6 (1996): 27–37.

Starkey, D.R., 'Ightham Mote: Politics and Architecture in Early Tudor England', *Archaeologia*, 107 (1982): 153–63.

—— 'Henry VI's Old Blue Gown: The English Court under the Lancastrians and Yorkists', *The Court Historian*, 4/1 (1999): 1–28.

—— *Henry: Virtuous Prince* (London, 2008).

—— (ed.), *The English Court* (London, 1987).

—— (ed.), *Henry VIII: A European Court in England* (London, 1991).

Stephenson, B., *The Power and Patronage of Marguerite de Navarre* (Aldershot, 2004).

Strong, R., *Art and Power: Renaissance Festivals 1450–1650* (London, 1984).

Styan, J.L., *The English Stage: A History of Drama and Performance* (Cambridge, 1996).

Suggett, H., 'The Use of French in England in the Later Middle Ages', *TRHS* (1945): 61–84.

Thirsk, J., *Horses in Early-Modern England: For Service, for Pleasure, for Power. The Stenton Lecture 1977* (Reading, 1978).

Thurley, S., 'The Banqueting and Disguising Houses of 1527', in Starkey (ed.), *Henry VIII: A European Court in England* (London, 1991), pp. 64–9.

Thurley, S., 'The Domestic Building Works of Cardinal Wolsey', in Gunn and Lindley, *Cardinal Wolsey, Church State and Art* (Cambridge, 1991), pp. 76–102 at pp. 94–6.

Thurley, S., *The Royal Palaces of Tudor England: Architecture and Court Life 1460–1547* (New Haven, CT, and London, 1993).

Toesca, I., 'Silver in the Time of François Ier: A New Identification', *Apollo*, 90 (1969): 292–7.

Tombs, R. and I., *That Sweet Enemy: The French and the British from the Sun King to the Present* (London, 2006).

Tomkinson, J., 'The Henrician Bastions at Guines Castle', *Fort, The International Journal of Fortification and Military Architecture*, 26 (1998): 121–42.

Vaux de Foletier, F., *Galiot de Genouillac, maître de l'artillerie de France (1465–1546)* (Paris, 1925).

Vellet, C., 'Entre légistes et ministres: Antoine Duprat (1463–1535), conseiller technicien de François Ier', in Michon, *Les Conseillers de François Ier*, pp. 211–27.

Walsby, M., *The Counts of Laval: Culture, Patronage and Religion in Fifteenth- and Sixteenth-Century France* (Aldershot, 2007).

Watts, K., 'Henry VIII and the Founding of the Greenwich Armouries', in Starkey (ed.), *Henry VIII: A European Court in England*, pp. 42–6.

Weary, W., 'La Maison de la Trémoille pendant la Renaissance: une seigneurie aggrandie', in B. Chevalier and P. Contarmine (eds), *La France de la fin du xvème siècle: renouveau et apogée* (Paris, 1985), pp. 197–214.

Wegg, J., *Richard Pace. A Tudor Diplomatist* (London, 1932).

Welch, E., *Shopping in the Renaissance: Consumer Cultures in Italy 1400–1600* (New Haven, CT, and London, 2005).

Wilken, D., *John Russell, First Earl of Bedford: One of the King's Men* (London, 1981).

Wilkie, W., *The Cardinal Protectors of England: Rome and the Tudors before the Reformation* (Cambridge, 1974).

Wolff, M. (ed.), *Kings, Queens and Courtiers: Art in Early Renaissance France* (New Haven, CT, and London, 2011).

Wooding, L., *Henry VIII* (Abingdon, 2009).

Woodward, D., 'Wage Rates and Living Standards in Pre-Industrial England', *Past & Present*, 91 (1991): 28–46.

Woolgar, C.M., 'Gifts of Food in Late Medieval England', *Journal of Medieval History*, 37 (2011): 6–18.

Youngs, D., *Humphrey Newtown (1466–1536): An Early Tudor Gentleman* (Woodbridge, 2008).

Unpublished PhD Dissertations

Helps, I., 'The Career of Sir William Fitzwilliam, Earl of Southampton: A Thematic Study', University of Southampton PhD dissertation, 2007.

Kisby, F.L., 'The Royal Household Chapel in Early-Tudor London, 1485–1547', University of London PhD dissertation, 1996.

Potter, D., 'Diplomacy in the mid-16th Century: England and France, 1536–1550', University of Cambridge PhD dissertation, 1973.

Richardson, G., 'Anglo-French Political and Cultural Relations during the Reign of Henry VIII', University of London PhD dissertation, 1996.

Index